Political Anthropology, Volume V

THE FRAILTY OF AUTHORITY

Political Anthropology, Volume V

THE FRAILTY OF AUTHORITY

Edited by

Myron J. Aronoff

Transaction Books
New Brunswick (U.S.A.) and Oxford (U.K.)

ISSN: 0732-1228
ISBN: 0-88738-091-3 (cloth), 0-88738-634-2 (paper)
Printed in the United States of America

Contents

List of Tables and Figures

Introduction

Myron J. Aronoff

Although the problem of establishing and maintaining political authority is as old as human civilization, the term *frailty of authority* is of more recent vintage. The late Max Gluckman (1956) attributed to the notion a very specific meaning in explaining the inherent constraints on the authority of political leaders. The essays in this volume analyze the social, economic, cultural, legal, and historical forces that shape and constrain the symbolic themes that give ideological legitimacy to collectivities ranging from dynastic American families to Communist party cadres in the Peoples Republic of China. The celebration of traditional religious and national secular Israeli holidays in kindergartens and national civil religious ceremonies are examined in analyses of early Israeli political socialization and of attempts by the recent Likud governments to resocialize the public to gain legitimacy for their regime and its world view. The roles of popular entertainment, ranging from traditional forms of Bedouin story telling to the political satire of Caribbean calypso and the radical musical message of the contemporary punk rock group the Clash, are examined as cases illustrating important aspects of challenges to and assertions of authority. Finally, the subtle manipulation of Moroccan elections is examined, including the response of King Hassan II to political change and challenges to his authority. While each contributor approaches the theme from a distinctly different vantage point, they collectively provide a multifaceted exploration of the inherent frailty of political authority.

Helen Siu artfully traces the rise and demise of the local party brokers who mediate relations between the peasants and the party-state in contemporary China. She shows how the communists replaced the "evil landlords" and their "local bullies" with new party elites who, after eliminating all possible opposition, controlled the lives of the peasants more thoroughly than had any previous regime. The reduction and isolation of the peasants' world led to their greater dependence on the local party cadres who were in turn increasingly (for more than two decades) dependent upon the national party bureaucracy. Dr. Siu explains the widespread peasant discontent following the party reforms since December 1978. The local party cadres were

1

blamed for the economic failures and the consequent suffering of the masses by both the peasants and the national elites (although the ruinous oscillation in policies partly resulted from factional competition among the elites). She contrasts the reaction of the older cadres and peasantry who had retained elements of their tradition on which they could fall back for support with that of the younger generations who, lacking traditional beliefs, became completely alienated and questioned the legitimacy of the regime and its socialist principles.

George Marcus analyzes the effect of dynastic trusts on the efficacy of authority expressed in family tradition or ideology among powerful elite families. He examines the conditions under which such traditions are created or invented in the face of countervailing cultural trends. Marcus emphasizes the period of decline of the dynasty during which, given the conditions structured by the trusts, self-justifying ideologies are reinvented (they may have been inherited from the first generation founder) or are created by second generation leaders and challenged by the third generation descendents. He gives contrasting examples of altruistic public-spirited and egocentric "robber baron" ideologies, but argues that both are equally impelled by the same structure of the Generation-Skipping Trusts.

In their study of representations of collectivity and family in holiday celebrations in Israeli kindergartens, Lea Shamgar-Handelman and Don Handelman effectively explore the state's role in early political socialization. The central theme, which is revealed through the analysis of symbolism and the architectonics of the ceremonial enactments of form and sequence, is the superordination of the collectivity over the family, and the proper relationship of the individual with, and responsibilities toward, both. Their analysis of the celebration of both traditional religious and contemporary secular holidays brings out themes which emphasize the victory of the Jewish people over enemies who sought to destroy them and their culture in ancient and in recent history. When this theme is exaggerated it can lead to the sense of national paranoia which I suggest (in my essay in this volume) characterizes the militant Israeli ultranationalists.[1]

The Handelmans also illustrate, through their analysis of the sequences of ceremonials, how very young Israeli children are taught the importance of history in understanding contemporary realities, which I contend is fundamental to understanding Israeli political culture. They suggest that the emphasis on such values survives primarily through inertia and has become detrimental to the interests of the state. In fact, these values were supportive of the worldview which the Likud sought to advance. The more critical perspective favored by the Handelmans would have undermined the ideological perspective the Likud government fostered. It would take a government far more secure and self-confident of its authority than were those of the Likud, or the present coalition of Labor and the Likud, to foster a critical perspective in the education of its youth. Genuine political authority can only be strengthened in a democracy through an educated and critical public, which is one of the reasons why Israeli society is currently undergoing a crisis of political authority and legitimacy.

In my essay I analyze two case studies to illustrate the manner in which the Likud government attempted to influence the perceptions of Israeli citizens to conform with its interpretation of political reality. I indicate why, in spite of its considerable success, it failed to establish ideological hegemony. Through elaborate memorialization ceremonies stretching over a period of nine months, Prime Minister Menachem Begin attempted to elevate his political mentor, Vladimir Jabotinsky, to the pantheon of Israel's greatest national heroes. This was done to rectify what he perceived to have been an historical injustice done by former Labor governments which he believed ignored Jabotinsky's place in Zionist history. However, this rewriting of history was also designed to establish the legitimacy, if not the ideological hegemony, of the government and the political movement which dominated it.

The elaborate state funeral given to what were reputed to be the remains of followers of Shimon Bar Kochba who led the Jewish revolt against Rome in A.D. 132 to 135 illustrates the central role of history and myth in the interpretation of contemporary political reality by the Likud-dominated government. Core values of the Likud elite, such as heroism, the indivisibility of the Land of Israel, and the conviction that the outside world is inherently hostile to Israel and the Jewish people, are analyzed in terms of the symbols and myths that were highlighted in this ceremonial. I conclude that the obvious manipulation of symbols, myths, and tradition calls attention to the socially constructed nature of political culture and undermines the frail fabric of political authority.

Smadar Lavie's analysis of allegory of experience and the paradoxes of occupation among the Mzeina Bedouin of the Sinai sheds yet another perspective on the frailty of authority. Caught between the vagaries of shifting Israeli and Egyptian military occupation and political suzerainty and the challenges brought by their exposure to economic and sociocultural influences which ignore traditional ways, the Mzeina Bedouin struggle to maintain their dignity, their sacred honor (a supreme value in Mediterrenean societies), and the integrity of their culture. By narrating a personal experience (involving her having been tricked by the local "fool," who is socially licensed to challenge authority, and having benefitted from Bedouin hospitality) in the traditional story-telling style, Ms. Lavie reconstructed Mzeina members' image of themselves and of herself. As a sensitive participant-observer, who as a Jew of Yemenite background shared cultural characteristics with which her hosts could identify, she had transcended her status of outsider and occupier (Israeli) and attained an accepted status as an adopted daughter among the people with whom she (literally as well as figuratively) lived.

The narration of allegories is at one and the same time a politically safe way of voicing protest against their situation and of reasserting continuity with their cultural traditions. By conforming to an "allegorical type" role which is immanent in the Mzeina culture, the anthropologist improvised on traditional forms while commenting on currently lived experiences as a metacommentary on Mzeina society and culture. Such allegorical roles are crucial in situations of social inconsistency because they can temporarily restore consistency and coherence in paradoxical situations. This restoration is accomplished through the dynamics of ritual play. Such rituals tend to "work" because, in spite of the erosion of many customs, tradition is still a compelling force among the Mzeina in these contexts, and because these rituals take place in intimate social contexts with multiplex relationships. In contrast, the national Israeli political ceremonies take place in much larger contexts with a socially and culturally more heterogeneous population related through the most contemporary division of labor. For the majority of Israelis, religiously sanctioned tradition is less obligatory than among the Mzeina.

Douglas Emery's analysis of the socio-political role of the punk rock group, the Clash, explores another dimension of the effect of the scope of social relations on the effectiveness of ritual authority. As products of the Brixton ghetto, the members of the group were able to make use of their experiences of social marginality and political alienation in their music, giving it a sense of authenticity. These experiences were combined with the worldview of the Situationalist International, a radical art school movement, to define a new identity for white working-class youth in Britain.

The Clash communicated their revolutionary message to their audience by redefining one of the dominant myths in popular music—that of the outsider. This was accomplished through the Situationist tactic of detournement which involved the combining of disparate cultural symbols to syncretically produce a new form. By linking the myth of the outsider with the myth of the revolutionary the Clash hoped to communicate a revolutionary identity that could be acted upon by their audience.

Instead, however, the punk community used this message and the concert setting only as a means to release aggression against the social system. The early punk community understood the Clash's message but used it in an unintended manner as a ritual of rebellion. When punk music increased in popularity a host of "part-time punks" entered the movement who did not understand the punk message at all, nor the use to which the message had been put. Hence the unintended use to which the earlier audience put the message of the Clash was undermined in turn. This undermining of the cathartic potential of the message combined with life cycle processes on the part of the original core audience to destroy the punk movement as a whole.

Frank Manning's analysis of calypso in the Caribbean offers an example of the effective use of musical performance as a means of challenging political authority. Manning shows how calypso, which emerged in Trinidad a century and a half ago, has spread throughout the eastern Caribbean to become the region's principal festival music. He compares the political role of calypso in Trinidad, St. Vincent, and Barbados. Calypsonians have traditionally played key roles as social and political satirists in Trinidad and were influential in the movement for independence from British colonial rule. Trinidad's Mighty Sparrow is the most famous of a long line of politically influential calypsonians.

Carnival is a much more recently invented tradition (Hobsbawm and Ranger 1983) in St. Vincent where it was first organized in 1950. Realizing its political significance, nationalist leaders wrested control of it from the business and service groups who started the Carnival. Subsequently, politicians have attempted to silence the calypso attacks on their authority by banning the playing of their songs on the radio. However, live performances, particularly at Carnival, are much more difficult to control or silence. In his analysis of the important role of the calypsonian Becket in defeating the Labor Party of the incumbant Prime Minister Milton Cato in the 1984 parliamentary elections, Manning relates the calypsonian to the traditional trickster figure in Afro-Caribbean culture.

The most detailed and dramatic case discussed by Manning is the case of Mighty Gabby, a consistent challenger of the authority of the regime and policies of Tom Adams, the Prime Minister of Barbados since 1976. Gabby, who combines calypso style with Evangelical themes, has become closely identified with the opposition Democratic Labor Party. Calypso plays such an important role in the politics of Barbados that it was debated in the House of Assembly in 1983. Manning suggests that calypso plays a major role in creating a special West Indian version of a theater state which, in the manner in which it is presented, sounds much like Caribbean musical comedy.

Dale Eickelman illustrates how a very different kind of regime, the Moroccan monarchy, deals with internal challenges to its authority which have included rural rebellions, violent demonstrations and riots in various towns in the interior of the country as well as in Casablanca, and aborted military coups. In spite of repeated predictions of its demise, the Moroccan monarchy, headed by King Hassan II, has managed to survive by adapting political tactics to changing social and economic conditions. Eickelman utilizes the analysis of recent elections to illustrate the resilience of the *Makhzan* (strongbox), as the regime is called. He argues that the king has demonstrated greater awareness of the long-term changes taking place in the society than have the leaders of the political parties.

Eickelman's analysis stresses the role of the "silent majority" in addition to that of the political elite. The monarch's role as "God's deputy on earth" has been effectively used to maintain his authority among the masses, and yet, Eickelman suggests that this use of Islam also places constraints on the regime in terms of changing popular expectations relating to the justness of an Islamic government. At the same time, following recent riots, restrictions have been placed on mosques and fundamentalist Islamic associations have been driven underground. In criticizing and refining the postcolonial vulgate view of Moroccan politics, Eickelman analyzes the role of the ramified network of patron-client ties that are the backbone of the political system in the context of significant changes which have characterized the society in the past two decades. His analysis of recent elections illustrates the successful subtle manipulative hand of the monarch, who has had to accommodate intensified political participation in the periphery which portends even greater challenges to his authority in the future.

Authority, be it ritual or political, has its strongest grasp in groups sharing a common experience and worldview. Symbolic meanings are most effective in legitimating political authority when they are morally compelling and believed to have a profound influence on the lives of the believers. This is more likely to be found in contemporary pluralistic societies within subgroups in the society. As the leaders of new nations struggle to establish and to maintain their authority over heterogeneous societies (many of which have been artificially created through colonial competition), it is imperative that they create salient symbolic universes of meaning. They frequently invent traditions which they hope will bind the nation together and transform their power into legitimate authority. To the extent that such ideological constructs are perceived to be manipulated, their effectiveness becomes undermined. Once the socially constructed nature of such traditions becomes transparent, they cease to be taken for granted and lose their power to compel belief. Similarly, as older traditions are exposed to novel interpretations of reality which challenge them, they can lose their compelling quality. When this happens revitalization movements commonly arise and attempt to restore coherence by reinventing traditions.

Notes

I wish to thank Professors John Middleton and Sally Falk Moore, my predecessors as President of the Association of Political and Legal Anthropology, who organized a panel on "Transformations in Politics and Property" at the 1984 annual meeting of the American Anthropological Association in Denver in which four of the contributors to this volume participated. I would also like to acknowledge the helpful comments on this introductory essay given to me by the contributors to this volume. Finally, I extend sincere thanks to Dr. Saliba Sarsar for his most valuable editorial assistance in the preparation of this volume as well as the entire series.

1. I am reminded of the story an Israeli colleague told about a discussion with his daughter who returned one day from kindergarten and said: "Daddy, I know that on Passover we celebrate our freedom from the horrid Egyptian Pharaoh who wanted to keep us as slaves. On Purim we are happy because brave Queen Esther convinced the King to hang the wicked Persian Hamen who wanted to destroy all of the Jews. On Hanukkah we celebrate our freedom from our Greek enemies. Daddy, tell me—who were our enemies on *Tu Bi-Shevat* (The New Year of Trees or Arbor Day)?

References

Gluckman, Max. 1956. *Custom and Conflict in Africa*. Oxford: Blackwell.
Hobsbawn, Eric, and Terence Ranger, eds. 1983. *The Invention of Tradition*. Cambridge: Cambridge University Press.

1

Collective Economy, Authority, and Political Power in Rural China

Helen F. Siu

Collective ownership means that the collective 'owns' us peasants as well as the resources we work on. The cadres who control the collective then do whatever they please with our lives. They behave no differently from the local bullies we heard so much in the 'recall bitterness' accounts of our fathers. However, the strongmen of the 1930s and 1940s had no legitimate claim on the peasants, who regarded them as excesses of the traditional society. The cadres, on the other hand, enjoy total authority given by the socialist system. Chairman Mao once said that the scriptures were good, only that they had from time to time been recited by priests with crooked mouths. I wonder about these scriptures; it seems that they have distorted the mouths instead.

This is a candid comment by a peasant in his late twenties who was once a member of the Party Youth League. During the land reform in the Pearl River Delta thirty years ago, young peasant activists recruited by the Chinese Communist Party (CCP) attacked the "evil landlords and local bullies" with a vengeance in the name of the revolution. It is ironic that three decades later they face the accusing fingers of a bitter and disillusioned young generation who are the revolution's eldest children.[1] Moreover, the statement points to a more serious political issue: for decades, the peasant activists turned party cadres had occupied the center of the political stage in the countryside, drawing legitimacy from their party affiliations. Peasant masses and party superiors regarded them as an integral part of the socialist system that was being created. While peasants attacked the "local bullies" of the 1940s as excesses and preserved their respect for the traditional order, those who denounced the rural cadres in the 1980s are questioning the ideological principles that gave the cadres legitimacy in the first place. To masses and leaders alike, the "socialist system" is at stake.

Peasant discontent that brewed in the countryside for three decades exploded when the winds of liberalization were assured by the CCP Central

Committee's third plenum in December 1978. To the dismay of the rural cadres, their ideological mentor had joined in the attack. Party authorities blamed the poor quality of rural leadership for agricultural stagnation and peasant alienation. Cadres who managed collective agriculture were said to have committed "blind directing based on poor information and uncritical following of ultra-leftist policies," and their "dictatorial leadership style" betrayed the party's mass line. Some theoretical journals started debates on the nature of agrarian socialism as well as the root problems of bureaucracy in "asiatic modes of production." The two debates address the contradictory nature of rural leadership—extreme egalitarian concerns imposed by the most dictatoral methods.[2] Recent official statements summarized the problems: some party leaders have not shed the extreme egalitarian mentality of small producers in China's feudal past; these leaders have found their agents in the vast countryside who accepted their mentors' ideological tune; although the nation has made progress in agricultural production to provide basic security for a majority of the peasants and workers, the history of trial and error exacted a heavy price; economically, the delicate balance between nature and cultivation was violated; some damage in the environment was irreversible, adding more pressure to the already limited material resources; politically, a generation grew up skeptical and alienated from the revolution because of personal sufferings; they now resent the party cadres and question both the legitimacy of the regime and the socialist principles.[3] The above official opinions are some of the most explicit admissions of failure and trouble in the countryside. Moreover, they blame the brigade cadres who actually enforced rural policies.[4]

This essay uses the case study of a commune in south China to illustrate and relate three dimensions of social transformation in the countryside from the 1940s to the 1980s: in the structures of production, exchange, and distribution; in the relationships of power between the state, the rural cadres, and the peasants; and in the changing world of meanings that crystalized a deep sense of cynicism towards the party and socialist ideology, for cadres and peasants alike. These three aspects of transformation intertwined to form a single but complicated structuring process. At the center of the process were individuals whose perceptions were shaped by cultural traditions that had been punctuated by the vicissitudes of socialist politics. Both rural cadres and peasant masses went about their daily economic activities, but they were also making moral and political choices. Their actions have created the historical process and the structures of relationships that continuously shape their real and perceived options.[5] Specifically, I want to trace the rise and demise of rural cadres: how they became agents for the state and party and helped to create and manage agricultural production collectives.[6] In doing so, they not only defined the relationship between the state and local communities, between the party and its cadres in the process of nation building, but also transformed themselves from peasant activists into local bosses who were eventually rejected by their fellow villagers and abandoned by their mentors.

This essay seeks to use a historically specific episode, a process of transformation, to illustrate how the changing macro-structures that encapsulated rural communities have penetrated the latter through rural agents. Parallel to these changes and often reinforcing them were the national ideological currents in which the peasants periodically found themselves engulfed but which they were able to manipulate from time to time.[7] These peasants were not mere spectators watching political dramas unfold afar; instead, through their actions, they helped shape their unfolding. What follows then is the story of many Chinese peasants who, in Madsen's words, "made themselves as they make history" in the second half of the twentieth century. In a short essay, however, I can describe only the events, the structural changes, and the personalities involved. To describe how these intertwined to create the structuring processes requires a great deal more ethnographic detail than I can provide here.[8]

Prerevolutionary Political Economy

The Huancheng area lies between Huicheng (Xinhui County Capital) and Jiangmen (a trading center) in the Pearl River Delta, 111 kilometers southwest of Guangzhou. By the early twentieth century, it already had a dense population and enjoyed good water transportation. Peasants grew two crops a year, rice and seasonal vegetables. The area was also known for palm and fruit growing. At the height of its development in the early 1920s, palm handicraft supported over 10,000 workers in Huicheng and was an important supplement for farm income.[9] Wholesale merchants of palm handicraft products in Huicheng and Jiangmen monopolized long distance and export trade and owned some of the best palm fields in the hinterland.

Two patterns of land tenure existed in the area. In the periurban communities land ownership was concentrated in the hands of merchants and ancestral estates whose headquarters were in town. Land use was fragmented, tenancy short-term and unstable. At least 20 percent of the farm laborers also engaged in petty trade and odd jobs in town, since the average household farm size was under ten mu.[10] Communities away from Huicheng oriented their marketing activities to a town farther south. Ancestral estates "owned" most of the land. Private landlords had relatively small land-holdings. The managers of the estates and the landlords were largely local residents who supervised the upkeep of their dikes and gave preferential, more stable tenure to lineage members. The average size of household plots (owned or rented) was 15-20 mu and few peasants engaged in petty trade or hired themselves out for long terms. The more self sufficient production orientation was reinforced by lineage ties, making these communities notoriously fierce and exclusive. Tianma Xiang, a single-surnamed township of over 5,000 residents at the southern tip of the Huancheng area was not only exclusive but also predatory at the expense of neighbors. Even today commune cadres in the area regard Tianma residents as "a breed of their own."

The xiang (township) was an important social-political unit for the peasants in the Huancheng area.[11] The traditional elite were the landed gentry who had connections with officials at the county capital, lineage elders, and lesser power holders such as the bao heads.[12] By the turn of the century, however, the landed gentry had moved to town and engaged in commerce and usury. The xiang, especially those in more peripheral areas, was dominated by local strongmen who ruled with their guns. These strongmen were uneducated "bandits and smugglers" who took control of lineage estates and the lands of absentee landlords residing in town. When civil war and the Japanese invasion racked the governments, and civic disorder became endemic in the first half of the twentieth century, the xiang strongmen rose to be local bosses—acting as protectors of their communities at times, but preying on their kinsmen and neighbors as well. Some collaborated with the Japanese military who occupied the region from 1938 to 1945. During the ensuing civil war between the Nationalist government (KMT) and the communists, from 1946 to 1949, the KMT relied heavily on these local strongmen to recruit soldiers, to extract taxes, and to uncover and exterminate those who sympathized with the communists. They held "official" positions that were lucrative and were auctioned to the highest bidder, facilitating their predations. When conflicts of interest arose, these strongmen dragged whole communities into mini-wars against one another. With arms and support from political patrons in the cities, local lineage feuds escalated in violence and destruction.[13] The excesses of these local bosses finally hurt their political patrons; peasants who felt deeply vulnerable revoked the regime's "mandate of heaven." By late 1949, when the People's Liberation Army (PLA) swept south from the northern provinces, all the signs for "the end of a dynasty" were evident in the peasants' traditional frame of reference. In a sense, the local bosses became powerful during a period of political decline and crisis, but their success eventually led to their undoing. It is important to note that the peasants did not regard them as legitimate power holders of the traditional order.[14]

Land Reform and the Recruitment of Peasant Activists

The KMT and the local bosses in the Huancheng area dominated until the very last days of the civil war.[15] There was little chance of political work by the CCP to prepare the area for the communist takeover. The People's Liberation Army swept into Guangzhou, Foshan, and the major cities in the delta as quickly as the soldiers could march. Local KMT armies defected in Jiangmen and declared the area liberated on October 23, 1949, while the peasants watched the drama and waited with cautious anxiety. As soon as the regular PLA forces joined with the local guerillas and underground workers, the campaign to disarm rural communities and to exterminate remnant KMT resistance began.

Most of the strongmen had fled the area before the communists arrived, some moving to Macao and Hong Kong. Many of their followers, however, whom peasants identified as "having blood on their hands," were swiftly arrested. The Anti-Bully and Rent-Retrieval Campaigns started in late 1950 in the area. Peasants were encouraged by party work teams to seek out landlords in their xiang and in the two regional cities to force them to pay back rent and rental deposits that had been given to them by the peasants. Furthermore, "landlords and bullies" were publicly tried for their crimes of exploitation. By such means the party sought to mobilize the peasants to recognize their own power in the process of creating the new political order. Work teams composed of party cadres, students, and workers from the cities came to the xiang and set up new peasant associations, which became the political centers in the xiang to conduct the land reform—to initiate the rent-retrieval campaigns, to organize the mass meetings to determine class statuses of every household in the xiang, and to oversee the division of land. Activists were recruited by the work teams to form the political nuclei within the associations. At first, the peasants were too timid to point accusing fingers. But after a few bullies in the xiang were "struggled against" and shot, some peasants started to attack with a vengeance. A record of the public trials in the county shows that most of the petty officials in the xiang, identified as "evil landlords and local bullies," received some form of punishment: public humiliation, beatings, confiscation of property, imprisonment or execution (Li and Hong 1952). It is important to note, however, that the masses made a clear distinction in terms of the nature of the crimes and punishment between the educated landed gentry who were "legitimate" merchants in town (they were called economic landlords) and the local bosses. The former were often treated leniently. When local activists indiscriminately harassed the economic landlords, the peasant often expressed uneasiness.[16]

The fan-ba (anti-bully) campaign is revealing in two aspects. First, it shows that the peasants acted according to their traditional value system. They attacked the local bosses who were considered to have committed "excessive bullying acts" by their blatant use of force; but the traditional elite (the landed gentry and merchants) were given some respect, indicating that the legitimacy of the old social hierarchy was not called into question.

However, the party saw the peasant anger as largely anti-feudal enthusiasm. Such misinterpretation led to future problems when the party tried to mobilize peasants to embrace socialism.

. Second, the problematic work styles of local activists, "authoritarianism mixed with leftist opportunism," is indicative of another party misinterpretation which led to future difficulties. The party work teams recruited poor peasants and hired hands on the assumption that they were downtrodden and would be determined to struggle against class enemies. They were therefore considered trusted allies of the party. The hired hands were particularly favored because they were supposed to have proletarian status and naturally its outlook. Such simpleminded economic determinism linking class exploitation to proletarian consciousness was a dominant trend in CCP thought, especially within the ultra leftist faction. It gave them an ahistorical view of human nature—namely that human nature and outlook can only be class based. In Maoist art and literature, radical portrayal of proletarian characters were noble and flawless whereas class enemies had no human feelings.

Nothing could have been farther from reality. The peasants' poverty was caused by many factors other than class exploitation. To understand what poor peasants considered unjust, how they viewed their poverty, what they perceived as options, and how they were motivated to act, one must take into account the historical weight of cultural tradition, and ideology promoted by the ruling elites, plus the actual social and political relationships in which individual peasants found themselves entrenched. The rigid economic determinism of the CCP in this period might be an expedient political strategy to distinguish friends from enemies, but it sadly left out, among much else, the forces of cultural tradition and individual imagination or creativity.

Two kinds of activists emerged from the rural landscape: the reluctant poor-middle peasant, and the opportunist protoproletariat. In the communities farther away from the two cities, the party work team had great difficulty recruiting peasant activists. In Tianma Xiang, for example, members of the poor peasants' association were reluctant to oppose their lineage elders. They were also afraid that once the work teams left, the local bosses would come back and seek revenge. Dividing the ancestral estates was another moral hurdle. Economic, religious, kin, and power relationships in this exclusive community were so intertwined in the peasants' world of meaning that it was hard to find a break in the structure. The party was only able to recruit some poor-middle peasants[17] who were more concerned with owning land and farming it well than with political struggles. As a matter of fact, after they had conducted the land reform with the help of party work teams, many refused to continue political work entrusted to them. Instead, they wanted to make it on their own with their newly acquired properties. For example, the chairman of the poor peasants' association in Tianlu Xiang refused to join the party or cooperatives until 1956. Like other poor peasants, he and his family had been given some good land. He grew rice for his own consumption and grew lychee fruits for the market. There was a period of recovery in the early 1950s and farm prices were reasonably good. The diked fields that had been under the management of ancestral estates were quite well kept, and crop yields were good. This man was motivated in his production efforts because he felt he could fully utilize his skills as a good farmer and enjoy the products of his labor.[18]

The activists from periurban xiang were of a different breed altogether. They seldom belonged to the dominant lineages in the communities. Too poor to rent a farm large enough to support their families, they engaged in petty account production for trade such as catching river shrimps or cutting wild grass to sell as fuel. They also hired themselves out to odd jobs as coolie or farm hands to supplement income. They were desperately poor but also politically shrewd. Many had travelled outside the county as migrant laborers and soldiers. In sum, they were marginal, mobile elements in their xiang, little respected by fellow villagers and often poorly treated. Many joined the party work teams with mixed motives. Some became party ideologues, as there was a ready way to acquire recognition, economic benefits, and assured political power. They knew also that the work teams were dependent on them to penetrate the villages. In following party policies, many overrode the concerns of kin and community since they did not belong to dominant lineages in the villages and felt that they had little to lose.[19] Party documents periodically cautioned against these "brave elements" but at the same time, given their "class" criteria, the party found them necessary and useful. Work teams often took these opportunist elements because they were unable to recruit others.[20]

The CCP's use of the local class relationships combined with individual peasants' motives and subsequent action created the beginning of a long-term party-activists relationship. With the organization of the party, the state interfered with society in an aggressive way, directing the peasant anger that it helped to arouse for the party's political purposes. On the other hand, individual activists were using the ideological power bestowed by the party to build their own bases and resources in the villages. While different types of activists were recruited from communities with different combinations of land tenure and social characteristics, a line can be drawn between periurban communities and those in the more peripheral part of the cities' hinterland. With different backgrounds, motivations, moral choices, and work styles, these activists formed different relationships with the party as well as with their fellow peasants.

The Taste of Bureaucratic Power: Activists Turned Cadres

During the land reform, political decisions were made by the peasant associations in the xiang (township), which also conducted meetings of representatives to nominally rectify the decisions. Activists who were members of the zhuxi tuan (chairmanship committee), the political nuclei of the xiang at the time, had a great deal of control over the livelihoods of fellow villagers in the xiang. When the committee assigned class statuses to each peasant household, everyone anxiously tried to avoid being labelled a landlord or rich peasant. The more affluent households pleaded and bribed. Being a poor peasant then implied legitimate power and future well-being.

The land reform was largely completed in the Huancheng area by 1953 and the xiang governments were set up. Activists in the peasant associations assumed important posts and were recruited into the party youth league branches. When party branches were set up in the xiang in 1954, the activists were the first group of local activists to be sworn in as members. Each xiang was given five salaried posts—whose holders were known to the peasants as the five leading cadres in their villages. The party members filled these posts. Those cadres who were busy with official duties often had their land farmed by former landlords and other disenfranchised elements.

Affiliation with the party enabled the activists to assume official positions. Their leadership roles in the countryside were thus institutionalized, and so was the ideological authority they drew from party and government. The two became increasingly inseparable. The new political reality altered the peasants' perception of political authority, which had traditionally been based on a combination of land ownership, education, age, lineage positions, and official status. From mid-1950s onward, authority was increasingly identified with officialdom buttressed by a party organization and ideology that were gaining a monopoly over potential challengers.

The Consolidation of Power in the Xiang

With the establishment of the xiang government and party branch, the xiang became a vital social, economic, and political unit in the Chinese countryside.[21] It was the local meeting point between state and society. Party policies were transmitted to the xiang through its cadres who were natives of the area and who were expected to enforce them in the villages.

In 1953, the national government laid the first foundation for a socialist economy. It took steps to nationalize the industrial sector, to control commerce by the state centralized purchase of grain and other major commodities, to impose a system of planned production, allocation, and rationing, and to collectivize agriculture.[22] The first three features changed the national political economy so that rural communities were encapsulated, whereas the last transformed the communities to accommodate the macro economy. These policies made peasant production dependent on the state sector for industrial inputs and for the sale of agricultural products. Collectivization enabled the state to control the countryside better—collectives with state agents in leadership positions were much easier to deal with than households each having their economic strategies and political expectations. Another government method in controlling the countryside was to maintain a steadily growing, balanced, urban economy sheltered from food price fluctuations and undisturbed by rural migration. The system of household registration and food rationing made it difficult for peasants to move to town though the disparity between rural and urban standards of living and the undervaluation of agriculture led many peasants to wish to leave the land.[23]

One side effect of limiting individual entrepreneurship and mobility was the shrinking of the peasants' social networks, as marketing activities were confined more and more to the xiang. Traditional social exchanges between communities were curtailed by the Great Leap Forward when periodic peasant markets in Guangdong were fixed on the same days to prevent roving traders buying at one market and selling in another.[24] While the xiang had been an important unit of identification for peasants in traditional times, other social and economic relationships cut across xiang boundaries and linked peasants from adjacent communities into wider district networks, such as higher order lineage affiliations, market communities. However, when these other ties were diminished and the xiang became the sole important local unit to relate to the socialist state, it also became all important for peasant identification. Membership in a xiang thus determined how the peasants made their livelihood and shaped the nature of social interaction and political pressure.

The party members of a xiang formed a political core to "elect" local cadres. If subdivisions of the xiang had more than three party members, a small party group was formed. However, the real power of decision lay in the party committee at the xiang government. Therefore, rural communities were encapsulated within a structure of administrative allocation and ideological monopoly. While the state consolidated its control over the new political economy, it depended on local agents for implementation of the new state-community relationship. Once formed, that relation deeply influenced the internal dynamics of the communities as well as the agents' perception of their unique relationship with the party-state.[25] With the grooming of local activists and party cadres at the xiang level of administration, the government developed the political framework for further penetration and control of the countryside.

Collectivization: The Peasants Lost Ground

When the national leadership decided to collectivize agriculture in a large scale in 1954, the party leaned heavily on its new cadres to set an example of embracing socialism by forming mutual aid teams (MATs) and cooperatives. The political intentions of the state were often modified by rural cadres to cope with local conditions, and a mosiac of realities emerged which embodied different motivations, meanings, and reactions of the participants. Many cadres took the lead in forming a variety of cooperative units with relatives and close friends. In periurban communities, ideologues sometimes went too far in their enthusiasm, as shown by the case of a party cadre in Chengnan Xiang who asked for permission to form a cooperative before results from experimental cases (shidian) in the county were evaluated. In xiang located farther away from the county capital, the enthusiasm of the cadres to embrace collective production was much lower.

Seasonal mutual aid teams formed by a few households were later upgraded to year-round groups that pooled some of their properties together.[26] Cooperative production was institutionalized by formation of the Agricultural Producers Cooperatives (Lower APCs) in 1955. The cooperatives consisted of forty or so households each subdivided into work groups that held shares which varied with land, tools, and labor contribution. In consultation with members, the head of the cooperative set production plans, saw to the payment of the unit's taxes, and administered its grain sales to the government. Members of cooperatives agreed among themselves on remuneration for property and labor contributions.

Enthusiasm for the cooperatives among various xiang was uneven. Households who were classified as poor peasants during the land reform were given priority to choose land and tools within the quota alloted. Many, especially those with strong laborers, decided not to join cooperatives. They were often protective of their new-found wealth and afraid of free-riders.[27] Cooperatives were given support by the government in the form of credit, seeds, and fertilizers; but as these items were still quite available in the mid-1950s in markets, and credit could be obtained from friends and relatives, peasants enjoyed some flexibility in the choice of their economic strategies.

The rural cadres were under great pressure to perform their role as enthusiastic state agents to implement socialism. Reluctant relatives, however, could be embarrassing. An old cadre in Meijiang Xiang told how his uncle was pressured to join the nephew's cooperative but withdrew three times. The stubborn old man was a poor peasant who obtained three mu of palm fields, six mu of orchards and one mu of rice paddy. With a household of seven, he decided to make it on his own. At the urging of his nephew, he reluctantly joined but immediately backed out on the ground that the cooperative evaluated his land at too low a price. Evidently he rejoined but quit the cooperative a second time over their evaluation of his labor power. Having rejoined again, he quit a third time after disagreements about the value of a boat he sold to the cooperative. "I was the laughing stock among skeptical villagers," complained the cadre, "because I could not even convince my own uncle."

By 1955, each xiang had a variety of cooperative units—seasonal and year-round MATs with various terms of distribution and collective properties—amidst a large number of households who produced on their own. Differences among members of the cooperatives over the valuation of property and labor shares threatened to paralyze production when dissatisfied members withdrew their participation. Tension between these differing kinds of production organizations is illustrated by an incident in late 1954. Angry fruit farmers in the adjacent area demonstrated in Jiangmen to protest against state agencies contracting to buy tangerines from some cooperatives and households and not others during a year of overproduction. Protestors publicly accused the cadres of favoritism and corruption. The incident is revealing in two aspects: it shows how peasants at the time perceived the forces that controlled their livelihood, and what they considered as effective action to change the structure of control. One of the aims of this essay is to describe and analyze how the changing structures of relations in the countryside changed peasants' perceptions of their economic and political options, with results that ultimately affected their actions. As one can now see, the demonstrations in 1954 contrast sharply with the the peasants' sullen diffused noncooperation during the mid-1970s, when resistance to state control was much more circumscribed and limited. Furthermore, cadres had greater freedom during the 1950s. For example, at that time, local cadres sometimes let personal grudges override party policies. A household classified as middle peasant in Tianlu Xiang refused to join a cooperative when invited. During the following season, a typhoon broke his dikes. He worried and finally asked to join. However, the cadres decided to teach him a lesson and refused his application.

It soon proved that such flexibility in peasant economic strategies was short lived, as Mao and his colleagues started their "high tide of socialism in the countryside" in 1956. Rural cadres were then told to organize local households into collectives (Higher APCs), which were ten times bigger than the Lower APCs, with remuneration rules favoring labor. The Huancheng area started its collectivization drive in 1956, when the mixture of individual producers, MATs, and Lower APCs in each xiang was grouped into one or a few collectives.[28] The transformation was abrupt and coercive, and individual production and exchange activities were thereafter restricted. The changes were brought about by xiang cadres working with their party superiors in the county capital and with a new group of activists they recruited in the villages. As directors of the APCs, the xiang cadres attempted to manage the economic and political lives of several thousand peasants. The collectives were subdivided into production teams, headed by the new layer of activist recruits. Many of these were later introduced into the party and became known as the collectivization cadres to distinguish them from those who had risen to power earlier during the land reform.[29]

Conflict between the cadres and the peasant masses in this period focused particularly on the lack of freedom for the collective members to use their own labor as well as to voice their opinion on the economic organization and strategies of the collectives. For example, a common complaint was that cadres in collectives constantly drafted labor for basic construction projects giving peasants little time to fulfill their household needs.[30] The cadres' primary concern to deliver the state grain quota also interfered with peasants' subsidiary activities and their need to grow cash crops for rural marketing. Locked up in their collectives, peasants had few alternatives to make a livelihood. Those cadres who were party political agents managing the collectives assumed tremendous power over people's lives, since they monopolized the transmission, interpretation, and implementation of rural policies. Some peasants resisted actively, as illustrated by an election of cadres reported in the county newspaper (*Xinhui Nongmin Bao,* 28 October 1956):

> Can "democratic elections" get good cadres? During the upgrading of the lower APCs in Wei Xiang, peasants raised issue with the cadres' past leadership style. Therefore many cadres were afraid that the masses could not distinguish between right or wrong, and decided that in the recent election, the committee members of the collective would be nominated by the party branch. The masses just needed to endorse by an open ballot. However, before the election, some peasants raised a protest to the party branch: We will not recognize any cadres we did not elect by ourselves. Some even said: We are not going to join the collective until we know who the cadres are.
>
> The party branch should not ignore the warning from the peasants. There was a similar case last year. When Weixi Xiang Cooperative Number Seven had an election, the masses did not wish Liang Dechen to be director, but the party branch ignored mass opinion and approved his posting. As a result, nobody listened to him and he was ineffective as a leader. Such a lesson made the party branch reverse their decision. They investigated among the masses. Members of the Cooperatives Number Three and Four told the cadres: Good production planning can only be implemented by good leadership. We have entrusted our property and livelihood to you. If you can elect good collective

cadres, so can we. After this investigation, the party branch realized that an election without prior discussions that is monopolized by an exclusive minority is divorced from the peasants. Those elected would not receive mass support.

Therefore, collectivization in the area can be seen as the outcome of actions taken by rural cadres who were increasingly drawn into the party bureaucracy by improvising national ideological tunes to implement party and state policies. Their role as local-level state agents was not always easy, since the national leadership was by no means united in composing the current ideological hit-tunes. In the mean time, conflicts between cadres and peasant masses hardened. Cadres found themselves accountable to their political superiors outside the communities who gave them authority and privileges, while the peasants, encapsulated in compulsory structures, felt that they were losing control over their lives and livelihood. The most common complaint by peasants during the process of collectivization, and especially during the time of the higher APCs, was that they had no time for themselves. After the land reform, most peasants had enjoyed a period of quiet prosperity under the new government, but they paid a heavy price thereon in the two following decades. Both cadres and peasants interviewed in the 1980s agreed that they reached a turning point in their attitudes toward the party-state when the higher APCs were formed. The peasants felt that before the APCs, joining the cooperative forms was voluntary, and they had other alternatives to make a livelihood without having to submit to political pressure. The cadres also felt that once they were locked into the party structure and had to prove themselves in the collectives, into which all the peasants were involuntarily locked, tension between them and the collective members intensified. Many rural cadres were sensitive to local sentiments and needs and at times had tried to cooperate with relatives and friends to resist state demands. However, they were increasingly absorbed into a web of political obligations and benefits that they had helped to create through affiliation with the party-state.

The People's Commune: A Bridge to Whose Paradise?

Twenty thousand people marched in Huicheng in August 1959 to celebrate the first anniversary of the establishment of Huancheng Commune (*Xinhui Bao,* 1 September 1959). The spirit of euphoria of the previous year still lingered in the minds of the organizers, though in reality, serious food shortages were already evident. In the previous year, a commune of nearly 35,000 members had been formed in the area, incorporating over twenty Higher APCs, which were then renamed Brigades. Each brigade supervised several production teams.[31] Young activists recruited by cadres during the collectivization campaigns became team and brigade leaders, many joined the party and were known as the Great Leap Forward cadres, while a few land reform cadres were transferred to the central commune administration. Under direction of county party organizations, commune cadres supervised practically every economic, political, and social activity of commune members. Party cadres were given virtually total power to draft and allocate the resources of the commune, including people's labor. Apart from making production decisions, the commune also organized large labor groups to transform the natural environment, for example, building bridges, roads, and dikes.[32] Every member was given a wage, food, and other rations set by the commune. Peasants ate in collective dining halls since food was allocated by the commune to such halls in accordance with the national trend to "eat rice from one big pot." Children were gathered in collective day care centers to free women for labor. Peasants were also obliged to contribute pots and pans, trees, furniture, and bricks from their houses to fuel the backyard furnaces and other commune enterprises. Furthermore, cadres were pressured to set examples of generous contribution: The manager of the commune's paper factory tore part of his house down in order to contribute bricks for a new factory building.[33]

The Great Leap Forward (GLF) and communization movement highlighted the power state organization had imposed on society, reinforced by the ideological power of the party agents in the countryside. Recent critics of the GLF have blamed the chaos of the GLF on the utopian political assumptions of Mao as well as on the type of rural cadres who found Mao's utopianism attractive.[34] In a self-critical moment, one old cadre I interviewed in the summer of 1983 described the cadres' mood at the time of communization:

> We were all caught in the spirit of euphoria, competing with one another, exaggerating and then believing our exaggerations. The state expected us to deliver, so we pressured the masses. Why did the peasants comply? Well, if they wanted to eat, they had to work; there was no alternative. One could not survive ouside of the collective. The cadres expected that the state would take care of them if things went wrong. We had a blind enthusiasm over the ideological power of the party. After all, it gave us what we had thus far, we did not want to let it down. But of course the party was acting on our exaggerated reports, so we fed each other wrong information that led to unrealistic estimates and waste. The peasants went along with the wastefulness for a totally different reason. They wanted to get at the resources before the latter were taken by freeloaders. This feeling was particularly strong in the rich xiang. So we ate up our year's grain reserve in three months! Then the hard times came, but the state told us that there was nothing they could do to get us out of the situation. We had to come up with food ourselves. The peasants hated us.

Everyone was watchful of who took more than their share of food. The culprits were pretty roughed up sometimes. Even today, people have a grudge over fellow peasants who were suspected of having hidden food 25 years ago. Cadres were accused of nepotism given their power of allocation. The hard times lasted until 1961. We rounded up those who were suffering from severe malnutrition and fed them nutritious foods. In one of the gatherings, the cynical patients "thanked" us and the party for making them so "bloated." We were all losers, including the party. Since the party enjoyed tremendous power to organize people's lives, then when things went wrong, people would not blame themselves; they blamed the party and the cadres instead.

The statistics of Huancheng Commune that I have collected show that from 1958 to 1961, there was dip in population, an increase in production costs, and a drastic drop in per capita income. For example, cost as per-

TABLE 1.1
Some Economic Statistics for Huancheng Commune

Year	Income Per Capita (yuan)	Cost as Percentage of Production (percent)
1953	135.9	29.3
1954	147.9	26.6
1955	131.4	25.2
1956	111.8	24.9
1957	70.7	32.1
1958	52.7	47.0
1959	88.6	26.3
1960	103.2	30.6
1961	106.1	29.4
1962	136.1	25.8
1963	129.6	29.6
1964	79.6	39.7
1965	99.6	35.0
1966	118.8	28.9
1967	129.3	28.2
1968	126.1	26.2
1969	117.0	28.1
1970	109.1	29.3
1971	118.5	28.0
1972	121.8	32.2
1973	111.5	39.9
1974	121.5	44.3
1975	102.2	37.0
1976	110.5	39.1
1977	149.2	32.9
1978	147.0	38.8
1979	139.3	43.5
1980	195.4	40.7
1981	220.4	49.0
1982	456.3	45.9

centage of production jumped from 24.9 percent in 1956 to 47 percent in 1958 while per capita income dropped from 111.8 yuan in 1956 to 52.7 yuan in 1958 (and 88.6 yuan in 1959). As shown in Table 1.1, such a trend started as early as 1957, when peasants were involuntarily incorporated into the higher APCs. It is sadly revealing that the cadres took more than twenty years to admit that reality, i.e., until the higher ups of the party had publicly denounced the GLF as a tragic mistake. This shows the ideological and censorship power of the party over the rural cadres. Though they were as much victims of the campaign as the masses, they had promoted the "lie" for more than two decades.

The consequences of the communization movement raise the following questions: Why were unrealistic policies pushed to such extremes and allowed to incur such heavy human costs before any revisions were made? Assuming that mass disincentive was seen and objections heard, why were they not reported and allowed to shape policy decisions? If such messages from the rural areas were transmitted but not acted on by party leaders, why had the party structure such insensitivity?[35] Another set of questions also needs to be asked concerning the motivations and actions of the rural agents: What were the structural positions of the rural cadres in the changing political economy? How did the ideological power of the party affect the cadres' moral and political perceptions? Did the cadres pursue strategies intentionally or unconsciously to protect their newly acquired legitimacy and economic interests?[36] The ultimate question remains: Why were the peasants unable to resist the transformations so detrimental to their lives? The GLF demonstrated the growing ideological power of the consolidating party state over its cadres, the corresponding power of the cadres over the peasant masses, and the dominating role of the state economy in shaping rural lives and landscape.

Power Struggle, Patronage, and Apparent Compromise

Moderate winds started to blow in the area in late 1960. Production responsibilities were then decentralized to teams and households. The state also promoted the revival of rural markets, relaxed the control over prices, and strictly forbade the brigade or commune officials to interfere with team autonomy. As before, brigade cadres were entrusted with the responsibility to enforce such liberalization.[37] In an effort to satisfy peasant demand, the rural cadres often confined team membership to a few households who were also close relatives. The "sanzi ibao" responsibility system was pushed with vigor and received by peasants enthusiastically.[38] In the county, many periodic markets were revived with their traditional schedules.[39] State agencies also paid high prices for most agricultural commodities.[40] The

TABLE 1.2
Average Annual Yield for Rice Grain in Huancheng Commune

Year	Yield (jin per mu)
1961	903
1962	909
1963	1144
1964	902
1965	971
1966	1057
1967	985
1968	946
1969	939
1970	842
1971	955
1972	915
1973	929
1974	1026
1975	879
1976	892
1977	1131
1978	917
1979	954
1980	1121
1981	928
1982	1111

Huancheng area with its traditional commercialized economy responded favorably to the liberalized policies. Peasant households that contracted with the teams had incentives to produce and the autonomy to make production decisions and keep the rewards. The unusually good weather in 1963 brought bumper harvests, reinforcing the spirit of revived prosperity for the peasants in the area. Rice grain yield in Huancheng was the highest since the revolution, reaching 1144 jin (1 jin = 1.25 lbs.) per mu (see Table 1.2). Collective income per capita had increased 21.7 percent from 1961 (not counting the income from subsidiary production and trading that did not enter into the team accounts).

Ironically, the cadres were doing even better. As a matter of fact, in 1983 they considered the early 1960s "the golden period" of their administrative experience. It was at first embarrassing for them to take the lead in demonstrating that the party was serious about liberalization. To convince the masses who had been made timid and skeptical by the preceeding decade of political vicissitudes, some commune and brigade cadres finally organized their own household members to trade at rural markets. That worked because peasants eagerly followed. The cadres no longer spent time allocating work, arguing about terms of remuneration, or watching out for items banned from the markets. They still supervised the payment of grain taxes and other state purchases for households under their jurisdiction, but they were now the unobtrusive middlemen between government agencies willing to pay and peasants who were eager to produce and sell.

By then, the presence of a growing state-owned industrial sector could no longer be ignored.[41] State agencies with whom the brigade cadres had official connections were important suppliers of fertilizers, seeds, credit, machinery, and consumer goods. The Leninist assumptions of the party under Liu Shaoqi (the official head of the state until his downfall during the Cultural Revolution) meant that all important production resources were still under state planning and allocation.[42] The brigade cadres were essential brokers between the state suppliers and peasant households, but were also subjected to bribery and corruption. Many had worked for the party for a decade and had built up extensive networks of connections with commune and county officials and links of patronage with lesser cadres in the production teams. Therefore, ironically, the commune and brigade cadres' ability to get ahead of the peasant masses in pursuit of market and price incentives was precisely because they had privileged affiliations with the party bureaucracy in the state industrial sector.

However, this golden period did not last long, as the successful maneuvers in implementing liberalized policies triggered reactions from high-level party leadership as well as from discontented peasants who lacked the cadres' opportunities to get ahead. An ideological battle was also brewing among the nation's top leaders. Mao was uncomfortable with the political implications of Liu's policies: Individualized production and profit motives defeated socialist spirit; furthermore, differentiation increased among the masses, and party cadres at all levels became entrenched in privileges. Therefore, in late 1963, Mao promoted the Socialist Education Campaign in selected rural communities. He intended to educate the masses about correct socialist policies and to rectify rural cadres "who had gone astray." More importantly, he wanted to discredit the rural supporters of Liuist policies and eventually focused his ideological attack on Liu to try to rectify the entire party bureaucracy.. Mao specifically wanted to create "professional" work teams that would train new party agents in the rural communities to carry out his policies.[43]

Liu countered the Maoist attack by directing an anticorruption movement against rural cadres, thus diverting attention from Mao's real concerns with the political nature of party policies.[44] From 1964 to 1965, many commune, brigade, and team cadres in Huancheng Commune were rounded up, severely criticized during confinement, and fined heavily. Liu devised a bureaucratic means of anticorruption attack. For example, each administrative level was assigned a quota of fines to be squeezed from the rural cadres. Then the work teams set up public criticism meetings where they urged a new group of young peasant activists to voice their accusations about cadre corruption.

"We were rounded up and kept at a 'guest house' in Huicheng," recalled an old brigade cadre in 1983. "No one in the brigade was spared. For a whole month we were made to study party documents and write confessions. I even had to confess how many free movies I had attended and how many pieces of sugar cane I ate while working in the collective fields. I was fined 46 yuan, but I refused to pay. Many cadres were scared stiff. If we did not have enough cash, we had to pay the party some of our personal belongings such as watches and furniture (evaluated at a very low price of course). Telling myself that the whole episode was but a farce, I took the opportunity to take a good look around in Huicheng. However, some cadres felt so humiliated that they refused to resume their posts afterward."

Despite such tough talk, most cadres I interviewed in Huancheng, agreed that the Siqing Movement was personally devastating. In a sense, they were used as pawns in a national power struggle over how socialism should be. The Liuist party organization that they benefited so much from turned around to victimize them in order to save its own neck from Maoist attack. At the same time, the cadres were confronted by internal cleavages that their previous maneuvers had created in the rural communities. Peasants who held personal grudges over what the cadres had done during "the three bad years" attacked with a vengeance. A group of younger peasants who felt left out in the period of prosperity rose to the occasion to claim a share of the privileges.

A new dimension was therefore added to brigade politics in Huancheng Commune. In 1965, the Maoist faction in the national leadership was gaining momentum. As the political winds were changing, rural production teams were consolidated into larger units, and market flexibility vis-à-vis state planning diminished. Brigade cadres were again given the responsibility to oversee and enforce the changing rural policies dictated from the commune and county administration. However, the brigade cadres no longer monopolized brokerage with party superiors. They now had to tolerate the presence of new peasant activists recruited to the political scene by work teams during the Siqing Movement. Some peasant activists were willing to be incorporated into the older cadres' patronage network. They became team heads and joined party youth league branches. With the old cadres, they maintained a united front vis-à-vis the peasant masses.

The ability of the old cadres to survive the retrenchment and the Siqing Campaign, attacked by both the Maoist and Liuist factions, demonstrated two rather paradoxical points. As a group of rural cadres, they consolidated their power position over peasant masses. Despite political factionalism within the national leadership, these local cadres held on to their privileges, using the ideological authority accorded them by Mao and the bureaucratic maneuvers encouraged by Liu. Incorporating young competitors into the elite structure was only an apparent compromise. Instead, by absorbing potential challengers and competitors into their patronage networks, they further buttressed their positions vis-à-vis the masses. The old cadres also participated in the elite network at the commune level administration. In the meetings of brigade cadres called by the commune to distribute grain and other production quotas, personnel matters were settled between old and commune cadres, who had sometimes been "revolutionary pals" during land reform and collectivization.

With increasing polarization of their party superiors in the mid-1960s, this united front of older and younger cadres in the brigades became more fragile. When conflicts of interests arose between them, each group sought the support of patrons at the commune party committee. The security of their positions in the brigade became much more fluid, depending on how political winds affected their party superiors. Only then were the masses able to find a break in the rural elite structure, taking sides with whoever served their interests best. Though the rural cadres solidly held on to their power positions, they were ultimately vulnerable by their relations with party superiors. As later events showed, although they could maneuver in political storms skillfully, they could not prevent their occurrence.

The Reign of the Radicals

Compared to the devastation in the cities, the countryside during the Cultural Revolution experienced only a few ripples. Huancheng Commune was separated from the county capital by a narrow waterway. The bridge that connected the commune to the city became the physical as well as the symbolic dividing line between the pro-Mao and pro-Liu factions. During the height of factional fights in the city, pro-Liu transportation workers moved their trucks to the commune side of the bridge for fear of sabotage by the radical red guards. Rural women from Tianma Xiang had been harrassed by radical red guards at the bridge because of their traditional attire and hair-styles. Under pressure from a divided party committee at the county level, the commune and brigades went through the "rituals" of political struggle. Most cadres were told to step aside, but those with very poor peasant status (e.g. brigade party secretaries at Dajiao and Chengnan, who were old activists) were quietly asked to fill the power vacuum. The commune mobilized and trained its militia to prevent factional fights from the city spilling into the commune area. This was considered a defensive maneuver, but it also gave support to the pro-Liu factions in the city. An old party secretary from Dajiao Brigade was made the "commander" of the militia.[45] When the "revolutionary committees" were established in 1969, old cadres in the brigades went back to their original positions with slightly different titles. For example, the brigade party secretary in Tianlu became the head of the brigade revolutionay committee, a common trend among the old brigade leaders I met. Although the commune cadres exchanged their posts, it was the same group of cadres as before, with a few newcomers. For example, an old peasant cadre in Chengnan Brigade was assigned to take care of commune militia. A younger women party member from Tianlu took charge of women's affairs. An old cadre from a neighboring commune became head of Huancheng. There were cases of old cadres in Huancheng being roughed up during the chaos of the struggle meetings in the earlier part of the Cultural Revolution. These incidents occurred in periurban brigades where city red guards participated. For example, the brigade party secretary in Dongjia at the time, whose brother was head of brigade finances, was beaten up by young red guards during a public criticism meeting on the charge that he and his brother monopolized the politics and finances of the brigade. Still the conflict was based more on personal grudges hidden under political rhetoric. Young activists recruited into party politics during the Siqing Movement were then defensive of their newly acquired privileges and were in no mood to tear down the party apparatus as the radical red guards in the cities had intended. As one old cadre recalled:

> It was an absurd drama with us both as audience and actors, but we did not suffer personally. The Siqing Movement hurt the cadres, but the Cultural Revolution hurt the institutions. We had to play the political game with different rules, but we were still the ones throwing the dice. Sometimes, the issues raised in the struggle meetings and the charges against us were so ridiculous that we did not know whether to cry or laugh (ku xiao bu de). I remember one sad episode with a commune teacher. In a hygiene lesson, he had told his students that in daily wear, the collar (ling) and the cuffs (zhou) of a shirt were most easily soiled. Unfortunately, the terms ling and zhou put together meant leadership (lingzhou), and he was severely beaten up by his students for speaking ill of chairman Mao. How dramatic!

What were the new rules of the game, to be played by both the old cadres and the young activists many of whom were recruited into the party only in 1969?[46] When the unifying party apparatus at the national and provincial levels was torn apart by factional and ideological struggles, cadres at the levels of commune and brigade could no longer use the rules of their bureaucratic organization. Mass elements who became important political actors in the county revolutionary committees were beyond the cadres' control. The evaluation of cadre performances and mutual expectations among cadres were more undefined, and more dependent on individual political choices. Sticking closely to whatever political rhetoric was pronounced by one's immediate superiors became the safest way to steer one's boat in the stormy political waters. Ideology thus became the safest way to legitimize one's actions. However, when ideological rules in the party were substituted for organizational rules,[47] political conflict became much more directly personal. In a sense, both cadres and masses were armed with a weapon—to condemn with political labels. "Dai Maozi" (dunning a political cap) was dreaded because it could lead to personally devastating political criticism and truncated career.[48] Since the Maoist faction emphasized the "criminal" nature of displaying wrong political attitudes, and since one's words and actions were held to indicate attitudes, people were much more cautious about what they said and how they behaved. As a result, everyone was toeing ideological lines transmitted from higher party cadres more closely than they really wished. Such effects were clearly illustrated by the fluctuating policies enforced by brigade cadres in the commune during the early 1970s following major ideological struggles between the reemerging old cadres and young radicals in the national and provincial leadership. As the radical followers of Mao gained influence in late 1975 until their fall in late 1976, radical rhetoric dominated the political scene. Commune and brigade cadres correspondingly pushed radical policies to the detriment of production, disregarding peasant resistance. Ideological domination was so strong that not until late 1978, two years after the fall of the Gang of Four, did commune cadres in Huancheng dare to relax their policies.[49]

Growing Grain as the Basis

During the reign of the radicals, several policies greatly affected peasant livelihood in Huancheng: the imposition of an increased grain quota, the "democratic evaluation of work points," "learn from Dazhai by thinking big and doing big," and the transition to brigade accounting. The grain quota in particular was a very sore issue for both brigade cadres and peas-. ants. In 1969, the brigades were urged to sell more grain to the government to build up state reserves to prepare for war.[50] The brigades in Huancheng reduced their own grain reserves to meet the demand. However, the state subsequently fixed the increased amount of sale as the brigades' "above quota grain" to be sold to the state. In order to not be accused of "not taking grain as the basis," a radical political slogan in the early 1970s, brigade cadres forced teams to take cash crops off their land to make room for growing grain and other food crops. When team leaders refused to cooperate, brigade cadres had to enforce the policies personally. Peasant subsidiary activities such as handicraft and petty trade were restricted in an effort to keep peasant attention to grain growing. During the height of the radical rhetoric in 1975 and 1976, cadres in Dongjia Brigade allowed each peasant household to raise a maximum of 10 chickens. In Chengnan Brigade, another periurban community, handicraft production was centralized by the team and workers were given work points. When violations occurred, team leaders often turned their heads away letting the brigade leaders enforce the unpopular policies. In Huancheng where cash crops were grown on half of the cultivated land and subsidiary activities had traditionally been an important source of peasant income, such radical policies deeply hurt peasant livelihood and production incentive. The tension was particularly great in periurban brigades where the traditions of handicraft and petty trades were strong but where the cadres were former activists/ideologues who were eager to toe the party closely. Cadres in Dongjia Brigade who had been recruited into the party around the time of the Cultural Revolution recalled that, in early 1976, they led a group organized by commune cadres, composed of party line youth league members in the brigade and the commune market town, to do political work in the teams. One of their jobs was to uproot cash crops in the collective fields to make the team members grow grain instead.

In the brigades farther away from commune headquarters, brigade cadres who were more sympathetic to the peasants would cooperate with them to cheat the commune and county officials.[51] For example, in 1975, the county government insisted on mizhi, the intensive planting of rice. Leaders in some of these brigades required the teams to apply this method only in fields along the main roads. When the county officials came to look around, they were shown only those fields. According to old cadres interviewed in 1983, such cheating would not have been easy if it were not for the implicit agreement of the commune head who was the brigade leaders' "old revolutionay pal."

Overemphasis by the party and state on grain growing often led to overuse of land, the disruption of crop cycles, and the disappearance of certain traditional crops. In Huancheng, tangerine growing nearly disappeared; spring vegetables gave way to winter wheat. In some years when commune officials pressured the brigade cadres to meet grain quotas, grain allowances for the peasants were cut, indicating that for fear of being reprimanded by their superiors, brigade cadres had 'offended' the peasants under their power. For example, in Tianlu each adult laborer was to be guaranteed fifty jin of grain distribution per month. Supposedly, brigade cadres would force team leaders to deliver grain to the state only after the peasants' minimum requirements were met. However, in most years, an adult peasant was guaranteed much less grain. Dongjia Brigade had a lower grain yield than

TABLE 1.3
Guaranteed Grain Allocation in Huancheng Commune and Selected Brigades

Year	Commune Average	Tianlu Brigade	Dongjia Brigade
	(jin per adult per month)		
1962	38.1		
1963	40.3		
1964	36.6		
1965	38		
1966	38.9	40.8	36.9
1967	43.8		
1968	41		
1969	37.5		
1970	33.3		
1971	36		
1972	39.1		
1973			
1974	47		
1975	37.9		
1976	37.8		
1977	44.4		
1978			
1979	39	38	36
1980	43	43	41
1981	34.7	36	28
1982	41	48	32

Tianlu, and there each adult was given a smaller amount of grain per month (see Table 1.3). In 1970, the amount of grain distributed to commune members was very low (33.3 jin per adult per month). This was probably due to a combination of bad weather and politics. Rice yield for that year was low (842 jin per mu on the average). Moreover, due to the government's call to contribute grain reserves in preparation for famine and war in 1969, brigade cadres had little grain left for maneuver. Most brigades cut the guaranteed amount of food to the peasants in order to meet their government's delivery quota on time. This heavy grain quota was an extremely sore issue for the cadres because they felt that the state put them in an impossible and unpopular position relative to their communities. Whenever I mentioned the issue to the brigade cadres interviewed, everyone, without exception, swore loudly and expressed their anger against the commune and county officials. In one interview in 1982, a couple of cadres shot up from their seats and pounded their fists on the table, and appeared embarrassed that they lost their composure in front of a guest.

Learn from Dazhai

Meanwhile, peasant labor was mobilized to "greatly change the landscape" in the spirit of "Learning from Dazhai."[52] In 1975, over 20,000 laborers were organized for over a month in winter to participate in the commune's highway-dike project. County officials were determined to make a model of it and ignored the protests of the eight brigades whose land was affected. After spending the labor time required and over 500,000 yuan (the commune's accumulated reserves), the project was abandoned half way through. Income producing fruit trees were cut, some brigades lost precious cultivatable land and labor power, the commune spent its reserves, but the peasants never got the electricity or the pumps from the county administration required to make the irrigation system work. The restructured canals blocked waterways that peasants in the area had always used for transportation, causing great inconveniences.[53] When asked why they allowed such a wasteful and unrealistic project to be conducted, old commune and brigade cadres interviewed displayed a general fear that their superiors would reprimand them, or remove them from office. It seems that the gap between peasants and cadres had widened greatly by the 1970s, and the cadres basically wanted to hold onto their privileges at all costs.

The Democratic Evaluation of Work Points

The democratic evaluation of work points was another sore issue for the peasants. Since the late 1960s, brigade cadres had been instructed to follow the Dazhai example and assign work points to each laborer based partly on their physical performance and partly on their political attitudes and activism. Meetings were held when each laborer presented his own evaluation of his work for approval or disapproval by his teammates. An example from Tianlu Brigade illustrates the problems. The old brigade leader recalled:

> In the beginning we instructed our team leaders to hold a meeting once a year. However, our teams were very large, the largest having over 1,000 people. Relatives and friends bickered over attitudes and worth. Nobody ever felt that they had a fair evaluation. The ones who talked loud and intimidated others got the most. We tried evaluation by work groups within the teams. Some met once a quarter, then once a month, once a week, and even once every three days. Nobody wanted to be stuck with a low value for any long periods of time. Women cried and men fought. Feelings were hurt and production was paralyzed.

Brigades tried the evaluation in different ways, and many reverted to the old system of piece rate. When radical rhetoric waned in 1972 and again in 1974, piece rates were officially enforced, but when political campaigns were pressing, the brigade leaders at least made the teams go through the radical motions. "We lost either way," commented an old cadre. "If we press hard on the masses, they complain, refuse to cooperate, or cheat. If we yield to their wishes, they said, 'we are all in this game together; don't give us lessons about socialism or claim moral superiority over us.' Being a party member in a sense became a stigma; it is only a means to some power and privilege that the party superiors care to hand down to us."

The Development of Brigade Enterprises

Another structural change that affected the political dynamics of the brigades was the development of brigade enterprises. Brigades started to develop small-scale enterprises in the early 1970s in response to the political calls for self-reliance. Brigade enterprises were those that serviced agriculture cheaply, such as grain mills, oil presses, machinery and tool repair; those that processed local cash crops, such as palm handicrafts, winemaking; and those that subcontracted with county industries, such as chemical processing of machine parts, sewing clothes for export, recycling industrial waste, etc. Brigade cadres considered the third type most desirable because it was least restricted by weather or crop conditions. It required little capital but introduced industrial knowhow and discipline to the workers. Moreover, its profit margins were high.[54] Periurban brigades were particularly endowed with connections to the county industrial and commercial complexes, and their surplus rural labor also needed employment opportunities. In many periurban brigades in the area, enterprises were taking an increasing number of younger, more educated women workers from the production teams. However much individuals were willing to work in brigade enterprises, the teams in the brigades were reluctant to give up their male laborers due to the demands of agriculture.[55] The teams were caught in a difficult position. Huancheng has been a very densely populated commune. In the late 1970s, cultivable land per capita was 1.2 mu. There was a serious problem of underemployment in the villages. However, the increasingly intensive agriculture (with multiple cropping, construction projects, etc.) also caused seasonal labor strains. On one hand, the teams welcomed the enterprises because they provided extra income for their labor surplus. On the other hand, radical party superiors could accuse team and brigade cadres of allowing nonagricultural activities to disturb grain production. Furthermore, brigade enterprises under contract with county factories were disturbed when their workers were called back to the fields periodically to meet agricultural work.

Conflicts also occurred between brigade cadres and workers as well as among team members over such issues as recruitment and wages, as illustrated by the experience of Dongjia Brigade, which had enjoyed the best enterprise development in the commune since the mid 1970s. Industrial wages were higher than agriculture income in the teams. Eager workers accused team and brigade cadres of favoring friends and relatives in the recruitment of enterprise workers. During 1976, brigade cadres in Dongjia tried to distribute worker's remuneration in the form of work points corresponding to the value of the teams in order to stop members from competing fiercely for brigade enterprise jobs. However, such measures created conflict among enterprise workers who came from different teams and who worked at similar jobs; but they were given different rewards due to the differences in the value of work points of their teams. Brigade cadres who had to make the decisions again found themselves entangled in accusations of personal favoritism and unfairness. Such accusations surfaced most acutely during political campaigns. Thus, while brigade cadres had acquired economic power at the brigade level to distribute favors to their peasant clients, their maneuvers around structural problems of reward and recruitment also triggered conflict between them and the team workers. Such conflicts sharpened during the reign of the radicals, when opportunities outside of the collective sector were not readily available. The resources in the collective sector were thus fiercely contested, and defended by whoever had access to them.[56]

The Transition to Brigade Accounting

Increase in the political power of brigade cadres over team workers associated with the development of brigade enterprises may be demonstrated by an account of Sancun, a brigade in Huancheng that made the transition to brigade accounting in 1978. The radical wing in the national leadership had often stressed the necessity to advance economic accounting from team to brigade and eventually to commune administration as part of the effort to socialize agriculture. They argued that brigade accounting would eliminate income differences between teams and centralize the use of land and tools, just as the transition to commune accounting would eliminate differences between brigades.[57]

Through personal connections, beginning in 1973, cadres in Sancun had developed a few prosperous enterprises. Consequently, the economic strength of the brigade over that of its six teams increased in terms of production value, labor force employment potential, and accumulated capital. In 1978, the county party committee, though disturbed by the political struggle in the national leadership, decided to make a limited effort to please some radical superiors. The county party committee applied pressure to the commune and brigade cadres to use Sancun as an experimental case for the transition to brigade accounting. Sancun's teams had much the same in resources and income, and the brigade enterprises were doing fine. The county committee calculated that if the brigade pooled its resources with the teams and set work point values for everyone, workers in the poorer teams would welcome the idea. They felt that workers in the richer teams would probably not object because they still came out ahead. In response to the scheme, the brigade cadres at first resisted, knowing well that most peasants would object to the likely loss of autonomy to use their resources. However, the cadres did not want to offend their superiors on the county party committee who could reward or sanction them. In consequence, the team members were notified of the new policy, which was implemented after very brief public discussions. The brigade contributed most of its enterprises' accumulated resources into distribution in order to raise team income. However, disincentive among team members prevailed. Moreover, in 1979 brigade enterprises began to feel the pressure from retrenchment in the state industrial sector. The normal sources of their contracts had closed, so that enterprise activities and income decreased sharply. As a result, the brigade's work point value dropped, confirming the fear of the skeptical team workers and exciting new anxieties. In 1980, the brigade quietly reverted to team accounting with the tacit approval of the commune party committee. In the team members' eyes, the experiment was merely one more example of the party cadres' lack of judgement and insensitivity to the villagers' opinions and interests. However unwilling the brigade cadres had been initially to undertake the task, they quickly yielded for political reasons to the county officials; but the speed with which the change was implemented also demonstrated the administrataive power the brigade cadres had over the lives of the villagers.

At the same time that brigades were developing their enterprises, the commune administration expanded the number and scale of its own enterprises. From 1969 to 1979, six new enterprises were added at the commune level, while the work force increased from 602 to 1355 and production value increased three fold.[58] The older brigade cadres were systematically transferred to the commune level to provide the political leadership of these enterprises.[59] The motives for the transfer of old brigade cadres to the commune differed in various periods. In the early 1970s, when the commune had to cope with radical rhetoric from the county party committee, old brigade cadres who were once very poor peasants were appointed to commune enterprises to ensure that the new commune enterprise would not "deviate from their agricultural orientations."[60] It was assumed that old cadres were loyal to their rural communities and would therefore make sure that the enterprises serviced agriculture. Moreover, radical elements in the county and commune leadership wished to replace aging brigade cadres with younger people who had been recruited during the Cultural Revolution and were presumed to sympathize with radical measures and aims.[61]

In the late 1970s and early 1980s, some old brigade cadres were also transferred to the commune level but for quite different political reasons.

Party reformers under Deng Xiaoping had assumed control of the national leadership by late 1978, and they insisted on removing old cadres who were considered technically and politically unprepared to administer the reforms. The national leadership wished to replace these old cadres with younger entrepreneurs who were technically more efficient and were willing to innovate. Brigade leadership in Huancheng and elsewhere underwent a structural change: Old cadres who had risen to power during the 1950s and became entrenched in the social and political networks of their communities were removed. Their work with commune enterprises increasingly drew their attention to politics at the county industrial and commercial complexes.[62] The removal of old brigade cadres from the rural scene broke whatever personal links the commune level cadres formerly had with the brigades. Hitherto, at commune and brigade levels, cadres who were old comrades from the land reform and collectivization campaigns could mediate and negotiate party policies and use personal influences. They had built particular ties based on sharing personal and institutional histories of party involvement and political work. These ties disappeared when the new brigade cadres replaced the old activists. Ideological pressure from the commune and county administration was applied to brigades with little mediation. On the other hand, when ideological pressure failed, there was little the commune cadres could do to influence the brigade cadres. Thus the brigades became more distant from the commune administration. When the national leadership started to push its agricultural reforms with increasing forcefulness after 1980, the countryside became a battle ground between those middle-aged cadres who had risen in the late 1960s and early 1970s and controlled the collective sector by implementing radical policies and the younger technical oriented peasant-workers who eagerly wanted the recent agricultural reforms, and who were cultivated by the new party leadership to become the next generation of rural cadres. However, in late 1978, two years after the radicals at the national leadership had been removed from power, rural cadres as a group held their positions and power unchallenged. The peasants' livelihood was still controlled by the collectives and thus depended on management by the cadres. Though talk of reforms was in the air, no one wanted to stick his neck out until the direction of the political winds at the party center had became quite clear.

The process of state penetration of rural communities had been mediated since 1949 by two generations of local activists who won their positions by combining personal charisma, skillful opportunism, ideological leadership, and party affiliation. Some peasants may have treated these cadres with the kind of awe and respect they used to give to officials in the traditional order. However, more awe than respect was given. In the eyes of the older peasants, the traditional landed gentry who acquired official positions were often feared and respected by peasant masses. They were educated, owned land they acquired by their wealth, and many became officials after passing difficult civil service examinations.[63] As mentioned above, such cultural assumptions about the legitimacy of the traditional landed gentry were not destroyed, when the "local bullies" who were regarded as aberrations of the traditional order were eliminated during the 1950s land reform. In contrast, the party cadres of the socialist period had come to power by participating in the Communist party and advocating an ideology that was alien to the peasants,[64] and remote from their social world. Moreover, after collectivization, cadres' actions were accountable more to their party superiors than to the communities from which they came and now controlled; and as the history of these two decades shows, state penetration into the communities by means of cadres brought continuous hardship to the peasants. The power of the cadres and their ideology were not accepted as legitimate by the peasant masses despite their prolonged compliance.

Reforms in the 1980s

A resolution of the central committee's third plenum in 1978 finally gave the signal for drastic rural reform. New systems of production responsibility were tried experimentally, and then actively implemented after yielding positive results. From 1980 on, increasingly bold measures were taken to decollectivize the rural economy and population. Not only were production resources and responsibilities transferred to households and individuals,[65] and rural marketing promoted vigorously to encourage specialization and entrepreneurship, but in September 1983, the commune organization was dissolved. Xiang (township) and cun (village) governments were set up to replace the former commune and brigade administration. Cadres in the xiang and cun signed and enforced contracts, supervised tax responsibilities and state purchases, but no longer managed peasant production. Former commune and brigade enterprises now became independent economic units (collective or taken over by individuals), creating their own business connections with state agencies. Rural labor was allowed more mobility and freedom to work in the reviving market towns.[66] Households having workers with specialized skills were exempt from grain quota obligations to promote further specialization and commodidization of agriculture production. The accelerating pace of the reforms was due partly to the party's reaction to their evidence of success, and partly to unexpected problems that arose along the way. Thus, the revival of old market towns was actively promoted to solve the problem of growing rural labor surplus under the more efficient agricultural system in densely populated areas.

Reactions to the reforms varied with local political history as well as the structural relationships between the brigades and the socialist economy. Amidst general enthusiasm for the reforms there were some mixed feelings.[67] Older peasants were at first more apprehensive. Many who had had rough lives in prerevolutionary days were more tolerant of the shortcomings of the socialist period. As they said, "We had seen worse times when we had no legitimate claim to anything," but now, "when we are old and weak, we are left on our own." This reaction was common in households with little labor power who knew that they would lose out in the open competition for limited resources and opportunities. After many years of compliance with party policies, such people feel they have been treated unfairly.[68] By this year, 1985, when specialized households (zhuanye hu) were relieved of grain quotas and allowed to prosper freely, older peasants having wide social networks and traditional craft skills have set up many new rural enterprises.[69] At the same time, young laborers are forming their own social networks. Households with young, strong workers are most enthusiastic about the reforms. In periurban brigades, young masses were moving to the county captial to work in construction and other odd jobs even before the brigade cadres were ready to implement the reforms.[70] As a result, when land and other resources were finally distributed to local households for use, women, old people, and children were left to take care of the fields. Some households therefore refused to take the land and the associated responsibilities and left the area altogether. In a brigade a short distance from Huicheng, a few households moved to a neighboring county to seek contracts for fish rearing and other opportunities arising in the special economic zones around Hong Kong and Macao. In 1982 thirty-five percent of the brigade's labor force commuted to Huicheng and Jiangmen to work, despite the unwillingness of brigade cadres to let them go. By then, most of the young male workers felt that they were no longer dependent on the collective for livelihood and therefore ignored the cadres' wishes.

There has been a trace of desperation in the ambitions and energies of these rural youths. Given past political experience, they are not sure how long such liberalization will last, and they know that they will not have the power to prevent its reversal. Therefore, they are "gambling with themselves" (pingming chu gan) to create at least some profitable niches before another political reversal confronts them. As the policies of the current regime have taken root, these young peasants have become bolder in their economic endeavors. Some have made long term moves.[71] Given the peculiar link between Huancheng and Hong Kong through emigration, the young peasants are contacting their friends who, one way or another, have gone to Hong Kong to work. The latter have become a major source of information on markets, captial, credit, employment, and technology.

Those old cadres who remain in the countryside not only share the apprehension of the old peasants but also feel doubly betrayed by the party they had served faithfully for three decades. They were forced to retire during the party "rectification" campaigns in 1982 when brigade and team leadership in Huancheng were trimmed, but they were too old and unused to field labor to make good use of the land allocated to them. The collectives that they built, directed, and profited from disintegrated in front of their eyes. As some said bitterly, "During the 1950 land reform, we took the land from the landlords and "bullies," now the peasants, together with the party, are taking the land from the collectives. It seems that all the effort we put in to transform the countryside vaporized into the air in such a short time. We made a full circle back."

The younger cadres who became brigade party branch secretaries in the radical mid-1970s were most vehemently against the reforms and came into open conflict with the young entrepreneurs who clamored for the division of the collective resources. Ironically, these cadres were made responsible for implementing the reforms since they were the party officials. To cope with the conflict between the new reform ideology and their own ideas and interests, they stalled and tried to sabotage the reforms in various ways, for which they were subsequently criticized by their party superiors.[72] These cadres are now demoralized. The economic basis of their power has been removed by their sponsor, the party, which had selected and legitimized them. They had followed the party line closely at the expense of their good relations with fellow villagers. The party had then turned around abruptly and called for entrepreneurship by younger peasants and workers who could afford to ignore them altogether. With the collective economy only nominally alive, they no longer had roles of managers and middlemen. Some peasants hailed these changes as "a second liberation."

To make matters worse for the cadres, they were sometimes blamed for not doing their job. During the recent party rectification, some cadres who had resisted the reforms were discredited. Unpopular cadres who were voted out of office during recent elections found it difficult to "be one of the masses." In some cases, villagers refused to include them in collaborative work projects. The former cadres have thus become outcasts, resented by the peasant masses as corrupt local bosses and now abandoned by the national party leadership who insist on different ideological principles. The stage is set for the induction of another generation of party cadres in the changing economic landscape. For the rural cadres, the recent reform program instigated by the national leadership is but another sad reminder that however "sheltered" they are from local opinion, they are always vulnerable to the vicissitudes of national politics and highly dispensable.

Rural and urban reforms are being pushed with increasing intensity. At the same time, the party bureaucracy at all levels has undergone one of the most thorough rectification campaigns in the party's history. The party leadership is by no means in agreement concerning the political direction of the country. However, the economic setbacks caused by bureaucratic ignorance and worker disincentives, and the ideological disillusionment of all sectors of the people, have forced the reformers to realize that they have to do something drastic to ensure the party's political survival. Current reform programs aim at reducing the power of bureaucratic control over economic decisions. Market principles are encouraged to allow competition and incentive among producers in order to achieve some allocative efficiency. Technical experts are respected. By recruiting these experts into the party, political leaders hope to eventually change the nature of the party itself. Who will throw the political dice next, and how, with what effect for the decades ahead. These are questions gnawing the minds of many.

Concluding Remarks

During thirty years of socialist experiment in the Chinese countryside, a few "political generations" of party cadres emerged in the creation of the collective structures that formed the basis of their power. They were successively recruited during the periods of land reforms, collectivization, communization, Cultural Revolution, and post-Mao reforms. By the late 1970s, the collectivized economy had drastically reduced alternative channels of material well-being and mobility for most rural residents. Accordingly, the stakes in the collective sector were high. As power relations between local cadres and their fellow villagers changed from community activism to ideological and bureaucratic domination of the latter by the former, the gap between these strata widened.

Peasants tried to influence their local leaders to protect them against state demands. At times, the cadres colluded with the community to cheat the state and to distribute favors to the local communities. However, the cadres were often more anxious to perform the wishes of their party superiors who held the ultimate power to assign them privileged positions or to dismiss them. Such anxiety largely explains why they would implement even the most unpopular policies transmitted by their party superiors, at the expense of their communal obligations.

The rural cadres therefore created an ultimate paradox for themselves. Their very monopoly of power and privilege over peasant masses in the collective economy were drawn from their vulnerable party affiliations. In their relations with the party-state, the rural cadres could never control the ideological tune their party superiors composed; they were always obliged to dance to it or to improvise. In the process, they made themselves villains in the peasants' eyes.

The dilemma of the rural cadres reflects larger issues of how the interaction between state and society has been structured in these three decades of socialism. With its ideology and organization, the party established a state that dominated society by eliminating the cultural, economic, and political bases for social groups that could challenge party authority. In traditional China, the state shared its power with regional elites who were both promoters of state ideology and representatives of their communities. The Confucian traditions also allowed that state power could be legitimately challenged by kin and community concerns, and recognized that the mandate of heaven accorded to emperors could be revoked. In the socialist decades, however, community and kin concerns were attacked as feudal and stigmatized. Socialist land reform eliminated the economic and political basis of the landed gentry. By the mid-1950s, the economic influence of private industries had been eroded by nationalization of their enterprises. By 1957, the anti-rightist campaign had silenced that section of the intelligensia who had formerly played the role of social and political critics. Thereafter in the cities, a young generation of students and workers were closely monitored by the units such as factories, schools, service organizations, neighborhoods in which they lived or worked.

Corresponding to the above changes, the party-state penetrated the countryside by grooming rural agents to collectivize agriculture. Peasants were thus frozen into collectives controlled by a new rural elite of cadres who found themselves acting more and more on behalf of the party-state, which granted them privileges but also made them vulnerable.

The dilemma of rural cadres also created another paradox for the party-state. Thirty years ago, the Communist party tried to discredit the traditional political economy and its ideological legitimacy by eliminating the landlords and local bosses. Most peasants, however, perceived the campaigns as merely removing "excesses." In the 1980s, in an effort to save its political leadership position, the party has tried to get rid of excesses—this time, the rural party cadres who were accused of having become corrupt, insensitive local bosses. However, the peasant masses, especially the younger generation who experienced the vicissitudes of socialist politics during the past three decades, not only denounce the cadres, but also challenge the political principles that have given the cadres privilege and power. As expressed in the quote at the beginning of this essay, the former member of the party youth league feels that the "socialist system" is problematic.

His skepticism is shared by old cadres who saw themselves as both culprits and victims. As one old brigade cadre soberly commented in the summer of 1983:

> Emperors throughout the centuries had never ruled the countryside, but the Communist party had succeeded in dong so by grooming us as agents. But we are merely agents. Our party higher-ups throw the dice. I followed the party and had my rewards and punishments. But I am also a product of the old society. When socialism no longer works for me, I fall back on the traditions I know. However, our younger generation of peasant masses had it rough. They were taught to believe that only socialism is worth fighting for, yet reality has continuously disappointed them. They had no tradition to hold on to because the party insisted that they should not learn those "feudal values." Whatever they learned about the old society was class exploitation that the party selected out to attack, and fragments that peasant masses retained without grasping where these traditions were rooted. Then they were told to embrace the socialism that has continued to cause them a great deal of personal agonies. After the drama of the Cultural Revolution, everyone grew cynical of political rhetoric. There might be a few true believers, but I think they believed in the ritual more than the content of the rhetoric (kouhao). Yet rhetoric was heavily imposed on our lives, because the national leaders were fighting about it as life and death issues. It became increasingly absurd for us to act out the slogans which were at best empty and at worst ruining our relationships with one another. I am not surprised that the young people feel so fooled (shou pian). Their desperate energy now is understandable. I feel sad that we cadres have been part of their problems. Now the villagers avoided us like a plague. We are stripped of economic control over the peasants, but we are still expected to carry out campaigns. Take birth control. When we go to the villages to try persuasions, all the women in the villages flee. Throughout this century, the Chinese peasants had fled the warlords, the KMT, and the Japanese armies; it is sadly ironical that three decades after the revolution, our fellow villagers are fleeing from us communists.

In a limited way, this essay tries to address debates among China scholars concerning the extent and the means that the party-state has penetrated rural communities. Moreover, by focusing on local activists turned cadres who maneuvered within structures of relations that they had helped to create, the essay addresses a general conceptual concern of the anthropological study of peasants: In complex agrarian societies where distinct hierarchies of power and ideological domination exist, to what extent have peasants contributed in the making of their world and the historical process?[73]

Notes

1. See Helen Siu and Zelda Stern, *Mao's Harvest* (New York: Oxford University Press, 1983) on the disillusionment of youth in China.

2. See Wang Xiaoqiang, "Nongye Shehui Zhuyi Pipan" (A Critique of Agrarian Socialism) *Nongye Jingji Wenti* (February 1980): 9-19; also see a special issue on the asiatic mode of production in *Zhongguo Shi Yanjiu* 3 (1983).

3. Wu Erren, "Bayi Nongmin Dangjia Zuozhu" (Eight Hundred Million Peasants Be Their Own Master) *Renmin Ribao* (December 27, 1982); He Zhiping and Yang Jianbai, "Guangyu Gaixian Dang Dui Jiti Nongye Lingdao De Wenti" (On the Problem of Improving the Party's Handling of Rural Collective Leadership), *Nongye Jingji Wenti* (April 1984): 2-9.

4. From statistics released by China, demographers estimated that between fifteen to thirty million peasants died from starvation-related diseases during 1959-1961. The Great Leap Forward is now officially denounced as a tragic mistake and rural cadres were blamed for making inflated reports about crop yields and peasant enthusiasm. See Mu Fu, "Zhonggong Zhiguo de San Da Cuobai," *Jiushi Niandai* 177 (October 1984): 41-46.

5. For the concept of structuring, see Philip Abrams, *Historical Sociology* (Ithaca: Cornell University Press, 1982); also works by Anthony Giddens, Myron Aronoff, Sherry Ortner, and Richard Madsen.

6. The essay will focus on administrators of xiang (townships) and brigade cadres in the postrevolutionary period. I believe that the xiang and brigade are the crucial points where state and society meet.

7. See Richard Madsen, *Morality and Power in a Chinese Village* (Berkeley: University of California Press, 1984) on a similar approach.

8. Such details may be found in the book manuscript I am currently preparing for Yale University Press.

9. Handicraft workers dried palm leaves to make fans, mats, baskets, etc. Most peasant households had family members working in the trade. Guan Xie Kuang "Jiefeng Qian Xinhui Kuiye Jingying Gaikuang" (A Survey of Prerevolutionary Palm Industry in Xinhui) *Guangdong Wenshi Ziliao* 28 (1980): 187-220.

10. One mu is 1/6 of an acre. The 20 percent figure is common among periurban communities in the Pearl River Delta. See Renmin Chubanshe, *Xinqu Tudi Gaige Qian De Nongcun (The Newly Liberated Countryside Before the Land Reform)* (Beijing: Renmin Chubanshe, 1961), p. 36.

11. It consisted of a cluster of villages or a large village with subdivisions. It somewhat corresponds to Skinner's descriptions of standard marketing communities or minor marketing communities. See G. William Skinner, "Marketing and Social Structure in Rural China, Part I," *Journal of Asian Studies* 24, 1 (1964): 3-43. In the area which later became the Huancheng Commune, there were fourteen such xiang.

12. They were petty officials who aided the county government to keep public order and collect taxes. See Hsiao Kung Chuan, *Rural China* (Seattle: University of Washington Press, 1961) for an overview of rural administration.

13. The famous cases were that between Tianma and Tianlu Xiang in the Huancheng area, and that between Sanjiang and Longcun Xiang farther south. See *Guangdong Siyi Qiaobao* (September 1948): 15-17. The resolution of conflicts in the latter case involved intervention from the provincial government.

14. See Frederic Wakeman Jr. and Carolyn Grant, eds., *Conflict and Control in Late Imperial China* (Berkeley: University of California Press, 1975) on the long process of replacement of landed gentry by local bosses in the Chinese countryside since the last century. Such sentiments in the local area are de-

duced from my reading of accounts of struggles against the bosses and "legitimate" landlords in Xinhui County. See Li Jian and Hong Tao, *Xinhui Zhonggong Baoxing Shilu (The Atrocities of Communists in Xinhui)*, (Hong Kong: Qiaoshing, 1952); see also Zhonggong Xinhui Xianhui Xuanchuanbu, ed., *Xinhui Xian Tugai Yundong Ziliao Huibian (Materials on the Land Reform in Xinhui County)* (Xinhui, 1960). The accounts were confirmed by interviews of old peasants during the last few years. The usual accusations against the bosses were: They were not educated, they engaged in unrespectable trades such as smuggling and extortion, they forcibly recruited laborers and cheated on wages and rent, they mismanaged ancestral trusts, and they had blood on their hands.

15. Guangdong Province, especially the Pearl River Delta, was one of the last areas to be liberated and was tightly controlled by the KMT.

16. See Li and Hong 1952:34 for the struggle of a landlord in Huicheng whom peasants in the area termed "charitable bully" (*xian ba*). He was a leading member in the town's chamber of commerce and was supposed to engage in respectable businesses.

17. Peasant classes were generally categorized as (1) landlords, (2) rich peasants, (3) middle peasants, (4) poor peasants and hired hands. See Zhongyang Renmin Zhengfu Zhengmu Yuan, "Guanyu Huafeng Nongcun Jieji Chengfen de Jueding" (Decisions on Determining Class Statuses in the Countryside), *Tudi Gaige Chankao Ziliao Xuanbian* (Beijing: Wushi Niandai Chubanshe): 29-50. Old cadres in these xiang whom I interviewed in the early 1980s repeatedly identified themselves as former poor middle peasants or part tenant farmers. They said there were relatively few full-time, mobile hired hands in their villages. Quite a few of these cadres also had a few years of education in the lineage free schools, indicating some economic well-being.

18. This kind of attitude was generally denounced by the party as "Wang Shuicheng Thinking"; see Zhongyang Huiyanhui Sheji Kaohe Huiyuanhui, *Gongfei Tudi Zhengce Yu Nongmin Zhuzhi Zhi Yangjiu (Research on the Land Policy and Peasant Organization of Communist Bandits)* (Taipei, 1953): 28-29.

19. These characters are repeatedly indentified by party documents as "brave elements" (*yonggan fenzi*). From the life histories of the old cadres in the periurban communities whom I interviewed, most of them fit such characterization. Their life experiences and quite often their outlook form sharp contrasts with old cadres in the xiang farther away from the cities. See chapter 3 of my manuscript for the life histories.

20. See articles in Huanan Chubanshe, *Tuizu Tuiya Chingfei Fanba Yundong Zongjie Yu Jinhou Renwu (Preliminary Summary and Future Tasks After the Campaigns to Return Rent and Rent Deposits, to Eliminate Bandits, and to Resist Bullies)* (Huanan Chubanshe, 1951).

21. In Huancheng, the prerevolutionary xiang often consisted of a few large villages, which later became higher APCs and brigades. The largest xiang in the Huancheng area had more than 5,000 residents. It was made into a brigade in 1958 and split into six smaller brigades in 1973. There were attempts to redraw xiang boundaries to make them smaller, with 1,500 to 3,000 residents. In the areas under the party's south central bureau, two levels of xiang were often set up (da xiang and xiao xiang), see Zhongyang Huiyuanhui Sheji Kaohe Huiyuanhui, op. cit.: 16.

22. See *Chen Yun Wengao Xuanbian, 1949-1956 (Selected Works and Drafts by Chen Yun)* (Guangzhou: Guangdong Renmin Chubanshe, 1982), and *Chen*

Yun Tongzhi Wengao Xuanbian, 1956-62 (Selected Works and Drafts by Comrade Chen Yun), (Guangzhou: Guangdong Renmin Chubanshe, 1981). Concerning the pace of implementing these policies, the national leadership was by no means in total agreement.

23. See Nicholas Lardy, "Prices, Markets, and the Chinese Peasant," Economic Growth Center, Yale University, Center Discussion Paper No. 428, 1982.

24. See G. William Skinner, "Marketing and Social Structure in Rural China, Part I," *Journal of Asian Studies* 24 (1964): 3-43. He claims that schedules of traditional markets were staggered to allow maximum trade and movement of participants. Since 1957-1958, Guangdong Provincial government, and especially the Foshan Prefecture, fixed the marketing schedules to the 1st, 6th, 11th, 16th, 21st, and 26th of each month. Old peasants interviewed during my fieldwork also claimed that the shrinking social world for the peasants forced them to take brides within the xiang. This occurred even in single surnamed communities; but I do not have figures to back up such claims.

25. Vivian Shue's recent works on center-periphery, state-local political relationships deal with similar problematic; see her paper "The Ghost of Feudalism in the Machine of State: China's Search for Adequate Forms of Local Governance," a paper prepared for the conference "To Reform the Chinese Political Order," June 1984.

26. The former was generally known as the MATs in which households helped each other's production during busy seasons. The latter form was locally known as the "mai chan zu."

27. An example of such mentality is given in the next paragraph. Indication of such mentalities can also be deduced from the difficulties cooperative cadres had in balancing remuneration between labor and property contributions. The more well-off households wanted more for their contributions in land and tools, whereas households with strong laborers wanted more for their work. For discussions of conflicts within the cooperatives, see Wan Nong, *Tantan Nongye Hezuohua Yundong Jeiji Zhengce de Jige Wenti (Discussing Several Problems Arising from Class Policies of the Agricultural Cooperativization Movement),* (Beijing, 1956), and Zhongguo Kexueyuan Jingji Yanjiusuo, ed., *Guomin Jingji Huifu Shiqi Nongye Shengcan Hezuo Ziliao Huibian,* vols. 1 & 2 *(Materials on Agricultural Cooperativization During the Period of Economic Recovery),* (Beijing, 1957).

28. In Xinhui County, 1210 cooperatives were upgraded and merged into 534 higher APCs. The average size of the latter was between 100 and 300 households. There were 24 cases where a xiang was converted into a higher APCs. See *Xinhui Nongmin Bao* November 4, 1956.

29. From the interviews, old cadres described the several "generations" of cadres being recruited in relationship to particular policy phases: They were the land reform cadres (*tugai ganbu*), collectivization cadres (*hezuohua ganbu*), Great Leap Forward cadres (*dayaojin ganbu*), Cultural Revolution cadres (*wenge ganbu*), and the younger, technically competent cadres who have been recruited since 1978 and who are generally categorized as the Four Modernizations cadres (*sihua ganbu*).

30. The government finally required collectives to grant rest days to the peasants. For example, each male laborer was granted 60 to 80 days a year and for the women it was 120 to 150 days. See *Xinhui Nongmin Bao* June 10, 1956. The government move was a response to peasant complaints. From numerous re-

ports in the *Xinhui Nongmin Bao* of labor intensive projects conducted by the higher APCs, one can imagine that peasants in the area were not left alone. In Tianlu Xiang, angry peasants cut down fruit trees to protest what they considered unfair terms of distribution (*Xinhui Nongmin Bao*, November 4, 1956). Anxious government documents warned that rigid restrictions on peasant subsidiary activities and marketing caused native products to have disappeared in rural markets (*Xinhui Nongmin Bao*, October 28, 1956).

31. This three-tiered ownership structure became the basic unit of production and administration in the Chinese countryside until 1983, when the commune was officially "dissolved." Members of production teams worked on the land allocated to the team and shared income from the products. The brigade and commune level of administration operated small-scale enterprises and recruited workers from the teams.

32. Jinniutou watergate and the commune highway were built at that time. So was the commune's major factory—the paper making factory.

33. These event were described to me by old cadres whom I interviewed during the late 1970s and early 1980s. Their stories were reinforced by reports in the *Xinhui Bao* (September 1959), and an article published by the Xinhui County Government in *Guanyu Renmin Gongshe Fenpei Wenti de Diaocha (Investigations into the Distribution Problems of People's Communes)*, (Guangdong Renmin Chubanshe, 1958), pp. 4-11.

34. See debates on agrarian socialism and the dangers of extreme egalitarianism among small producers (Wang Xiaoqiang, 1980).

35. See He Zhiping and Yang Jianpai, 1980. Also see Yu Qinghe, "'Bu Weishang' Yu Tong Zhongyang Baochi Izi" (Not Relying on the Higher Ups and Agreeing with the Party Central) *Fendou* (June 1984): 13-14.

36. See an excellent study by Richard Madsen, *Morality and Power in a Chinese Village* (Berkeley: University of California Press, 1984) on how both cadres and masses created their moral character as the cadres improvised party and state ideology to create the material changes in the countryside and as the masses reacted upon the changes.

37. See the party document "Nongcun Renmin Gongshe Gongzuo Tiaoli" (draft), known as "The Sixty Articles" (1961).

38. The "three freedoms and one guarantee" gave the autonomy of production decisions back to the households. Peasants were allowed to keep their surpluses. These maneuvers were later criticized by the radical faction in the party as deliberate corruption of party policy.

39. See *Xinhui Qiaokan (Xinhui Overseas Chinese Journal)* (1963-65) for descriptions of different market towns in the county: peasant marketing activities, items sold, prices, etc.

40. While prices for cash crops were raised greatly, those of rice and other food crops were quite stable. See *Xinhui Qiaokan*, 1963-65, on prices of agricultural products in the county.

41. See Chen Zhengxiang, *Guangdong Dizhi (An Economic Geography of Guangdong)* (Hong Kong, 1978) on the industrial development of Guangdong Province, especially pp. 103-16.

42. See Dorothy Solinger, "Marxism and Market in Socialist China: The Reforms of 1979-80 in Context," in Victor Nee and David Mozingo (eds.), *State and Society in Contemporary China* (Ithaca: Cornell University Press, 1983) pp. 194-219. One cannot differentiate between Mao and Liu's policies by using the

dichotomies of centralization/decentralization and administrative allocation/ market. Mao centralized ideology, though decentralized organization. Liu depended on state planning and allocation, centralized the state and party organizations, but gave much autonomy to the factories in production management.

43. See the party document known as the Ten Articles "Zhonggong Zhongyang Guanyu Muqian Nongcun Gongzuo Yuegan Wenti Jueding" (Draft); it was revised by the Liu faction in 1964 which in turn was revised by the Maoists. See also a detailed account of the Socialist Education Campaign and the Siqing Movement in Richard Baum, *Prelude to Revolution* (New York: Columbia University Press, 1975).

44. For example, the "Taoyuan experience" was organized by Liu's wife, Wang Guangmei, as a model of rural cadre rectification, emphasizing party discipline.

45. The militia was jokingly known as the 107 worker-peasant militia. The 1 was the pole peasants used to carry cargo, the 0 represented the wide rim hat peasants wore, and the 7 was the hoe they carried. The old militia head was still nicknamed "the commander" today.

46. It is important to note that unlike city cadres recruited into the party during the same period, these young rural cadres were not allied with the radical factions. Old cadres today repeatedly emphasized that these were not followers of the Gang of Four, though they were categorized as the Cultural Revolution generation of cadres. The old cadres to some extent put up with these young activists because the latter had no ideological differences with them. They recommended the activists to be cadres when radical factions in the county administration required the creation of a leadership structure that included younger cadres.

47. See Franz Schurmann, *Ideology and Organization in Communist China* (Berkeley: University of California Press, 1970) on how the CCP uses both ideology and organization in managing the country.

48. Apart from class labels (such as landlord, rich peasant, reactionary, criminal elements, rightist) that denied victims economic and political access as well as socially ostricized them, new ones were invented by factions in the Cultural Revolution, such as "Capitalist Roaders," "counter-revolutionaries," etc. See Hong Yung Lee, *The Politics of the Cultural Revolution* (Berkeley: University of California Press, 1978). See also Anita Chen, Jonathan Unger, and Richard Madsen, *Chen Village* (Berkeley, University of California Press, 1984) on village struggles and their devastating effects on participants. Cadres in my commune also talked about being labelled, but emphasized the highly ritualized nature of the processes.

49. The third plenum of the party's 11th Central Committee in December 1978 signified the winning of the reformist faction in the national leadership. However, in late 1977, a year after the Gang of Four were arrested, the commune still promoted winter wheat, a policy associated with the radicals. Peasants were also hesitant because they were afraid of another policy reversal. Restrictions on rural trade were not relaxed until after 1980.

50. It was the time when the United States was increasingly involved with Vietnam, and China was anxious that she might be drawn into it.

51. Scholars who have done work in other rural communities have observed a certain degree of cooperation among team and brigade cadres to cheat commune and county officials on grain yields and sales.

52. It was a model brigade in Shanxi for the radicals since 1964. The legacy continued under Hua Guofeng until the end of 1978.
53. In Huancheng, like elsewhere in China, there were rising production costs and diminishing returns. In the 1950s and 1960s (except for 1958) costs over production were on the average under 30 percent. In the 1970s and early 1980s the average went over 40 percent.
54. For detailed descriptions and analyses of commune and brigade enterprises in Huancheng, please see my unpublished Ph.D. dissertation, "Economic Development and Institutional Change in a Chinese Commune," Stanford University, 1980.
55. The conflicts of interest among the three administrative or ownership levels of commune, brigade, and team were unique with China's collective agricultural economy. The teams (basically village hamlets) were entitled to work on the land and resources alloted to them since the formation of the commune, and member households shared team income. The brigades and commune were administrative bodies which also operated enterprises. The party cadres in these administrative levels had continued to interfere with team autonomy concerning agricultural production and distribution.
56. In a way, the brigade cadres, through developing brigade enterprises, created a local basis of power independent of their party affiliations. The enterprises allow them to grant favors to peasant clients on their own terms. However, this does not, as some scholars believe, reduce their vulnerability in relation to the state. Brigade enterprises eat the crumbs off the urban state industries, the production and management of which have fluctuated with political campaigns. Huancheng's competitive advantage in the development of collective enterprises (due to its periurban location) also made the cadres extremely anxious about campaigns that could harm the operations of brigade enterprises and their urban patrons.
57. See *Nongye Xue Dazhai*, vols, 1-22 (*Learn From Dazhai*), published throughout the 1970s. Such policy preferences are criticized by the reformers in the 1980s as extreme egalitarianism, as they see disincentive from members of richer teams who feel victimized by the less productive members. The transition, as the moderates insisted, must be voluntary among peasants with the proper economic basis of mutual benefit. The transition cannot be imposed from above by administrative means. With the recent decollectivization procedures, the issue of transition to socialism is no longer raised in party documents or academic journals.
58. The value increased from 1,973,600 yuan in 1969 to 6,380,000 yuan in 1979.
59. See Helen Siu, "Rural Leadership and Socialist Transformation in China," paper given at the 1981 AAA Meetings.
60. In periurban communes like Huancheng, enterprises often took more profitable urban contracts than provided cheap services to the brigades and teams. Huancheng's enterprises, such as the agricultural machinery factory, the construction team, and the transportation team had. been accused of "deviating from the proper tracks."
61. Young party youth league members in commune enterprises (whom I interviewed in the early 1980s) described how they were systematically sent to county "political work camps" in Huicheng throughout the 1970s to learn political skills and then sent to rural brigades in Huancheng and surrounding communes to "tuan dian" (squat in a community). This was to prepare them

for future political work in the countryside. Such training was discontinued in 1978.

62. Again, Huancheng's periurban position caused its enterprises to orient very much to urban contracts. For example, its palm handicraft factories were linked to foreign trade corporations at Huicheng, its construction team contracted itself out to the city's housing bureau, so did its brick factory.

63. See works of Etienne Balazs, Ho Ping-ti, Chang Chung-li, on the imperial civil service examinations and officialdom. "Respect" for education and officialdom penetrated to the peasant masses through official ideological education, and informally through classical novels (e.g. The Scholars), accounts by market town story tellers, folk religious beliefs, lineage rituals, etc.

64. The CCP concept and method of class struggle are examples.

65. See Helen Siu, "The Nature of Encapsulation: Responses to Production Responsibility Systems by Two Rural Brigades," a paper given at the Workshop on Recent Reforms in China, April 1983 (Harvard University). The production responsibility systems were introduced by stages. Bao chan dao hu was tried since 1979, but bao gan dao hu was not introduced until 1982-1983, when work point systems were abolished and households were responsible for production costs fully. In September 1983, the commune and brigade administration were dissolved. In 1984, a central party resolution confirmed that tenure contracts for peasant households should last at least 15 years, thus giving only a nominal existence to collective ownership in the countryside. See articles in Nongye Jingji Wenti (Problems in Agricultural Economy) from 1980-83.

66. They were called peasants who left the land but not the xiang, since their household registration is still rural, and they do not depend on the state for grain rations. They are either supported by grain from their family plots or they buy grain in the market at a higher price.

67. See Siu, op.cit. for composition of two brigades, one in periurban area and the other located slightly farther away from Huicheng.

68. Note the timing of my last round of interviews (summer of 1983) when specialized households were in the process of being promoted.

69. The idea came from conversations with Deborah Davis-Friedmann concerning economic strategies of different age groups in China.

70. The construction workers were getting 10 yuan a day in Huicheng compared to the 25 yuan a month average income in the countryside (1981). The county factories were also ready to hire cheaper temporary labor from the villages because they were undergoing reforms which made them totally responsible on their own profits and losses.

71. For example, some young residents in Huancheng contacted relatives in Hong Kong to buy motor-tricycles to extend the market of their thriving quail-rearing business. An informant who emigrated to Hong Kong four years ago and who learned his skills as a baker has returned temporarily to help his friends set up a western style bakery.

72. I think the party put them in impossible positions and expects these cadres to actively erode the basis of their own power. See official articles against the cadres in Fendou, 1984, Xuexi Yu Xuanchuan, 1984, Renmin Ribao (December 27, 1983), and Nongye Jingji Wenti 1983.

73. This idea originally came from a colleague, William Kelly.

2

Generation-skipping Trusts and Problems of Authority: Parent-Child Relations in the Dissolution of American Families of Dynastic Wealth

George E. Marcus

The generation-skipping or dynastic trust has been the venerable and widely used legal device for preserving private concentrations of wealth in American society since the early nineteenth century. Lawrence Friedman has written (1964) the most thorough account of this instrument from the perspective of legal scholarship. A dynastic trust consists "of a chain of life interests, enjoying income rights, while enjoyment of principal is postponed until the Rule of Perpetuities forces distribution to relatively remote descendants" (p. 548). The Rule Against Perpetuities would limit the life of such an instrument to about three generations or a century. The trust is implemented when the accumulator of wealth dies, and typically affects relations between second generation parents, who receive income, and their third generation adult children, who will receive the principal. The trustee is the representative of the ancestor among the living; who the trustee is and how this position is filled are crucial factors in the politics of the extended family and fortune emanating from the founder.

As Friedman goes on to point out, the generation-skipping trust (Gst) favors lineal and future relatives over collateral living ones, and involves the inclusive distribution of benefits but the exclusive distribution of control of the collectivized wealth (in the position of the trustee). The Gst thus formally marks out a lineage organization in the typically loose-knit network of extended family relations that have characterized American middle-class life and imposes a schedule or program of dynastic longevity upon it as well. While it is commonly supposed that the primary rationale for the use of this trust is the avoidance of taxes, Friedman persuasively demonstrates the dynastic effect of the use of this device, whatever motivates its

51

implementation. As he writes (p. 549): "A well-drafted testamentary trust lasting several generations is subject to only one estate tax, upon the death of the settlor. The intervening deaths of life beneficiaries do not constitute taxable events. But none of the tax savings accrues to the estate of the settlor himself. These savings redound to the benefit of later generations, while the immediate family gives up the right to enjoy unrestricted use of principal. In short, the dynastic trust saves taxes, but for itself, as an entity, rather than for the immediate income beneficiaries." The key point for us here is that second generation parents have little or no control over the inheritance of their wealthier children, vis-à-vis the shared patrimony, and this condition is of crucial importance in the shaping of a dynastic tradition and authority relations within the descendant families.

One reason why the Gst deserves more treatment than it has gotten among social scientists, concerned with elite organization and systematic relationships between property and power, is the increasing frequency of its use (although the Tax Reform Act of 1976 has effectively constrained, but not eliminated, its use in the future). The trust itself is an old instrument of the English common law which was developed on American soil in the courts of early nineteenth-century Massachusetts. The social context for this refinement in transplantation had to do with the consolidation of the colonial merchant elite into the Boston upper-class of Brahmin families, cultural institutions, and corporations (see Marcus 1983 and Hall 1973). The frequency of use of the Gst then increased nationwide during the late nineteenth century period of family capitalism and the expansion of the American economy. Trust companies and the corporate management of private wealth rationalized the dynastic dimensions of affluent middle-class life which the use of the Gst imposed. By 1949, among estates valued at less than $300,000, about 44 percent of their total value was held in Gsts. The percentage increased to 65 percent of the value of the estates of $1 million or more. In 1959, 52 percent of the gross estates worth $1-$1.25 million created trusts; the percentage rose to 77 percent for gross estates worth $10 million or more (these statistics are cited in Tuckman 1973:70).

I offer an ethnographic rather than formally legal or economic account of the Gst; that is, I explore the cast that this device gives to intergenerational relations during a decisive phase in the historic short-term cycles of dynastic organization among American wealthy families. I have found that in some such families, ties among a body of descendants seem much stronger and more organized than in other such families, and that in these former cases, the beneficiaries of wealth have been in much firmer control of their patrimonies for much longer than in the latter cases. A distinctive feature of the stronger families is a dynastic tradition or ideology that seems to have an emotional and cognitive hold on descendants, however ambivalent about it some may be; it preoccupies them. The emergence of a Durkheimian collective representation establishes the psychological conditions among descendants for their active participation in managing their wealth, of which they would otherwise be passive recipients.

I am not so much interested in the content of such traditions (this is a separate topic that concerns the recurrent themes which characterize a quite diverse and idiosyncratic array of dynastic microcultures), but rather in the conditions under which they are recreated or invented after the first generation, and particularly in the factors that make them compelling to descendants. These latter are otherwise thoroughly absorbed in the countervailing trends of mass middle-class consumer culture, which have historically undermined the traditional kinds of family sentiments and sanctions through which classic dynastic tendencies are thought to have flourished. From the perspective of Victorian mores and pretensions about the family, parent-child relations have increasingly become marked by permissiveness and the suspicion of authority.

If the politics of kinship of a former era and the founding generation (e.g., the arrangement of marriages, the choice of children's careers, and the maintenance of functional gender boundaries) is no longer vital, and if the posture of patriarchal authority and the value of family solidarity rituals (annual meetings, etc.) are suspect among self-conscious descendants, then what stimulates the elaboration of and considerable psychic investment in the ideologies which make strong dynastic families active rather than passive in the management of their bureaucratically organized ancestral wealth? I would suggest that one interesting place to look for the source of such dynastic vitality is in the predicaments of parent-child relations, emerging from the distinctive way that the Gst instrument mutually as well as differentially links parents and children to a mature organization of ancestral wealth.

In most contemporary cases of the use of the Gst, its ethnographic or sociological aspects are only of limited interest, because the dynastic dimension of its use is diffused in the administration of property and does not impose or cultivate a distinctive culture within the families involved. Thus, a self-consciously dynastic family does not necessarily follow from the implementation of a dynastic trust; lawyers, bankers, investment advisors, and trust companies through an impersonal division of labor—in short, professional fiduciaries—often become the caretakers of dynastic functions conducted in bureaucratic routines. Their client families are largely free of dynastic authority in everyday life, save for occasional restraint on their spending and consumption behavior, which appears to them, not in the guise of the ancestor, but in that of the formal rationality of the lawyer, the banker, or the accountant.

In contrast to this routine and predominant use of the Gst among the ordinary wealthy, so to speak, I am interested in the role of Gsts within statistically rarer, corporately organized dynastic formations which are major sources of political and economic power in their areas of activity. Internally, such formations append three or more generations of a family to a complexly administered fortune, consisting of ownership and management interests in a number of interlocked "going concerns," as the law calls them—businesses, private corporations, and most notably in mature formations, philanthropic and cultural institutions. These are the archetypal dynasties in American society, self-consciously understood as such by the families involved and by their publics. On a national scale, they are the Rockefellers, Fords, Guggenheims, and Mellons, among others, and on a local and regional scale, they are, for example, the Kempners and Moodys of Galveston, Texas, my particular ethnographic subjects.

Such formations typically last for three to four generations as organized entities, and then gradually dissolve until by the seventh or eighth generation there is a body of moderately well-off descendants who share a privileged belonging to a particular locale or community, which is ensured by the resource of an association with a famous name. This is the resource that is perhaps the most durable of all a dynasty's assets. Until they dissolve into upper-class establishments, situated usually in urban settings (see Jaher 1982), such families are little worlds unto themselves that sustain ambivalent relationships with the institutions of such upper-class establishments, composed of families and individuals, sometimes more wealthy than dynastic formations, but certainly less independently organized than them.

My general project has been to understand the rise and particularly the process of dissolution of such American dynastic formations. There have been two marked periods of dynastic organizing among the wealthy in American history. One originated with the colonial gentry elite, among whom dynastic formations evolved after the Revolution and played out as organizations after the Civil War. The second period originated in the late nineteenth century with the accumulation of massive fortunes from post-Civil War industrialization of the American economy, and the formations resulting from this period of entrepreneurship and accumulation are just playing out in the 1970s and 1980s. Each period of about a century is associated with important moments in the legal history of trusts, as noted above. Each period likewise has distinctly different characteristics, and within each, formations themselves vary a good deal, influenced by the idiosyncrasies of family culture ("as little worlds unto themselves"), by the influences of ethnicity and regional culture, and by the kinds of enterprise in which the fortunes were made. Nonetheless, the use made of a more or less uniform set of perpetuating and consolidating instruments of organization, offered by a national legal system in response to the problem of inheritance, constitutes identifiable cohorts for systematic study of these oddities of American social organization. They are essentially middle-class families, made dynasties by their associations with complex organizations of wealth.

My specific research interest is in the dynastic formations which have developed since the late nineteenth century. First-hand work with two surviving dynastic formations of Galveston, long in the process of dissolution, led me to see them roughly in the comparative context of all other such organizations nationwide that shared their historic experience. It is likely that formations originating after them, in the mid twentieth century up to the present, will have quite a different experience. Economic organization has become much more corporate in character, thus more rapidly dissociating families from functions in founding enterprises as well as cultural institutions. The challenges of public policy to the viability of dynastic wealth have grown much more sophisticated, thus creating still more dependence on the expertise of professional fiduciaries and managers. The cultural underpinnings of the middle-class family, of which dynastic families are largely hypostatizations resulting from the imposed continuity of patrimonial property, have shifted in the direction of what culture critics have called the narcissistic or therapeutic self, suspicious and critically reflective about socialization and authority within family contexts.

For mature old wealth, going through a climactic process of dissolution, like the Kempners and Moodys of Galveston as well as the Rockefellers and Mellons, the temporal insight of the saying, "shirtsleeves to shirtsleeves in three generations," seems to have some validity. From the two periods of their proliferation, dynasties as organized entities *do* seem to last three to four generations, but often they have not begun in shirtsleeves, and certainly, massive concentrations of wealth with their appended families rarely return to shirtsleeves so quickly. There are two prominent and obvious moments that mark cultural conceptions of the three to four generation cycle of organization in American dynasties—the upside, the period of formation, and the downside, the period of decline. For very important cultural reasons the upside has gotten far more attention than the downside both in the scholarly and popular literature on dynasties and in common conceptions of them. For one thing, Americans tend to be more optimistically progress oriented than decline oriented, more interested in the origins of things than in their death. Decline is definitely part of the story, and it reinforces the democratic notion that budding aristocracies *should* not last. Yet, the story of rise from obscurity and dynastic hopes for the future, characteristic as a theme of the first and briefer moment in dynastic development, speaks more strongly to certain aspirations and fantasies of middle-class thought. And it is, after all, the broad middle class who are the main consumers and composers of the cultural narrative of dynasty which permeates the scholarly and popular expressions about them. These middle-class longings consist in hopes for continuity of family, against a reality which makes it difficult. Dynastic sagas, particularly focused on first to second generation relationships, play out these hopes in a way that at least would be realistic for people in middle-class situations to imagine—the self-made person or couple keeping the family together well into the children's adulthood and perhaps beyond.

In contrast to this emphasis in the pervasive cultural narrative on dynasties, I place my emphasis on the period of decline, the long slide downward from the second generation on. Far from signalling decadence or loss of power, I would argue that in dissolution, a dynastic formation generates its most enduring and forceful legacy in its urban and regional environments and in its arenas of economic activity. Complex internal processes of dissolution during this poorly understood phase—the post-entrepreneurial, patrician period of dynasties—leads to powerful and lasting external effects. During this long period, a dynastic formation is a chrysallis for institution building and support; increasingly institutionalized and fragmented itself, it leaves corporate forms in its wake that are shaped by its own internal process of dissolution through the decoupling of going concerns from dynastic management, on the one hand, and by increasing assertions of independence from dynastic caretaking among the body of descendants, on the other.

Dissolution as the direction of dynasty is programmed by legal design and paralleled by the evolution of a family dynastic tradition or ideology, which while not necessarily pessimistic, understands the path of dissolution. In dissolution, the collective wealth becomes a much more complex resource, the control of which is subject to internal factionalization and contestation among its descendants and professional managers in their varied attempts to gain independent use of all or parts of it. Dynastic climax has thus been not only the ethnographic present for my research among Galveston old wealth from the late 1970s onward, but I suggest that it is also the critical period to focus upon in order to understand the most decisive effects of these organizations as particular kinds of elite operators in American society.

My interest here in the role of Gsts as the source of the distinctive dynastic quality in relations among descendant families within mature formations helps me to solve a conceptual problem that I have faced in my Galveston research. This concerns how to grasp the level and nature of organization within loosely structured extended families, in contrast to the tight bureaucratic organization of their collective property. It became clear to me that, at base, what has held most aging dynastic formations together—what has bound families to fortunes—has not so much been a positive, internalized conception of authority emanating from an ancestor or current leader, as the mere entanglements of sharing and benefitting from complexly organized wealth that is given reality through the esoteric knowledge and practice of various kinds of financial and legal experts (see Marcus 1980 and 1983). As a family ages, dynasty becomes more and more a bureaucratic matter of the family office—a coordinating unit which most large fortunes have. Whether or not family leaders retain control over such a bureaucracy, it is the manipulations of wealth performed by experts that at critical junctures present descendants with explicitly dynastic family problems, in the experts' attempt to resolve periodic disputes and challenges that arise both from within and without the dynastic organization, and in so doing, hold the dynasty together, permitting the long-term playing out of the founding ancestor's will in an orderly and predictable process. Thus in many formations, the bureaucratic caretakers of dynastic organizations are the true heirs of the founder, and effectively exercise a surrogate authority for him.

From the point of view of dynastic fiduciaries, the Gst is merely the mechanism for organizing the wealth shares of segment descendant families in terms of the complex arrangements of property, often including the bank which administers the trusts. While descendants themselves may come to share this instrumental, rational view of the Gst, they experience its formal schedule of interests quite differently in their relationships. In particular, the Gst shapes a morality in parent-child relations in which different sorts of linkages to ancestral wealth establish mutual orientations that encourage such conditions as dependency, suspicion, ambivalence, demands for accountability, and sometimes, rebellion. In short, Gst-mediated intergenerational relationships are the crucible in which a dynastic family's self-justifying and self-glorifying ideology is both forged by second generation leaders and challenged from within by descendants. The formal structure of Gst interests has conflict built into it and assures that contestation rather than solidarity will be the environment for assertions of authority and tradition during the mature and dissolving phases of dynastic organization. The challenge for the anthropologist of dynastic formations, in which their appendaged families take active rather than passive roles, is thus to put flesh and blood on the bones of the Gst instrument.

The second (sibling) to third (cousin) generation transition is perhaps the best moment to capture analytically the process by which the ancestrally imposed Gst interests are integrally absorbed into parent-child relations.

The founder is deceased, and second generation leaders and parents are dealing with third generation adult children in the context of the full operation of trust and other organizational instruments. Family relations, then, are set against the relation of the family in general to a complex of trustee and fiduciary positions, which at various loci constitute the structure of control over the collectivized wealth. From the cases that I have reviewed, mature second and third generation relations are the critical phase in the long decline of dynasty. The course of the inevitable conflicts over control and collective arrangements in the third and later generations of dynastic formations are distinctively set in the relation of the second generation to the third, after the founder has become an ancestor. The Gst is the formal mold for intergenerational relations replicated from family unit to family unit among descendants during this critical phase, and thus it provides a focus and leverage for analyzing dynastic culture in the conceptually "messy" familial side of formations, which parallel their neat bureaucratic structures of wealth shares.

The GST in Parent-Child Relations during the Second to Third Generation Transition

The penetration of the structured interests of the Gst into the content of descendant relations might best be understood as a case of the general role of mediations within dynastic families. If there is one feature that does distinguish the lives of the rich, and especially those involved in dynastic formations, from middle-class experience, it is the extent to which they rely on the personal services of others. The rich live in worlds in which their relationships within the family and beyond are pervasively monitored, guided, and represented by third parties, who are in one capacity or another functionaries of the wealth of the family. For example, lawyers, accountants, and investors mediate the relations of the family as whole to its wealth; teachers, servants, and later, therapists mediate relationships within the family, between parents and children, and among siblings and cousins; personal assistants and public relations specialists become gatekeepers between the world at large and members of the family. Finally, and most importantly for the purposes of this essay, the Gst mediates relationships between parents and their adult children.

Hegel's classic discussion of the complex dialectical relationship between master and servant, Simmels' sociometric exercise of reconceptualizing the basic relationship dyad by the introduction of a third, the tertius gaudens, and Toqueville's ethnographic observations about the relationship of masters and servants in early nineteenth-century America all provide suggestive ways for thinking about the nature of mediated relationships among the dynastic rich. But the following points seem the most important to me in the study of descendant relationships. First, whatever the form the mediation takes, it is always some communication about the fact of wealth, of possessing it, or being possessed by it. The mediator, be it a person such as a servant, lawyer, teacher, psychiatrist, or an instrument such as the Gst, is after all only present in the activities of a descendant because the particular organization of wealth in which he or she is implicated makes it possible or (in the case of the Gst) commands it. The pervasiveness and subtlety with which the fact of wealth enters the experiences of the rich are perhaps most vividly represented in the fiction of Henry James, especially *The Golden Bowl* and *The Spoils of Poynton*.

Second, a major argument of my research on dynasties is that as a dynastic organization ages, in relative terms, the force of dynastic motivation and belief moves from the flesh-and-blood descendants themselves to those in the various categories of mediators. While a particular lawyer may not himself express a pro-dynastic ideology, the division of labor of experts, administering the wealth and the family's relationship to it, embodies a commitment to continuity (first of wealth, and then of family), which may be far more enduring and unambiguous than any such similar feeling among descendants from the second generation on. Furthermore, the various sorts of servants and assistants that come between descendants themselves and between the family and the outside world are often stronger proponents, or at least amplifiers, of family reputation and glory than are the people they serve, whose preoccupation with family ideology is fraught with ambivalence. They can be hired and fired in relation to the dynasty whereas descendants cannot be, but as part of their jobs, they tend to reinforce the kinds of images and ideas of family which come to be doubted and contested among family members themselves. Such mediators are middle-class penetrators into dynastic organization, and as such, they bring the middle-class fascination with dynasty to its heart, as an ironic source of support for it in its long dissolution.

Third, and last, the lives of descendants in their relationships as parents, children, siblings, and cousins can be understood as a coming to terms with these sources of mediation, or in different ways attempting to overcome them or see beyond them. To understand the classic notion about the mystifications of wealth in the lives of the rich concretely is to focus on the mediation of relationships that I have described and the attempts of descendants to relate to each other through them. Not only can the internal conflicts that typically occur in the dissolution of dynasties best be understood in this context, but so can the efficacy and compellingness of family ideologies and traditions, characteristic of strong families within dynastic organizations. These conflicts, which are played out in the terms of family ideologies, are decisive in determining the long-term disposition of dynastic wealth in its institutional and corporate legacies.

The specific kind of mediated relationship I shall consider is the imposition of the Gst on adult parent-child relationships. While the Gst does involve the periodic intervention and counsel of human fiduciaries, it meditates through its scheduling of interests as an internalized part of the dialogue between parent and child. The Gst is in a sense the direct and ever present representative of ancestral wealth in their relations.

We can now look at the predicaments of parents in relation to children, as they are tied to shared wealth by the Gst. However, dealing with such shared interests does not usually result in mutuality or a meeting of the minds. Rather, it is likely to produce conflicts, ambivalence, and suspicion in the framework of strong emotional attachments of both parents and children to the objectified idea of family. The conflicts surface as the challenges to dynastic organization and continuity from within that typically arise from the second generation on in American dynasties. At the heart of such conflicts is a dynastic tradition or ideology that is never fully authoritative, but derives its emotional power and compellingness from its being contested and debated in different versions by descendants differently positioned in relation to the collective wealth. While the mediation of the Gst cannot explain the content or particular shape of ideologies that characterize strongly organized families, it does locate the process which motivates the construction of such traditions and stimulates their cognitive hold, that is, the interest that descendants take in stating and contesting them. In many rich families, descendants become indifferent or are only mildly concerned with family traditions. In strongly dynastic families, they worry about them with passion, and this passion, not the authority of patriarchs or parents, gives the body of descendants power over their wealth. The source of this passion about family, however conflictual, is in the differentiation of interests that the Gst comes to impose in second to third generation parent-child relationships.

The predicament of second generation parents is that they have very little authority which is not derived from the considerably autonomous organization of ancestral wealth, yet they are burdened with full accountability for the rule of this organization over themselves and their children. Dynastic authority, as noted, is securely programmed in legal instruments and the work of professional caretakers, and to the extent that some parents emerge effectively as family leaders, it is because they have established for themselves a position of management and knowledge within this complex and technical structure of capital. Authority relations in dynastic families are very much a matter of those who have esoteric knowledge of the inner workings of family capital and those less knowledgeable who become dependent on the former. Often this distinction divides along parent-child lines, and the former (or a subset of leaders within this category) are effectively authoritative as managers in relation to the latter, their descendant constituency.

This familial reproduction in effect of the manager-owner/stockholder distinction, so important in the development of the modern corporation (see Berle and Means 1932), is not registered overtly in the discourses of internal family relations (until disputes lead to embarrassing and painful episodes of litigation in the public arena). Rather, what descendants demand of leaders and children of parents is accountability in the more substantive terms of idiosyncratic family history. The professional bureaucrats of family wealth, who de facto exercise much more ancestral authority in their specialized practice than do parents and actual family managers of wealth, are really not accountable to the family other than in the narrow sense of technical competence (see Marcus 1983). It is rather the second generation parents and leadership who bear the weight of accountability in rich, persuasive terms in response to continual descendant queries about the way that ancestral wealth (and memories of the ancestor) intrudes in their lives. The bind of parents is thus that they become accountable in the sentimental language of kinship for the perturbations of a structure of wealth from which they have a partial, derived authority in family affairs at best.

It is interesting to understand this accountability of parents in both senses of the word—they must give an accounting of wealth management (the defense of decisions made behind the scenes that influence the state of the collective wealth), but they must also give it through an account of dynasty that is more vivid and normative than just columns of figures, that is, through the promotion of a particular sort of ideology for the family. The details of this ideology are in part inherited from the first generation founder, but they are also reinvented by the second generation caught between the superior and autonomous authority of the legal management of the ancestor's will and the burden of doubly accounting for this wealth and its meaning for the third generation descendants.

Conversely, the special predicament of third generation children is their adult socialization into wealth, which involves an acquisition of some degree of knowledge of the dynastic organization in which they are implicated through the structure of Gsts, followed by efforts to change or modify their positions relative to it, as both they and their parents age. Early socialization of the rich, as Robert Coles has shown (1977), has much to do with the inculcation of a distinctive sense of entitlement. Children learn from parents and third parties, such as servants and teachers, fundamental lessons of inequality, that they are special and privileged. Adult socialization involves a growing awareness of family wealth and the controls it exercises, which is the behind-the-scenes source of the earlier more existential lessons about entitlement. This later lesson is often more problematic, since it emphasizes, just as one grown into adulthood, a certain continuing childlike dependency on parents and the more mysterious control by the family office of one's present and future interests. Some descendants are happy with the convenience of such dependency; others are more dissatisfied with these conditions. Any attempt to do something about it means learning about the inner workings of the bureaucratic administration of wealth, challenging second generation versions of family ideology, or both. The second generation of course selects some third generation descendants to know more about the wealth than others in the interest of succession, but other descendants attempt to learn more on their own in order to break the hold of dependency and the convenient caretaking it offers. Demystification of family affairs sometimes occurs through the formal training of descendants in business schools and law schools, sometimes through the independent hiring of counter professionals.

Perhaps the most decisive growing into consciousness of the structure of wealth behind the privilege that a child learns in early socialization occurs when she realizes the different formal configuration of personal interests in the collective wealth between her parents and herself. Depending on the nature of family ideology, this does not always lead to open conflict or immediate rebellion, but it does create an atmosphere of ambivalence and suspicion that becomes increasingly consequential in the negotiations, if not conflicts, that bring about the dissolution of dynasty and the decoupling of shares of wealth and controlling ownership of businesses from collectivized family interests.

The related and combined predicaments of parents and children should thus be seen in the context of Gst interests in order to appreciate fully the potential for suspicion, challenge, and conflict that exists as a third generation reaction to the strong motivation of the second generation to promote a family tradition or ideology. The weight of the ancestor's gift does not fall upon his own children through the Gst, but upon his grandchildren. They will bear the burden of using this wealth and also of the final taxation of it. This creates a linkage between the third generation and the founder from which the second generation is excluded. The independent parental authority of the second generation thus tends to be overshadowed, since they have little ability to influence either their children's access to the collective wealth or what it means to them symbolically.

Between the bequest of the founder and its ultimate receipt by the third generation, second generation parents receive the income from the Gsts, not particularly as wealth with the moral associations and burdens of a gift, but as capital which they can use in any number of ways. They can build their own fortunes with it (and thus initiate new Gsts which will put the third generation in the middle of a legacy, as they themselves were), they can spend it on themselves, or they can spend it on their families. The point is that third generation children will receive a portion of wealth, independent of their parents' will or control, which has a different moral and symbolic significance than that of the wealth as income which their parents enjoy (most receivers of trust principal rather than income think in terms of philanthropic or monumental uses of it, for both tax and sentimental reasons). The second generation's mode of inheritance is more flexible and essentially less responsibility laden than the form in which patrimonial wealth comes to their children. Yet, dynastic accountability, as previously discussed, rests with the parents, and not with the children who will come into wealth in a way that ironically seems more suitable to one who has to account for dynasty. While other factors of socialization in parent-child relations often serve to head off conflict, this difference in the way patrimonial wealth is received, place against the function of accountability of the second generation in relation to the third for an organization that the family does not fully control, shapes distinctive kinds of conflicts that typically arise in the dissolution of a wide variety of dynastic formations which append strong families preoccupied with their own character and tradition.

We must finally view these particular conditions of intergenerational relations in terms of the distinction between leadership and collateral lines that usually emerges in a dynastic family after the founder dies. Gst mediated parent-child relations are repetitively played out in each descendant family unit within a dynastic organization. In some dynasties with strong family traditions, no clear leadership line arises in the second generation, and the history of the dynasty is one of enduring competition for relative power positions (as in the case of the Moodys below). In such families organized by competitive relations, the particular parent-child dynamics, described above, are played out with a more or less even intensity across descendant families without the semblance of an authoritative version of family history.

In contrast, in dynasties where there is a marked distinction between a leadership line and collateral lines among descendants (often the line of the eldest male child, as in the case of the Kempners below), the intensity of focus in the development of dynastic authority and tradition skews toward the leadership line. These appear to the casual outside observer to be the classically strongest sort of dynastic formations, where hierarchically organized and cooperating families control the administration of their own wealth. However, I would argue that the conflict/competitive alternative model of dynastic family organization exerts just as powerful a hold on descendants and their involvement in dynastic wealth as does the cooperative/hierarchical model.

In dynastic families with strong leadership lines, the Gst settles into parent-child relations differently within the leadership line than it does within collateral lines. The problem for second generation parents in the leadership line is how to make successors out of their third generation children. The parents are very much in the middle between the ancestral legacy and their children's independent relationship to it through the terms of the Gst; yet, as leaders of the formation, they have assumed responsibility for reproducing leadership roles in their children. Thus, without highly motivated efforts to create dynastic mystique and authority for their own children, as they promote it generally for the formation, the leadership parents are likely to be overshadowed by the legally programmed alliance between their children and grandparental wealth. The dynastic impulse of strongly active families within formations, manifested in the concern with and promotion of a particular family ideology or tradition, does not derive from something intangible in family character or collective psychology, but rather is powered in its intensity by the working out of the structural implications of the Gst.

The same structuring implications of the Gst play out differently in collateral family lines. Here, parental authority is undercut by the effective management control which the leadership line has over the wealth in which parents and children of collateral families are mutually interested through the Gst structure. It is not the shadow of the ancestor which threatens to undercut the parents in these collateral families, but the active management of the leadership line. In a sense, the children in collateral families are more interested in dynastic affairs than are their parents, since their literal interests in the wealth are both greater and future oriented. Parents in collateral families are thus often mere conduits for dynastic authority and culture to their children who look to an uncle, aunt, or cousin for patrimonial accountability. In collateral lines, then, the Gst tends to have a subversive effect on parental authority, within the confines of the immediate family unit; but from the perspective of overall authority relations among descendants, it reinforces the impact of dynastic ideology intensively developed within the leadership family line.

Two Variations: The Kempners and Moodys of Galveston

I want finally to ground the above arguments in necessarily telegraphic interpretations of the dynastic cultures within the two Galveston families of old wealth, which were the major subjects of my research (for fuller descriptions of these families, see Marcus 1980). I have neither the space nor the inclination (having not yet satisfactorily solved the problem of how to present the content of specific relationships in ethnographic detail[1] to lay out here the process by which dynastic ideology is shaped in these families. I merely want to connect in a general way the fact of a distinct ideology in each case, which was elaborated after the first generation, with the particular configuration of intergenerational relationships.

In the late nineteenth century, the port city of Galveston was a flourishing community of merchant wealth. The city and the port declined dramatically during the twentieth century, and the society of wealth disappeared save for three families which continued to prosper primarily in cotton trading, banking, and insurance. These became corporate dynastic formations, which economically dominated their stagnant native city until the 1960s, and then became more detached patrons, self-absorbed with their own internal problems of dynastic dissolution. Even today, the prosperous financial institutions established by each of these families stand in sharp visual and symbolic contrast to their shabbier downtown surroundings.

Two of these families sustain an active presence and interest in the city. The Kempner family originated with a Jewish immigrant from Poland who died in the 1890s leaving a million dollar fortune, a widow, and eight surviving children—four sons and four daughters. Through a series of successful ventures in the early twentieth century, the four brothers greatly expanded the fortune. The eldest brother and his family assumed the position of leadership in a developing formation, the ownership of which was legally formalized in the 1920s. This legal constitution emphasized equal distribution of ownership shares down the eight descendant lines and collective management by the brothers. Reproduction has been much greater in the leadership line than in the collateral lines, meaning that the children of the eldest brother and their descendants have less personal financial ownership of the collective patrimony which they manage for their collateral constituency of cousins.

In this situation, the leadership line from the second generation on has elaborated a family ideology or tradition of altruism. Family stories play up the themes of sacrifice, lack of pretension and conspicuous consumption, good citizenship, and the putting of family values above business ones (although good business sense has certainly been emphasized in the family). There are indeed the elements for this story in the background of ethnicity (being Jewish means, in essence, being clannish) and the personal character and talents of actual family figures, but the compellingness of these stories in their role as legitimizers of dynastic leadership has much more to do with the predicament of accountability that second generation leaders onward have faced in relation, particularly, to their sisters and their sisters' descendants. Suspicion of self-dealing has always been present, though understated. Appeals to altruism, backed up by the manifest fact of the unfavorable financial position of the leadership line in relation to the whole, have always served to temper any suspicions among the descendant constituency (until a recent painful litigation over precisely the fiduciary responsibilities of family leaders emerged in the mid-1970s).

This tradition of altruism may now be wearing thin as the formation moves into fourth generation leadership, but it has not only been an internal matter. It has colored the image of the Kempners in the community, which they have in turn tried to live up to in their projects. The internal ideology of altruism translates into a classic patrician posture in relation to the community. They have always been portrayed as leading citizens of the community, not extravagant in their philanthropy, but personally involved in it, as well intentioned stewards of the public good. This is quite a different image from that of the other major surviving dynastic family in Galveston, the Moodys, who have a history of rivalry with the Kempners (and other families now gone). This rivalry is kept alive in memories and current feelings, but it is effectively subdued, now that both dynasties in the climax of dissolution influence community events with a less determined motivation of domination.

The Moody dynasty also derives from a late nineteenth-century cotton factor and merchant, whose son and namesake greatly expanded the fortune during the early twentieth century. This man operated in the style of a socially distanced patriarch in relation to his children. After the son who had been his chosen successor died prematurely, he established at the death of his wife and in preparation for his own death an elaborate institutionalized structure for his wealth, which would operate autonomously from his descendants, leaving them to compete for commanding positions within this structure. Much of the third and fourth generation history of the dynasty has thus been the struggles among descendants to control the patrimony, not out of sentiments for dynastic continuity, but to gain access to capital for personal business projects.

The centerpiece of the Moody dynasty is a large foundation, which before federal regulation, held the major ownership shares of operating businesses and trusts of the fortune. Internal family politics has focused on ensuring the family's control of the foundation board. Now professionally managed, the foundation operates according to rationalized principles of philanthropic ideology, even though family members are still quite influential in selecting projects. The philanthropic presence and activity of the Moodys in Galveston is much grander than that of the Kempners, but it is also less personal and less integrated into the history of the family. This has to do with the strategic role that the philanthropic institution played in the Moody family of securing the perpetuation of the fortune amidst uncertain relations of trust and power between the generations.

Without a firm leadership line, the parents in descendant families, most active in competing for control of the fortune, have in a sense tried to free themselves from their ancestral legacy rather than to fade smoothly into it. They have thus been actively engaged in making their own fortunes, in reproducing their own father's entrepreneurial achievements, rather than committing themselves to the latter's institutional legacy into which he did not welcome them anyhow. This descendant orientation has led to the creation of a family ideology with a distinctly individualistic, opportunistic, and "robber baron" character. The emphasis for ambitious descendant parents has been not to work for the ancestral legacy but to renew it in their own terms. This involves both trying to be like the father, as a self-made man, but also violating the collective legacy which he left and which, through the Gst, vests directly in their children. Such parents move to siphon off as much capital as possible from the fortune for their own projects—e.g., by attempting to have earnings on capital declared as income rather than principal. This of course results in conflicts of interest with their own children. But the accountability (and the account of family tradition) that they offer is of the promise of their own efforts to renew and create wealth in an active way rather than just preserving it, so as to place their own children structurally in the position they were in relation to the ancestral accumulator by creating new trusts.

The general point here is that the different way the Moody descendants have related to their ancestral wealth from that of the Kempners has resulted in very different kinds of dominant family ideologies. I would argue further that the predicaments of sharing wealth within the Gst structure has had much to do with the direction these ideologies took and with their intensity of interest and expression. Both dynasties are now in dissolution: the Moodys have been marked by overt (and newsworthy) internal conflicts all along, but this is a much more recent and disturbing phenomenon for the Kempners.

Finally, the relationship between the politics of dissolution within these mature formations and the impact that they have had on Galveston has been quite clear. Patrician and robber baron styles, each arising from internal problems of sharing wealth, have respectively dominated the projects of these two dynasties and, in sometimes ironic and indirect ways have affected the dispositions of wealth in their final resting places—the businesses, banks, and charities that will long outlast the familial organization which spawned them.

Conclusion

This essay has explored the utility of the Gst as a framework that permits the ethnographer of dynastic formations to capture or analytically fix systematic intergenerational relations among descendants that are otherwise difficult to grasp. The problem of accounting for strong independent dynastic cultures emergent among bodies of descendants followed from my appreciation of the primary controlling function of the administration by professionals of property in most formations. In total, I conceive of this project as a prolegomena for ethnographic readings of the histories of American dynasties. Dynasties are just one distinctive kind of elite process in capitalist political economy that can be so read. Such projects of ethnography involve special problems of conceptualization, which must expose the intimate connections between interpersonal and impersonal processes, or of men and machines, as Pierre Bourdieu has put it (1981). The crucial problem for this essay in this regard has been the manner in which a particular formal mode of holding property (the Gst) became absorbed into family relationships.

The broader contribution of the ethnographic study of dynastic formations is to the revitalization of elite theory itself. This theory had the potential of demonstrating the systematic connections between wealth and power in capitalist societies, and thus, of filling in the lacunae of the great social theories of Marx and Weber. As theory, reflection on elites became discredited by the heavily, and eventually consuming, ideological atmosphere in which it occurred. As an empirical research tradition, the study of elites has debated apparently intractable issues of social architecture about the cohesiveness, origins, and structure of elite positions and relationships. Their content and consequences are far less understood. This research tradition has likewise had primarily normative motivations and implications. Only with the insight (see Hall 1982) that much of the contemporary structure of mass institutions has evolved from elite sources—from the bowels of elite cultures, so to speak—has the way been cleared for ethnographic studies of the complex transformations of property and power in the routine lives of those caught in the grip of corporate wealth and its power fields, such as the dynastic families discussed here.

Note

1. Interesting differences (as well as methodological and ethical problems) are posed for the ethnographer of American dynasties compared to one of similar lineage phenomena in tribal societies. Rarely in tribal ethnography is there the identification by name of specific personalities and characters in the discussion

of interpersonal relationships within descent contructs—the discourse is generalized. It is Tallensi or Nuer tribesmen who interact, not a specific named X or Y. It is just the opposite with the discussion of dynastic formations—the emphasis is on particular identifiable individuals and idiosyncratic conditions rather than on a standard form of relationship or organization. Dynasts are always specifically a Shrub Kempner or a Mary Moody Northen. While tribal ethnography might have developed differently (and is being so in contemporary experimental ethnographies which tend to identify particular persons in the dialogue of fieldwork), it is difficult to imagine how the subjects of ethnographic work among American dynasties could be generalized or made faceless. This has not been a problem for the journalistic and popular accounts of American dynasties, but it has been a nagging one for me, brought up in a research tradition which has always been uneasy about individualizing the behavior and thoughts of persons in ethnographic accounts.

References

Berle, Adolph Jr., and Gardiner C. Means. 1932. *The Modern Corporation and Private Property.* New York: Macmillan.

Bourdieu, Pierre. 1981. "Men and Machines." In *Advances in Social Theory and Methodology: Toward an Integration of Micro- and Macro-Sociologies.* Ed. K. Knorr-Cetina and A.V. Cicourel. Boston: Routledge & Kegan Paul.

Coles, Robert. 1977. *Privileged Ones: The Well-Off and the Rich in America.* Boston: Little, Brown.

Friedman, Lawrence M. 1964. "The Dynastic Trust." *The Yale Law Journal* 73:547-92.

Hall, Peter D. 1973. "Family Structure and Class Consolidation among the Boston Brahmins." Ph.D. dissertation, SUNY, Stony Brook.

———1982. *The Organization of American Culture, 1700-1900: Private Institutions, Elites, and the Origins of American Nationality.* New York: New York University Press.

Jaher, Frederic C. 1982. *The Urban Establishment: Upper Strata in Boston, New York, Charleston, Chicago, and Los Angeles.* Urbana: University of Illinois Press.

Marcus, George E. 1980. "Law in the Development of Dynastic Families Among American Business Elites: The Domestication of Captial and the Capitalization of Family." *Law and Society Review* 14: 859-903.

———. 1983. "The Fiduciary Role in American Family Dynasties and Their Institutional Legacy: From the Law of Trusts to Trust in the Establishment." In *Elites: Ethnographic Issues.* Ed. G.E. Marcus. Albuquerque: University of New Mexico Press.

Tuckman, Howard P. 1973. *The Economics of the Rich.* New York: Random House.

3

Holiday Celebrations in Israeli Kindergartens: Relationships between Representations of Collectivity and Family in the Nation-State

Lea Shamgar-Handelman and Don Handelman

The object of education, contended Durkheim (1956:71), "is to arouse and to develop in a child a certain number of physical, intellectual, and moral states which are demanded of him by . . . the political society as a whole." Mechanisms of education, he added, are among the major means through which "society perpetually recreates the conditions of its very existence" (1956:123). Durkheim conjoined two themes that are salient for the modern Western nation-state. First, that the political economy of education, especially formal education, is a crucial expression of the ideology and authority of the state. Second, that the reproduction of social order depends, in no small measure, on the exercise of the power of education through the requisite apparatus of the state.

In the case of Israel the tasks of formal education were less the replication of social order than the construction of an ideological blueprint that contributed to the very creation of the state. The fusion of political ideology and formal organization, in order to influence the maturation of youngsters who were the future generation of citizenry, began in the kindergarten.[1] For example, a veteran Jewish kindergarten teacher[2] reflected, as follows, on the intimate ties that developed between the Jewish community, the *yishuv*, in pre-state Palestine and the kindergarten system. These were bonds, she enunciated, between a form of early-age education and "the ideas and aspirations that lifted the spirits of those parts of the nation that rebuilt the ruins of its homeland and rejuvenated this." The Zionist dream of returning to work the land of Israel, she added, "brought the garden into the kindergarten" (Fayence-Glick 1957:141). As in numerous other aspects of the nation-building of Israel, that of the kindergarten was linked closely to the practice of proto-national ideology.

Very young children experience and learn the lineaments of personhood and world through the family arrangements into which they are born. In these contexts they are enculturated into a sense of hierarchy and status, of order and division of labor, of sentiment and loyalty, through notions of kinship and familism that come to be the natural ordering of things. Only later is the child made to realize that parental superordination is itself subordinate to the idea of a wider social order; and that on numerous occasions loyalty and obligation to the collectivity transcends that of familial ties. This transition, however obvious, is crucial to the reproduction of the social orders of the state. It clearly is in the interests of representatives of the state to recruit the cooperation of the family in order to achieve societal goals; and thus they phrase its relationships to the family in terms of cooperation and consensus. Politicians and officials commonly liken the state and its citizenry to a great family; while the idioms of kinship and familism are used in cognate ways.

Yet this relationship between state and family is fraught with tension. This is evident in times of crisis, should officials intervene in the affairs of family; and especially when they insist that organs of the state are mandated to fulfill functions of social control and affect that the family considers its own (Shamgar-Handelman 1981; Handelman 1978). With regard to children and their maturation, state and family do have overlapping and congruent interests; but their concerns also differ and are continually negotiated.

Bluntly put, all children must learn that their parents are not the natural apex of hierarchy and authority; and that the rights of the collectivity can supercede those of familism. This is integral to the process of maturation in the nation-state. In present-day Israel the young child's entry into the kindergarten is the onset of extended periods in educational settings that are regulated and supervised by organs of the state. The youngster is moved slowly during this lengthy transition from his embeddedness within home and family until, at the age of 18, he enters the army for compulsory service. At this time he is given over wholly by his parents to the authority and service of the state. The transition is one from offspring to citizen.

With regard to this transition, kindergartens in Israel are of especial interest, since their annual round is punctuated by numerous ceremonial occasions that, on a wider scale, are of import to the religious and civic cultures of nation and state. Anthropologists are very well aware that ceremonials, whether sacred or secular, are concentrated foci of the explicit and implicit, yet selective, production, display, and manipulation of symbolic forms and sentiments (Turner 1982; Manning 1983; Moore and Myerhoff

1977). During such occasions other themes and qualities of the everyday lived-in world are held in abeyance (Handelman 1982, 1983, 1984). Whether an analysis stresses the semiotics of ceremonial structure (Geertz 1972), or the dramatistics of enactment (Turner 1974), the ritualism of ceremonialism is patterned to communicate in enhanced and pointed ways, regardless of the size or scope of the occasion.

Holiday celebrations in Israeli kindergartens are in keeping with these attributes of ceremonialism. Given the early ages of the young participants the messages of these celebrations, at least the explicit ones, are presented in quite clear-cut ways. Through such occasions children are involved, outside of their homes, in focused representations of culture that, in general, are considered to be of significance to aspects of the nation-state. On an explicit level many of these occasions celebrate versions of tradition and historicity of the Jewish people, and of the renewal and coherence of the Jewish state. Scenarios emphasize the joint effort, the consensus of cooperation, between kindergarten and parent, state and citizen, in order to inform the maturation of the child with experiences that begin to situate his personhood in relation to directives of the past and expectations of the future. On a more implicit level the "hidden agendas" of such scenarios unearth the more problematic relationship between state and family.[3] Thus numerous celebrations can be understood as versions of the relationship between representations of collectivity and family, through which youngsters are shown, and are encouraged to experience, that the superordination of the former supplants that of the latter. This sort of exposure is especially important for children in urban locales where different spheres of living are quite compartmentalized, where settings of home and work are separated, and where the access of children to the world of adults, of hierarchy and equality, is limited. The kindergarten is the first location where children learn of hierarchy and equality outside the home.

This paper discusses four cases of kindergarten ceremonials in relation to the symbolic loads they convey. It is surprising how little sociologistic analysis has been done on questions of whether and how kindergarten youngsters are exposed to the focussed manipulation of symbols and of symbolic formations of a supra-familial character, whether in Israel or elsewhere. Studies of kindergartens tend to emphasize the learning of competence in daily interaction (Jones 1969; Shure 1963; Shulz and Florio 1979). However, our argument is closer in spirit to that of Gracey (1975), who contends that the task of teachers in American kindergartens is to drill children in the role of student and, by extension, to prepare them for the rigid routines of bureaucratic corporate society. Nonetheless, work on ceremonialism in kindergartens is minimal (Heffernan and Todd 1960; Moore 1959); while there are only bare traces of such discussion on higher grades

(Kapferer 1981; Burnett 1969; Bernstein, Elvin, and Peters 1966; Waller 1932; Fuchs 1969; Weiss and Weiss 1976).[4]

We have chosen to interpret and to explicate a small number of cases, from our larger corpus of descriptions of such events, for the following reasons.[5] First, ceremonials have their own integrity of internal structure that conveys the significance of the occasion as a viable performance. This is violated if the event is not described in and of itself. The celebration, at least in part, should become the context for its own interpretation. Second, detailed description and discussion permits the reader to form interpretations alternative to those that we argue for. We hardly would insist that there are singular constructions of significance in such celebrations. Third, with so little attention given to kindergarten celebrations, it is advantageous to have available concrete examples. These may lay out some parameters of discourse for future discussions.[6]

Nonetheless, our interpretations will focus on certain structural aspects of these ceremonials that are related more specifically to our argument of explicit and implicit levels of communication in versions of the interplay of collectivity and family. In particular we give attention to the sequencing of enactments. Sequencing in ceremonial, and in other activities, probably is of signal import in cultures that, according to Lee (1959), are made coherent through lineal codifications of reality, and that have a strong sense of chronology in history and biography. Thus those acts that are placed, for example, "before" and "after" implicate the logic of organization of the whole sequence of enactment. Whether it is put together this way consciously or not, a planned occasion becomes embued with a symbolic load that, in keeping with lineal thinking, takes on much of its significance through its sequencing: through the additive accretion of symbolic acts, and so through the emergence of a more-or-less coherent story line. In addition we discuss the significance of social formations in enactments, and that of prevalent symbols. These structural aspects of enactment will be related to the three categories of person—teacher, child, and parent—whose positioning in relation to one another implicates the rudimentary conceptualizations of collectivity and family that are enacted in the kindergarten.

Therefore the next section takes up the relationships among these three categories of persons, in terms of the ideologies and goals of kindergarten educators in Palestine and Israel. In the context of this discussion, the following section discusses the celebrations themselves.

Kindergarten and Celebration in Israel

The first kindergarten in Palestine was established in 1898, and it was intended as a preparatory class for elementary school. The language of instruction was German, translated into those of the pupils. The first Hebrew-speaking Zionist kindergarten was opened in 1911. Unlike its predecessors it was an autonomous unit for early-age education. In the context of Zionism this kindergarten, its successors, and local seminaries for kindergarten teachers, all freed Hebrew early-age education from the domination of foreign theories of pedagogy. These kindergartens gave especial attention to the cultivation of the Zionist spirit: for example, to the values of working the land and building the nation (Fayance-Glick 1957:141).

By 1919 there were thirty-three Jewish kindergartens in Palestine, with a total of 2,525 pupils. Some coordination of kindergarten policy and curricula was instituted during the period of the British Mandate, on the part of the educational department of the Zionist governing bodies of the *yishuv*. Nonetheless, the prevalent pattern was of a variety of kindergarten frameworks, Zionist and other, that were subsidized in part by numerous sources, and whose programs of instruction were supervised in varying degrees.

With statehood, in 1948, kindergarten education was centralized. The Law of Obligatory Education, promulgated in 1953, made kindergarten mandatory for children at age 5, and placed the supervision of kindergartens under the aegis of the national Ministry of Education. Numerous kindergarten classes were opened for children from the age of 2 and above. From the 1920s until the present the demand for places in kindergartens almost always exceeded those available. In 1982-83 some 250,000 children, between the ages of 2 and 5, were enrolled in 2,035 kindergartens. Of those aged 2, 63.6 percent were enrolled; while for those aged 3 and above the equivalent proportions were over 90 percent (*Statistical Abstract of Israel* 1983:654).

Throughout the period of Zionist early-age education teachers insisted that the kindergarten was to be used to inculcate the meaning of Zionist existence, and to teach somewhat vague notions of Israeli "culture," not only to children but also to their parents, many of whom were recent immigrants from diverse cultural backgrounds. The kindergarten was conceived of as an instrument of national purpose: one that would help to transform the child into an Israeli person different from that of his parents. Moreover, a person who would re-enter the home to influence parents to alter their own attitudes towards the rearing of children.

Writing of the Mandatory period, Katerbursky (1962:56), a veteran educator, stated: "The obligation of the kindergarten is to uproot bad habits that the children bring from home." This was attempted, for example, through parent-teacher meetings and through instructional sessions in preparation for holiday celebrations. Katerbursky (1962:58) added: "We understand that the parents, especially the mothers, are still very distant from understanding many of the educational . . . [and] social problems of education; and we will have to educate them as well." When the occasion allowed, mothers were given instructions on how to behave towards their children, on correct attitudes towards the development of the child, on how leisure time with children should be spent, and on the kind of cooking that children would enjoy eating at home. Although such exercises were phrased in the idiom of mutual understanding between teachers and parents, it is clear that the former regarded these goals as integral to their pedagogical mandate (Katerbursky 1962:64).

These themes of inculcation hardly changed after statehood. If anything they intensified with mass immigration and a more centralized educational bureaucracy. Numerous books of instruction and advice for kindergarten teachers were published. These attest to differing perceptions over aims held by kindergarten and home: although these were ameliorated by the rhetoric of mutual cooperation disseminated by educators. We note again an emphasis on the need to educate parents as well as children (Rabinowitz 1958), and, for that matter, to enlist the youngsters as allies in this endeavor. For example, one educator put this forcefully: "Our influence on the surrounding can be great with the help of our faithful partners, the children, if only we will know how to inject into the home one common version of customs. . . . It is not the first time in the history of this country that the child fulfills an important role in educating the nation. . . . That is why we can hope that in the new assignment of the 'ingathering of the exiles' (*kibbutz galuyot*) . . . the child will fulfill his mission and will not disappoint us" (Zanbank-Wilf 1958:57). Less direct but cognate sentiments are expressed in other such didactic manuals (Naftali and Nir-Yaniv 1974; Shemer 1966; Ministry of Education and Culture 1967).

During the *yishuv* period and after, the celebration of holidays in the kindergarten was understood by educators as a signal device through which to inculcate children and parents in what Rabinowitz (1958) called the embedding of traditional contents in new patterns. Writing primarily of the *yishuv,* Fayance-Glick (1957:141) noted: "Special stress was given to holidays as a way of teaching tradition, concepts of history, and Israeli folklore to babies through the pipelines of pleasure and joy saturated with experience. And many kindergartens reached a high aesthetic level through forming the holiday and the party." Many weeks were spent in preparations that, "filled, and are filling today, most of the teaching year . . . and it is as if the kindergarten life is one long holiday with intermissions for pieces of secularity and intervals of reality" (See also Katerbursky 1962:153).

Parents were integral to these celebrations. They were lectured on the meaning of holidays; and were taught songs and dances of the kindergarten, so that they could participate fully in the celebratory education of their children (Katerbursky 1962:72). The implicit effect of such didactics was to bring parents and children together under the tutorial direction of teachers.

In more recent instruction books the teacher is featured as a touchstone of tradition. Parents, however, have undergone the traumatic social and cultural dislocations of immigration that destroyed the traditional atmosphere of holidays in the Jewish home. The teacher also is a source of modernism: of the creation of new patterns of celebration through the borrowing of elements from different Jewish traditions, in order to bring the holiday anew, through children, to homes bereft of such ceremonial occasions (Rabinowitz 1958b). No matter how naive such attitudes appear to be, they reflect the cultural melting-pot notions of Zionism. These often emphasized that immigrants would have to begin again to build a tradition in common, in order to create anew Jewish personhood in the resurgent homeland (Ben-Yosef 1957).

In such books, parents often are delineated as persons who have little information of value on ceremony in the new State. Along with their young offspring, they must be taught how to prepare the material of ceremonials (food dishes, costumes, etc.), and they must learn the symbols, songs, dances, and stories of holidays that are used and are narrated in the kindergarten (Rabinowitz 1958b). Holidays are understood by the advisors of teachers as special foci for the enculturation of the family as a whole.

In general the young child is understood, if dimly, by educators as a small-scale mediator of relationships between state and family, between public and private domains, and between "general" and more particularistic notions of culture. All of these relationships have built into them potentially conflicting loyalties, obligations, and rights—but these rarely are recognized by educators. Hidden in their writings is the premise that the control of the child, as a resource, is crucial to the reproduction of the nation-state. On the one hand the child is the citizen and culture-bearer of the future, and on the other the child as parent-to-be is essential to the formation of the family to come.

Therefore serious thought is given to the planning of ceremonials in the kindergarten; and instructional books offer various scenarios for their enactment (Rabinowitz 1958c). These are designed less to instruct didactically or to encourage reflection. Instead emphasis is placed on the arousal of emotion through symbolic forms that evoke collective sentiments. In general there is a profusion of what Langer (1953) called "presentational" symbolism: media that engage the senses more than the critical faculties of mind. Participants should experience enactments by living through their symbols, rather than as spectators. Instruction books note, for example, that the kindergarten child needs the emotional experience of a holiday, not a logical explanation or historical exposition. Ideally the celebration should be a "common experience" that "uplifts the spirit" and that encourages feelings of togetherness (Rabinowitz 1958a, 1958b).

In the views of kindergarten educators the arousal of such sentiments is induced if scenarios are well-designed, so that their enactment is left less to chance. The architectonics of celebration should be logical and holistic, with defined segments of opening, elaboration, and closing (Fayence-Glick 1948). Attention should be given to one or more major ideas or motifs, to scheduling in relation to calendrical cycles, to the sequencing and progression of the program, and to overt symbols. Often these symbols are both "living" and "lived through," such that the physical positioning of the participants itself creates symbolic formations. The symbol comes alive, and participants live through this both as a collectivity and as individuals. Such devices powerfully invoke a metonymy between motifs of celebration and their being experienced, and a synecdoche in which each part of the collective entity replicates and signifies the coherence and unity of the whole. Educators appear well aware of this more explicit level of symbolic manipulation. Yet since teachers are quite autonomous in how they plan celebrations, there is a good deal of variation in their enactments among kindergartens.

But kindergarten educators often deny that, at a more implicit level, symbolic formations in celebrations actively manipulate versions of relationships between teacher and parent, collectivity and family. Nonetheless we argue that each category of participant—teacher, child, and parent—has significance beyond the immediate persons who participate in celebrations. The teacher is a statist figure, a "gardener" whose task it is to cultivate, and so to enculturate, her young charges. In Durkheim's (1956:89) words, the teacher "is the agent of a great moral person who surpasses him: it is society . . . the teacher is the interpreter of the great moral ideas of his time." Licensed by the Ministry of Education, and subject in part to its curricula and supervision, the teacher is the first official-like figure with whom the little child comes into continuous contact outside the home. Her structural position is, in no small measure, in opposition to that of parent and home. For four to five hours a day, six days a week, she is in charge of a collection of children, indeed of a small collectivity, in which each child in theory is equal in worth and status to every other, and where she has no vested interest in the particulars of any one. Her criteria of sentiment are "objectified" in terms of more universalistic criteria, like those of a child's capabilities, capacities, and behavior. Her mandate is to help to mold the child and, through the youngster, to affect his current family of procreation and his future family of orientation.

The child's experience and knowledge, sentiment and loyalty, derive almost wholly from the encompassing primary group of the family. In the course of years of attendance in educational institutions, he ideally will be reconstituted in the image of citizen: one whose ultimate loyalties will be to the abstract idea of the nation-state. Although his attachments to family are neither attenuated nor diminished, there must occur a shift in the positional hierarchy of family and state, with the latter coming to encompass the former. This transition also is about the standardization of the biographical uniqueness of the individual and of the individual family. These processes, we believe, are begun in the kindergarten, and perhaps are most concentrated in its celebrations.

Kindergarten Celebrations

The occasions to be discussed are representative of the range of Jewish holidays celebrated in Israel, in terms of their traditional or modern roots. Given the paucity of information available on kindergarten celebrations, we prefer to inform the reader with a sense of the variation among such occasions, rather than to limit our focus to one or two categories of holiday. The first two of our cases, Hannukah and Purim, are traditional holidays, but not holy Days of Rest. Both commemorate victories: Hannukah of the Maccabees and of the rededication of the Temple in Jerusalem, and Purim the saving of the Jews of Persia through the influence of Queen Esther. Both are celebrated, in varying degrees in home and synagogue, and Purim also in the street. Our analysis of a Hannukah celebration demonstrates the implicit manipulation of hierarchy, such that the family unit is shown to be encompassed by the collectivity. The case of Purim that we discuss brings out an implicit assumption that the maturation of children moves them from a condition closer to nature to one of civilization, and so toward their assumption of citizenship in the future. The third case, Mother's Day, is borrowed from modern Western popular culture, and is a wholly secular occasion of no official standing. The implications of our case suggest that it is the collectivity that mandates the legitimacy of the family unit, and not the reverse which is closer to the viewpoint of the family. The fourth case, Jerusalem Day, is a secular state commemoration of the reunification of Jerusalem following the 1967 Six-Day War. Our analysis of this case points to the symbolic forging of direct links between the collectivity and the child as future citizen, without the mediation of the family. All of these cases offer implicit versions of hierarchical relationships between collectivity and family that should reverse the early-age experiences of the child. However, we stress here that, in the first few years of education, youngsters experience dozens of such celebrations. Explicit themes, contents, and organization vary within and among kinds of celebrations. Yet the types of implicit relationships between collectivity and family that emerge from our cases likely have a cachet of relevance that extends to numerous other kindergarten celebrations. While, for the child, it is the cumulative accretion of such experiences that has enculturative impact.

All the celebrations described took place on the kindergarten premises (although others, not discussed here, sometimes were taken outside). The kindergarten is defined as "the child's world," and the only adult that has a legitimate place within it is the teacher—the representative of the collectivity. Parents (and other adults) always are only guests in the kindergarten. Nothing better symbolizes this attitude than the chairs in the kindergarten. In all kindergartens visited, no more than one or two full-size chairs were found. That is to say, as a rule, the teacher sits in a full-size chair and, "at her feet," as it were, the children on small chairs. When parents are invited to the kindergarten, be it to a celebration, to a parent-teacher meeting or to their child's birthday party, they always are seated on children's chairs. Thus a parent in the kindergarten always occupies a child's place.

Prior to the celebrations, the children were given explanations in their respective kindergartens with regard to the character of the holiday concerned, its significance for the people of Israel or for the children themselves (as in Mother's Day), its dominant symbols, and some rudimentary historical background. Where the celebration involved more complicated enactments by the children, these were rehearsed beforehand. All the actions that took place in these celebrations were in accordance with the explicit instructions and orchestration of the teacher, unless otherwise specified.

Hannukah: Hierarchy, Family, and Collectivity

Hannukah, the Festival of Lights, commemorates the victory of the Maccabees over the Seleucids, and their rededication of the Temple in 165 B.C. According to the *Talmud,* in the Temple there was only enough undefiled oil for one day of lamp-lighting. Miraculously the oil multiplied into a supply sufficient for eight days. Hannukah is celebrated for eight consecutive days in the home, primarily by the lighting of an additional candle each day, in an eight-branched candelabrum, the *hannukiah* (pl. hannukiot). An extra candle, the *shamash,* is used to kindle the others. Hannukah celebrates liberation from foreign domination: it is a triumph of faith, of the few over the many, of the weak over the strong. In present-day Israel the martial spirit of this holiday casts reflections on the struggle of the Jewish people to create a unified national homeland.

Books of instruction suggest that the major motif be heroism in'Israel. The enactment should evoke the emotional experience of the occasion. The central symbols of the celebration should be the hannukiah, candles, tops,[7] and, according to some, the national flag. The locale of the party should be filled with light, just as the shirts or blouses of the children should be white, to create an atmosphere of joyous luminosity. The best time is late afternoon or early evening, for these hours evoke the uplifting illumination of the holiday from the midst of darkness and the depths of despair; and they connect the kindergarten to the home, where candles may be lit soon after. Scenarios suggest that a central hannukiah be lit by an adult; that the parents light the small hannukiot made by their children; that the children form "living hannukiot"; and that parents and children dance or play games together (Rabinowitz 1958c). Certain of these elements were incorporated into the example described below.[8]

Description. The party began at 4:30 P.M. Thirty-two children, aged 4 to 5, and their mothers sat at tables placed along three walls of the room. Only a few fathers attended. A name-card marked the place of each child. The tables were covered by white tablecloths. At the center of each were a vase of flowers, bags of candies, and candles equal to the number of youngsters at that table. Before each child stood a little hannukiah made by that youngster. On the walls and windows were hung painted paper hannukiot, oil pitchers, candles, and tops, all of which had been prepared in the kindergarten. Against the fourth wall was a large hannukiah, constructed of toy blocks covered with colored paper, which supported eight colored candles and the shamash.

An accordionist played melodies of the holiday, and the mothers joined in singing and in clapping. The teacher welcomed all those present and, at a prearranged signal, her helper extinguished the lights. Each mother lit a candle and aided her child to kindle his own little hannukiah. The room lights were turned on. A father lit the large hannukiah of toy blocks, and recited the requisite prayers. As he did so, the teacher told the children: "Remember, when father says a blessing, you must sit quietly and listen to the blessing." More holiday songs followed.

The teacher announced: "Now we want to make a living hannukiah. A living hannukiah that walks and sings, a hannukiah of parents and children." She arranged the mothers and their children in a straight line, so that each child stood in front of his mother. An additional mother-child pair, the shamash, stood some feet to the side. Each mother held a candle, and each youngster a blue or white ribbon. Each child gave one end of his ribbon to the child-shamash. In this formation all children were attached to the shamash by their ribbons, and each mother to her own child. The mother of the shamash lit the candles held by the others. The lights were extinguished, the room lit by the living hannukiah in the gathering darkness of late afternoon. The accordionist played a melody of the holiday, "We came to chase away the darkness," as each mother walked around her child. The lights were turned on. The mothers returned to their seats as a group, followed by their children.

The children and mothers of one table returned to the center of the room and were told by the teacher: "The children will be the spinning tops. Get down, children." They fell to their knees, bent their heads, and curled their bodies forward. Each mother stood behind her child. The teacher declared: "The whole year the spinning tops were asleep in their box. From last year until this year, until now. And the children said to them, 'Wake up, spinning tops. Hannukah has come. We want to play with you.'" To a background of holiday melodies the teacher moved from child to child, touching their hand. With each contact a child awakened, stood up, raised his arms, and began to spin. Each mother spun her child, first clockwise, then counterclockwise. Next the mothers became the tops, spun by their children in one direction and then the other. The teacher told the second table: "You'll also be spinning tops. Each mother will spin her own child and when I give the signal, change roles. Alright? Let's start. . . . The children are the spinning tops . . . the parents are the spinning tops." Those at the third table followed.

Mothers and children held hands, formed an unbroken circle, and danced round and round the teacher. Only one father joined the circle. More singing, and food, followed. As 6 P.M. approached, the teacher gave the participants permission to leave; and the party broke up.

Discussion. This ceremonial is composed of three major segments, the overt symbolism of which is quite explicit. The first focuses on the serious traditionalism of the holiday, primarily through the emblem of the hannukiah. This segment brings out the connectivity between past and present. The second works through the make-believe of the spinning top, and evokes the relationship between present and future.

The initial segment proceeds through a series of candle-lightings: mother helps her child to kindle the small hannukiah, father lights the large hannukiah, and the candles are lit on the living hannukiah. These actions and others are embedded in the melodies and songs of the holiday that tell of heroism, victory, and the illumination of darkness. These themes weave together emotion and experience to carry the past into the present. The blue and white ribbons of the living hannukiah are the official colors of the modern state, and of its flag. In the living hannukiah ancient triumph is fused with modern renaissance. Collectivity is dedicated to temple, temple to collectivity.

Here the idea of family is central. The enactment replicates symbolic acts—the kindling of candles and prayers—that should take place within the home, and that delineate familial roles and an elementary division of labor. Thus it is apt for mother to help her small child, in this instance to light the hannukiah. Moreover, it is appropriate for father, the male head of household, to recite the prayers that accompany this act, on behalf of the family. Here one father does this on behalf of the assembly. The symbolism of this enactment then transcends the level of the family. The "living hannukiah" encompasses all of the mothers and children, while respecting the singularity of individual families, represented here by the dyads of mother and child. Each mother stands behind her child; and walks around and encompasses the latter, delineating the family unit. This living hannukiah is a collective symbol that also is a symbol of collectivity; while this collectivity itself is constituted of smaller family units.

The living hannukiah projects into the present the significance of past heroism and dedication. This is done through the living bodies of mothers and children, who themselves compose the shape and the significata of this central symbol. Thus the collectivity is presented as living through family units, just as the latter live within and through the former. Each is made to be seen as integral to the other. However the connotation is that the collectivity is of a higher order than the individual family, since here it encompasses the latter.

In contrast to the seriousness of the first segment, the second is playful. Its motif is the top, a child's holiday toy that itself is inscribed with Hebrew letters that denote the miraculous—the multiplication of oil, and perhaps the victory itself. But in this segment commemoration and tradition are not marked. Instead the make-believe is evoked, slumber is shattered, and the participants act joyously in the holiday mood. Again the focus is that of the family unit, represented by dyads of mother and child. The hierarchy at the close of the first segment is kept. The teacher activates each child, and the latter performs under the direction of mother.

But in this make-believe segment, mother and child reverse roles: the former becomes the sleeping top that is awakened and directed by her child. Unlike the inscription of tradition in the first segment, the playful is full of potential, as is the youngster who eventually will exchange the role of child for that of adult. As a mature adult the child will become a parent, bringing into being and controlling children of his own. This segment projects the child, as parent-to-be, towards a future in which he will replace his parents and will replicate their roles and tasks. Through the two segments past and future are joined together wilth a sense of the movement of generations. Whereas the first segment recreates family and collectivity in the images of tradition, of the enduring past, the second segment demonstrates the transitoriness of particular parents and the direction of succession. For the child the experience may evoke some feeling that his own parents are not timeless monoliths that will continue to structure his world indefinitely.

The second segment closes and the third starts with an unbroken circle dance of mothers and children who revolve about the axis of the teacher.[9] This formation is a restatement of the relationship between family and collectivity. The circle dance, however, blurs the distinctiveness of particular families and, within these, of parents and children, adults and youngsters. The delineation of family units has disappeared. Instead, all are closer to being discrete and egalitarian individuals who themselves are part of a greater and embracing collectivity. This formation connotes the connectivity of present and future citizens, and their orientation towards an axial center.

In this and in other kindergarten celebrations the teacher is the sole arbiter and the ultimate authority. She is seen by children to control parental figures before their very eyes. We argued that the teacher is a statist figure, perhaps the earliest representation of authority outside the home that very young children encounter. In these celebrations she is not an alternative source of authority to that of parents, as she may be perceived by children in the daily life of the kindergarten. Instead she is the pinnacle of hierarchy that supercedes and that subsumes the family. Thus the whole enactment is framed by the architectonics of hierarchy that are external to, but that act upon, the family unit. All actions of such celebrations, regardless of their explicit content, are embued with this quality of hierarchy.

The implicit messages of this Hannukah celebration are about hierarchy from a more statist perspective. The first segment constructs a version of the superordination of roles within the family, and then embeds the latter within a version of collectivity. The second deconstructs the centrality of family status and transforms hierarchical relationships among family members. The third emphasizes equality among citizens, all of whom are oriented towards the statist figure of the teacher.

In the first segment the child is dependent upon, and subordinate to, his mother in order to light the little hannukiah. In turn, both of them are dependent upon the figure of the father in order to light the large hannukiah and to recite prayers on behalf of the whole family. This series is an accurate rendition of the comparative status of elementary roles within the family. Family units then are made to constitute a symbol of the collectivity, the living hannukiah. The collectivity is seen to exist as a coordinated assemblage of families. Here individual families are dependent upon and are subordinate to the collectivity in order to relate to one another, and in order to create an alive and enduring vision of tradition and belief. The first segment builds up the symbol of the hannukiah in increasing degrees of encompassment and hierarchy. The apex is the living of this collective emblem. Integral to this are the ribbons, in the national colors, held by the children. Thus the hannukiah itself is embued with the symbolism of statehood; while implicit in this more traditional collective emblem is a more modern version.

The second segment begins with an expression of hierarchical family roles. The dyad of mother and child delineates the coherence of the family unit. The mother directs the movements of the spinning top, her child, in an accurate depiction of status and authority in relation to her offspring. But their reversal of roles is, at one and the same time, a representation of independence and of equality. The autonomy of children, and their founding of families, is expected to be an outcome of maturation. Through this process children partially are freed of their subordination to their family of procreation, and thereby are inculcated in their obligations of citizenship to the nation-state. As citizens, all Israelis are the theoretical equals of one another and are subordinate to the state without the intervening mediation of the family. In the third segment, the circle dance, there is no characterization of the family unit: the unbroken circle evokes egalitarianism and common effort and all the dancers are oriented towards their common center. Orchestrating their actions stands the teacher, just as the state stands in relation to its citizens.

Like the hannukiah alive, the circle dance is a living collective symbol. But each is in structural opposition to the other. The hannukiah depends on the family and on its internal hierarchy for its existence. The circle dance eliminates the specificity of the family unit and simultaneously relates each participant in equality to all others and to a statist apex of hierarchy that is not representative of family. In the sequencing of this celebration the unbroken circle with its apical center supplants the cellular hannukiah; just as, for children, with time the state will supercede their parents as the pinnacle of authority.

Purim: The Evolution of Maturity

Purim commemorates the deliverance of the Jews of Persia from the evil designs of their enemies through the persuasions of Esther, the Jewish queen of the Persian monarch. This story is read in the synagogue; and the holiday is celebrated by a festive family meal, and by the exchange of gifts of food among relatives and friends. An especially joyous holiday, it is the only time in the ritual calendar when some license in dress and behavior is encouraged. Secular celebrations take the form of dressing up in costume and attending parties.

Instruction books designate the holiday as an entertainment, with children in costume and parents in attendance. Little mention is made of the traditional significance of the holiday; and scenarios for its celebration rarely are given. It is left to the teacher to decide on the measure of organization desired. The example we discuss is in keeping with such advice. Its explicit enactment is intended to entertain and to amuse the youngsters and their mothers. However, in this there is a degree of implicit patterning that connotes the role of the kindergarten in the maturation of children. Of this the teacher denied any conscious knowledge.

Description. This celebration was held for three year-olds. Some two weeks prior, at a meeting of mothers and teacher, the teacher requested that the children be dressed in animal costumes. Her reason was that such figures were closest to the world of the child, and therefore more comprehensible to the youngsters. If this were not possible, then the child should be dressed as a clown. A few days before the party each mother informed the teacher of the costume her child would wear, so that the teacher could prepare her program.

The party took place in the late afternoon, at the onset of the holiday. Mothers and children were arranged in a wide semi-circle, facing an open area where the teacher stood. Mothers sat on the tiny kindergarten chairs, their offsprings on the floor before them. Music of the holiday played in the background.

The celebration consisted of two loosely articulated segments, separated by an intermediate segment of an unbroken circle dance. In the first the children showed their costumes before the assembly in a set order of presentation. In the second, five mothers who were dressed as clowns performed a rehearsed dance and song. The teacher, dressed as a clown, organized the presentation of costumes in terms of a simple narrative. Many years ago, she said, there was a king, and she called out a boy dressed as a king. He was joined by a girl dressed as a queen. In their court, continued the teacher, there was a zoo full of animals. She called out the inhabitants of the zoo. As each kind of character came forward a song that described its typical movements or activities was sung. The following was the order of appearance. Five cats walked on all fours and meowed. Then three rabbits hopped out. A bear fiercely lumbered forth and was introduced as a "teddy-bear." Three dainty dolls came forward and were described as living in cardboard boxes. All of these dwelled in the royal zoo. The teacher told a soldier, a policeman, and a cowboy to come out, introduced them as the "royal guard," and marched with them around the semi-circle. This ended the narrative of the zoo within the royal court. The remaining children, all dressed as clowns, were called forth. After this, all the mothers and children formed an unbroken circle, with the teacher in the center, and danced to the melody of a song about a little clown.

The teacher announced that the performance of the children had ended. She requested the performing mothers to sing. Each of their costumes was of a single color, and their song described the activities of clowns dressed in each of these colors. They sang in a line, with the teacher at their head. Food followed, and the party ended.

Discussion. Unlike the previous Hannukah celebration, this one of Purim was not considered to have any coherent scenario or explicit significance. The intention was to have fun and to give the youngsters the opportunity to play make-believe characters. The teacher had hoped that all of these characters would be animals—in her view, close to the world of the child. Faced with a mixed bag of costumes, she used a simple narrative to order their appearance. On a more implicit level this ordering is of direct relevance to our contention that kindergarten celebrations, in various ways, are engaged in the symbolic representation of rudimentary socialization, in the direction of adulthood and citizenship.

The teacher recasts the kindergarten as the court of a king and queen. This role-play is in keeping with the story of Purim, of Queen Esther and her Persian monarch. But from this point on there are no further connotations of the text of the holiday. Nonetheless, monarchy and court are emblematic of hierarchy, of moral order, and of social control. In short, these are symbols of maturity and of statehood that exist above and beyond those of home and family. A zoo is situated within the court and is filled with characters. In Israel, zoos are institutions where wild animals, instinctive and unconstrained in their nature, are locked in cages, artifacts of civilization that place external restraints on these creatures. This is a popular view of the zoo. In the teacher's view small children are close to the world of animals and so are driven by their instincts and are not governed by the obligations of maturity and by the norms of civilization. In the enactment children-as-animals are placed in a zoo, itself within a court. Through these metaphors the kindergarten is represented, on the one hand, as a locale of moral order with connotations of ultimate authority and so of statehood, and on the other as a place of confinement for those who have yet to learn internal restraint.

The order of appearance of the inhabitants of the zoo suggests strongly that the more "natural" state of youngsters is conditional. Their sequencing projects a developmental image of enculturation, of moving towards maturity within metaphors of hierarchy and control. The first animal to appear is the cat. Although cats in Israel sometimes are pets, the cities of the country are pervaded by a profusion of alley cats that are undomesticated, fierce, and wary of humans. Even as a pet the cat is a comparatively independent and autonomous creature. These are the primary stereotypes of the cat in Israel. In her narrative the teacher describes the children-as-cats as "looking for friends." That is, these make-believe cats desire to establish relationships, with the connotation of becoming more domesticated through sociation.

The next is the rabbit. In Israel this creature usually is found in the wild, and sometimes as a pet. In either case it is thought of as a timid, passive, and docile creature—a vegetarian in contrast to the more predatory cat. Although wild, the rabbit is more easily caged and controllable than is the cat. The rabbit is followed by a child dressed as a bear. However enthusiastically he plays this gruff bear, the teacher turns this wild and fierce creature into a "teddy-bear." Unlike cat and rabbit, the teddy-bear is a child's plaything. As a toy it is the human product of its natural counterpart—that is, a copy. Its animalism is man-made. A product of culture, it is a fully-controlled and domesticated creation, in contrast to cat and rabbit. Still, the teddy-bear retains its animal form.

The doll appears next. This is again a child's plaything and is man-made. Yet, unlike the teddy-bear, it is created in a human image, and its attributes of behavior are largely those of a person. According to the narrative the doll lives in a cardboard box, its own enclosure that is somewhat more akin to a home than is a cage. Where the teddy-bear is a play upon nature, the doll is a reflection of humanity and civilization. Of all the zoo creatures to appear, the doll is the most domesticated and restrained. These controls are inherent in, and emerge from, its human form and its attributes of culture. They are not a shell of strictures imposed from without, as in the case of cat and rabbit, nor an intermediate being, a domesticated animal, like the teddy-bear.

Left with a soldier, a policeman, and a cowboy, the teacher organizes them into a "royal guard." These are not inhabitants of the zoo, but stand outside it, and close and complete the framework of social control introduced by the royal figures. Like the latter the royal guards are fully human figures whose roles embody a regimentation of maturity and order. They are guardians of moral codes against the predations of more impulsive natural beings. Such associations are reinforced as the teacher takes these guardians by the arm and they march together. As she had not done with those within the zoo, the teacher identifies herself with children who, by being given roles of control and order, play themselves as they should become in the future—as mature adults.

Wittingly or not, the teacher has brought into being a small drama about the evolution and the enculturation of humanity and hierarchy that leads to maturity and the assumption of responsibility beyond that of the familial. Framed at the outset and at the close by human figures with statist and hierarchical connotations, the characters of the zoo are transposed from the wild to the tame, from creatures of instinct to artifacts of culture. Just as their mothers watch this encoding from the periphery, these youngsters see their mothers watching this happen to them. The children experience a brief metaphor of how they are perceived to be by the teacher and of what they are expected to become.

The figure of the clown was intended by the teacher as a fall-back costume for the children. Clowns were not included in court and zoo, but were presented afterward. On the face of it, these residual figures have no logical connection to prior actions in the sequence, nor to those that followed. In overt terms these clowns, like those of the clown-stereotypes that they copy, are simply unabashed figures of fun that are in keeping with the good humor of this holiday. Nonetheless, the deeper structure of the clown type likely makes these figures the most complex of the celebration (Willeford 1969).

These clown costumes, like those of numerous clown stereotypes, are composed of variegated elements that do not compose any simple pattern of symmetry and homogeneity, as do the other costumes. The elements of these clown costumes are without gender; they contrast with one another to a degree; and so, in theory, this kind of configuration should encourage an attitude of reflection toward the complexity of the overall composition. The clown is a human figure, but it is an experimental one that is constructed more self-consciously. In other words, the clown figure plays with potentials, and with the axiomatic and the taken-for-granted in human existence (Willeford 1969; Handelman 1980). Ironically, clowns are more figures of maturity than are authoritarian monarchs and regimented guards. The maturity of the clown is, in part, related to a freedom of action that accrues when self-discipline is more assured; and when one is well-aware that one is not that which one plays at. This is the maturity of adulthood, of the teacher and the performing mothers, all of whom are dressed as clowns. In our view, the appearance of the clowns, following on the characters of court and zoo, represents the completion of maturation. In a way, it signifies a reward that maturation carries with it—the freedom of action.

The appearance of the child-clowns is followed by a circle dance of all mothers and children. As noted, the connotations of this formation are of collectivity, egalitarianism, and joint effort. But there is no delineation here of the family unit, nor of the special bond between mother and child. Thus the teacher reunites the children with persons who first and foremost are adults, rather than mothers, after these little people have been represented as trained and developed in an idiom of social order. This process is validated in the second segment of the celebration. The teacher and clown-mothers perform a dance and song. The figure of the clown appears here as the apex of authority and maturity, with the teacher at its pinnacle. On this note the celebration ends.

In our view the entire enactment is an extended metaphor of a process of maturation that the child will undergo in order to turn into an adult member of a wider collectivity. The children are presented, through court and zoo, in different stages of development. These characters are superceded by the more complex figures of the child-clowns. The character of the clown, with its connotations of freedom tempered by self-discipline, is used to free all the children to rejoin the adults in an egalitarian circle dance. Thus the enactment is projected towards a future in which youngsters take their place of equality alongside their parents. The child-clowns also bridge the two segments. They share their figuration with teacher and performing mothers. The child-clowns blend fairly easily into the figures of the clown-mothers, who are adults indeed, and with that of the teacher-as-clown who here is at the apex of adulthood.

Mother's Day: The Creation of Family and Intimacy

This party was celebrated together by some forty children aged 3, 4, and 5, who belonged to three separate classes of the same kindergarten. The explicit aim of the teacher was to have the youngsters demonstrate their love and respect for their mothers. This included the giving of gifts by the child to his mother. However the sequencing of enactment conveys a more implicit pattern: that it is the collectivity, represented through the teacher, that brings into being the affective bonds of the mother-child relationship.

Description. During the prior week each child prepared a present for his mother: a piece of shaped dough, decorated, baked, and lacquered. A small hole allowed this to be hung on string, like a pendant. Each gift was wrapped, together with a greeting card. On the morning of the celebration vases of flowers were placed on tables, as well as an additional flower intended for each mother. The children arrived at the usual early hour; their mothers were invited for midmorning. The small kindergarten chairs were arranged in a large unbroken circle. An accordionist provided music.

Each mother was seated, with her child before her on a cushion. The teacher stood in the center of the circle. From the outset she instructed the children on how to greet and to behave towards their mothers. "Come children," she cried, "let's say a big 'hello' to mother! Let's give mother a big hug! Let's sing together, 'What a Happy Day is Mother's Day'." After the singing each child was handed a flower. They sang together, "A Fine Bouquet of Flowers for Mother." "Give the flower to mother," said the teacher, "and give kisses to mother." Each child turned, gave his mother the flower, and kissed her.

The mothers stood and were arranged in pairs. Each pair faced one another and together held their two flowers. The children formed a large circle and, holding hands, walked around all the pairs of mothers and sang. Mothers and children sat and sang together. The teacher said a few words to the youngsters on the importance of being nice to mother. The children stood, faced their mothers, and sang: "Let's bless mother, blessings for Mother's Day. Be happy in your life, for the coming year. Arise and reach 120 years."[10] The teacher instructed: "Give mother a big hug and sing, 'My dear mother loves only me, yes only me, yes only me'." After they had done so, she added: "Now smile at mother."

The mothers closed their eyes and each child gave his mother the present made especially for her; and according to instruction, gave her "a very warm kiss." The children sang together, while the mothers hung the pendants around their necks. Each mother and child formed pairs and danced and sang together. The lyrics concerned physical coordination of the "look up, look down" variety. The teacher enunciated the lyrics, so that they became instructions for movement that were followed with accuracy. All returned to their places. Since the day was Friday, said the teacher, she and the children were going to teach the mothers a song with which to welcome the Sabbath. After this singing the teacher announced that the "ceremony" was completed.

One mother stood and declared: "We want to say that it's true that we're the children's mothers. But we want to thank and to give a present to the real mother of the children while they're in the kindergarten. We want to give her this bouquet of flowers." A youngster was given the bouquet and presented it to the teacher, while the mothers applauded. Snacks were offered by the teacher, and the party closed.

Discussion. The explicit scenario of this celebration is clear. The children show their affection for their mothers in order to honor them. These qualities of emotional closeness are expressed through various media: song, dance, gifts, and numerous tactile gestures. According to the teacher the use of different media was intended to declare emphatically the strength and the vitality of the mother-child bond. The sequencing of these numerous acts was not meant to convey any implicit significance. Instead their purpose was to lengthen the celebration, and so to give the children many opportunities to demonstrate their appreciation.

In our view there is a more implicit patterning in this sequence: one that projects the creation of the familial bond out of collective formations, under the supervision of the teacher. The major social formation consists of an outer circle of mothers, an inner circle of children, and the teacher in the center. Each concentric circle constitutes a category of person—that is, mother and child. The child is situated between mother and teacher. Although each child is placed close to his mother, the affective expression of this dyad is orchestrated wholly by the teacher.

The initial stress in the ceremony is on the delineation of the social category of motherhood. Mother first is welcomed as something of a "stranger," and the youngsters are told exactly how to show affection towards her ("Let's say a big 'hello' to mother! Let's give mother a big hug!"). Such instruction may well be necessary to coordinate the actions of participants, especially when half of them are little children. Yet such directives also impress that an acquaintanceship is being formulated, that the category of children is being introduced to that of mother. It is as if, within the kindergarten, the abstract category of mother is being made real for that of the child. The intimate affection of the mother-child bond, one that precedes the kindergarten experience, is re-presented here as the creation of the teacher.

The first gift follows: a flower given to the child by the teacher, that he in turn presents to his mother. This gift is standardized for all of the mothers. Like gifts generally, its symbolic value establishes a relationship. Of common worth, this gift forges the same kind of relationship between each child and each mother. This rather impersonal gift serves to mediate into existence the category of mother and to articulate it to that of the child. This gift accords motherhood to each woman, through the proof of her status—her child who is the giver of the gift. In contrast to the developmental cycle of the family, here it is the alliance of teacher and child that forms and activates the category of motherhood. But the source of the gift is the statist figure of the teacher, and so the category of mother, and its articulation to that of the child, is shaped at her behest.

Subsequent actions support this line of interpretation. After the first gift the seamless circle of seated mothers is fragmented. The mothers form pairs: each couple holds jointly their gifts of flowers, and is connected through these. In other words, through the medium of the gift each mother is transposed: from being a member within the category of mother to becoming individuated, a person and a mother in her own right. As such she represents the motherhood and the nurturance of a family unit. Moreover, connections between families as discrete entities are delineated, as mothers jointly clasp their gifts. Yet these particular families still are denied children of their own. The youngsters are kept in their categorical formation that encircles these mothers. This implies that, from a more collectivist perspective, personhood develops within categorical boundaries: that, first and foremost, people are members of social categories, and only then are they accorded the status of persons with their own unique attributes.

The participants resume their original formation. The children stand as a category, face the mothers, and sing their blessings. They then sing, "My dear mother loves only me, yes, only me, yes, only me." This act marks the beginning of a transposition whereby each child is told to recognize the especially intimate and affective bond between himself and his mother. This shift is realized through the personalized gift that each child had prepared especially for his mother. This second gift mediates the creation of a unique relationship between a particular youngster and mother. Just as previously the mother was accorded personhood in her own right, so now is her child. The category of child is fragmented; mother and child are united, and the family unit is delineated.

This intimate bond is represented further as the concentric formation breaks up, and as each mother and child form pairs and dance and sing together. Each pair, like each family, is a separate and distinct entity. However its unity depends on the teacher, who tells each pair exactly how to coordinate their movements in unison. The special bond that is crucial to the existence and to the reproduction of the family is under her control. This is emphasized as teacher and children teach the mothers a song with which to welcome the Sabbath. The ceremony to welcome the Sabbath within the home, on behalf of family and household, is exclusively the domain of the wife and mother. Her expertise, should she do this rite, likely is garnered from sacred texts and from having watched her own mother. No external intervention is required. Here she is treated as if she were ignorant of one of the essential ritual elements that maintain the integrity of the traditional home. Instead it becomes incumbent on a representation of collectivity in alliance with its wards, the children, to impart such knowledge to mother and home.

The next occurrence is an addendum to the planned celebration, decided on by some of the mothers. It complements well the preceding sequence. One mother, on behalf of the others, thanks the teacher and calls her "the real mother of the children while they are in the kindergarten," and presents her with a gift of flowers, via a youngster. Motherhood, the special bond between mother and child, is returned through the figure of a child to its source in the enactment, the teacher. She is described as a mother and, by extension, the kindergarten becomes akin to the home, a locus of socialization that prepares the child for adulthood. Yet, in terms of this ceremony, it is through the kindergarten that the home comes into existence. And through this final gift it is to the kindergarten, embodied in the figure of the teacher, that this right is returned. The teacher is a representation of collectivity, and it is to this wider collectivity that authority is arrogated to mold these youngsters.

In other words, motherhood was delegated to the collectivity by a representative of the mothers attending the party. In Hebrew, the words "state" (*medinah*) and "motherland" (*moledet,* literally, land of birth) take the feminine form. Phrases like, "I gave my child to the state" or "I sacrifice my child for the good of the motherland" are common in describing the relationship of family-collectivity. Against this background the delegation of motherhood to a representative of the collectivity gains in depth of meaning.

From the perspective of family and home the implicit patterning of the whole ceremony recasts and reverses the normal progression of the domestic cycle: for it is the collectivity that creates the family. The usual view of parents, and the one that the little child first experiences, is that in the beginning there is the family; that into this nexus the child is born and within it matures; and that with time he leaves and establishes his own home. But here the progression is as follows: first the collectivity exists and is composed of social categories of people. Links are forged between categories, and from these there emerge discrete social units, or families. These are accorded the right to bear and to raise children; and from this there emerges the special bond between mother and child. In this process the rights of, and obligations to, the collectivity are shown to be paramount.

Jerusalem Day: Statehood and Citizenship

After the 1967 Six-Day War, Jerusalem Day was promulgated as a civil state holiday to commemorate the reunification of the capital of Israel. It is celebrated primarily through official receptions and other functions, which include a festive mass march around the environs of the city. The major thoroughfares are decorated with the national flag and with the banner of Jerusalem, a golden lion (the emblem of the ancient kingdom of Judah) rampant on a white background with blue borders. Jerusalem is the central place of the Jewish nation and state. The city was divided, from 1948 until 1967, into western and eastern sectors, the former within Israel and the latter controlled by Jordan. Within the eastern sector is Mount Moriah, the Temple Mount, the site of the first temple built by Solomon, and of the second, destroyed by the Romans in 70 A.D. This defeat spelled the onset of the Diaspora, the widespread dispersion of the Jews into exile from ancient Israel.

Circumventing part of the western and all of the southern borders of the Mount are walls that survived the Roman sack. These remnants of the outer ramparts of the second temple complex are all that was left of that edifice most sacred to Judaism. A short stretch of the western rampart is called the Wailing Wall, but is known in Israel as the Western Wall. For reasons overly complicated to discuss here, the Western Wall, long a site of worship, has become since 1967 the most significant symbol of the State and of Judaism. The Wall has become evocative of a nation whose florescence as a state awaited the return of its people. It is symbolic of a continuity that is perceived to have endured throughout the absence of Jewish sovereignty for close to 2000 years. Therefore it connects and condenses, as does no other physical presence in modern Israel, the glory and then the desuetude of the past and the national redemption of the present. We raise these points because much of the symbolism of this kindergarten celebration is focused on the Western Wall.

Description. Three classes of 3, 4, and 5 year-olds, totalling some sixty youngsters who belonged to the same kindergarten, participated. The celebration took place in the open courtyard of the kindergarten on the morning of Jerusalem Day. Parents were not invited. The courtyard was decorated with national flags and with cut-outs of the lion of Jerusalem. Most of the children were dressed, as asked to, in blue and white clothing. Each was given a small lapel pin that depicted the lion. Each class was seated along one side of the courtyard, with the teacher in the center and an accordionist nearby.

The ceremony opened with songs whose respective themes were: the ancient kingdom of Israel, rejoicing in Jerusalem, and the re-building of the temple. In a brief peroration the teacher declared that Jerusalem was and always would be the capital of Israel; that this day marked the liberation of East Jerusalem and the reunification of the city by the Israel Defence Forces; and that this day was celebrated by everyone throughout the country.

Four children of the oldest class recited a lengthy poem that told of two doves who dreamt that the people of Israel would arise. The two doves flew to Jerusalem and alighted on the Wall. The closing lines stated: "The children of Israel are singing a song; next year the city will be rebuilt." The assembly sang of the ancient longing of the Jewish people to return to Jerusalem. As this melody continued, six of the 4 year-olds danced, each holding blue and white ribbons. During the dance each child gave the ends of his ribbons to two others. As their performance ended the children were joined by the ribbons in the form of a six-pointed Shield of David (the *magen david*, commonly translated as the Star of David), the emblem on the national flag.

The teacher told a story taken from a booklet of legends about Jerusalem. The narrative spoke of a lonely wall, dark with age, and laden with the memories of the great temple, and of the free nation that dwelled here. Enemies burned the temple and drove out the Jews. They tried to destroy the wall, but their tools broke. The gentiles used the wall as a rubbish heap in order to obviate its presence. For centuries, in their hatred of the Jews, they dumped their garbage about the wall, until it disappeared from sight.

One day a diaspora Jew came to see the wall, but all denied its existence. He came to a great mound of rubbish and there learned of the custom of obliterating the Jewish wall. He swore to save it. A rumor spread that precious metals were buried there. The populace swarmed to sift through the garbage, found some coins of value, and uncovered the top stones. Happy, the Jew kissed the wall. The next morning another rumor spread that treasure was buried at its base. People excavated the rubbish and gradually the whole of the wall was revealed. No treasure was found except for that of the Jew—the Wall itself. Yet the Wall still was filthy; but a miracle occurred. Clouds gathered and rain poured, cleansing and purfying the Wall. And the Jew gave thanks for this salvation.

Dancing, and carrying toy blocks, the 3 year-olds built a wall of roughly their own height. The other youngsters formed a circle, held hands, and revolved singing and dancing around this model. With this the celebration ended.

Discussion. Unlike the previous three celebrations, in this one no reference is made to the family, nor for that matter to any social units that may mediate between nation-state and citizen. Their relationship is direct, immediate, and hierarchical. Here the family unit of the child not only is superceded but is rendered irrelevant to the nation-state. The nation is presented as the redeemer of the state, and the state as the protector of the nation. Both depend on the faith and loyalty of the citizenry.[11]

The courtyard is decorated in emblems of statehood; and it acquires the semblance of an official locale. The outfits of the youngsters are standardized through colors that shape these children into living emblems of the state. Thus their bodies are inscribed with signs of citizenship, of belonging to the collectivity. Each child appears as a small part that embodies the greater whole, itself composed of many such components. In other words, the ideal relationship between citizen and collectivity is one of synecdoche. This relationship is not manipulated during the ceremony, but is repeated in various ways.

The ceremony is divided into a preamble of songs and speech, followed by the formal enactments. The preamble enunciates themes and sentiments that are developed through the enactments. The opening songs lay out the connectivity of past, present, and future; although the words of each have in common references to verities that are held eternal. The first is about King David, who made Jerusalem the capital of ancient Israel. The second rejoices in Jerusalem eternal. The third tells that the temple, a metaphor of the nation in its reborn homeland, will be rebuilt. The words of the teacher situate these sentiments within the reality of present-day Israel. The assembly celebrates the reunification of the eternal capital of the nation-state, as do all of its citizenry on this day. Moreover this deed was accomplished by citizens in the people's army of the Israel Defence Forces, in which all these youngsters will serve on their completion of high school. Collectivity and citizenship are presented in and through one another in mutual interdependence.

The enactments begin with a poem that evokes a feeling of prophecy. The doves dream that the renewed people of Israel will rebuild the city around the central focus of the eternal Wall. In Israel the dove is an emblem of peace that harks back to the biblical story of Noah's Ark and the dove that returned with an olive branch, signifying an end to God's wrath. The poem connotes that the people of Israel will accomplish their task with God's blessing. The next song expresses the longing of people and nation to return to Jerusalem, and so to carry out this endeavor. The sense of prophecy is mated with feelings of deepest desire.

In turn, prophecy and desire are realized as six youngsters create a living Shield of David. This is a complex multivocalic symbol used by the Zionist movement to signify rejuvenation and attachment to a national homeland (See Scholem 1971). Here it is sufficient to note again that it is a preeminent emblem of the State. In this ceremony, children who sat in a loose assemblage create the precise and coordinated pattern of the emblem. As in other living symbols, just as they bring the emblem into being through their collective efforts, so its shape ties them to one another and incorporates them within a greater and encompassing design. The aesthetic and emotive effect is one of a symmetrical blending of part and whole, of the blue and white coloration of dress and of connecting ribbons. The implication is that the citizens of the future will continue together to carry out the design of the emblem, which signifies the actualization of the collectivity.

The primary message of the narrative of the rediscovery of the Wall is that the Jews must defend their patrimony, otherwise they will lose this. The tale is an allegory: the world of Israel, signified by the Wall, must be demarcated clearly from that of non-Jews who threaten its integrity and viability. This is the logic of nation and state, at their boundaries, and it is one that resonates strongly with aspects of the historical Jewish experience. In terms of nationhood then, one either is a Jew or one is not. In terms of statehood, one either is a citizen or one is not. In the ideology of the nation-state these two dimensions of inclusion-exclusion become almost isomorphic. The outer boundaries of the permissible are set by the collectivity, to which the desires of the citizen are subordinate. This is perhaps the highest level of contrast between "inside" and "outside" that is set for the Jewish citizen of modern Israel; and this is a lesson that youngsters will have reason to learn in numerous contexts beyond that of the family in years to come. At this level of contrast the hierarchy, values, and relationships of the family always are of lesser relevance.

The tale posits a series of contrasts between Jew and gentile that derive from a simple postulate: that the Wall, and by analogy the nation and state, are indestructible and enduring despite all the depredations of enemies throughout the centuries. This is its internal and eternal truth. By comparison all else is transitory. The Jew who returns to his source, across the gap of generations, is motivated by ideology. His is the wisdom of spirituality. The gentiles who try to destroy his roots are driven by materialism. He uses their cupidity to reveal the glory of the Wall; and his spirituality helps to bring about its cleansing. In the context of the celebration the qualities of Wall and Jew are those of the nation-state and its citizenry. The attributes of the gentiles are associated with all those who would deny to the Jews their homeland. The tale is at once a metaphor of renewal and a parable about boundaries of protection and national salvaton that, in the modern world, the state views itself as best able to uphold.

The closing enactment brings the message of the story into existence through the cooperative efforts of the children, just as the living Shield realized the prophecy of the poetic doves. The youngsters build the Wall from the ground up, just as modern Israel was redeemed through the joint efforts of its citizenry. The simulated labors of the children signify that which will be expected of them when they attain adulthood and full citizenship. The children dance in an unbroken circle around the completed Wall. Again their formation evokes egalitarianism, synchronization, connectivity, and perhaps the outer boundary of statehood that must be drawn and protected by its citizenry. Once more the center of the circle is filled, here by the model of the Wall—an emblem that is hierarchical and authoritative and, above all, a symbol of the Israel nation-state.

Conclusion

In the world of the little child the kindergarten celebration is among the very few categories of occasion when the order of things that structures the wider social environment directly intersects with, and dominates, that of the home. In part this is evident through explicit symbolism. Yet perhaps more profound in their impact are the architectonics of enactment. Their significance derives from the very ways in which people in unison are mobilized, organized, and synchronized in social formations in order to accomplish the more explicit scenarios of celebration. The lineal progressions of such formations constitute their own implicit sets of messages; and it is these that we have addressed here.

These celebrations, and numerous others like them, make extensive and intensive use of living formations. Some of these take the shape of explicit symbols, like the hannukiah and the Shield of David. Others, like the unbroken circle and the dyad, remain more implicit. In either instance these are highly powerful media. Through them the meaning of things is turned into the shape of things. The shape of things is graspable by the senses, as is the case of icon and emblem. Yet in such latter instances these shapes still are largely external to the human body, to the source of emotions and feelings. But one grasps the shape of things in living formations by living through them. This is a more sensual experience; one that engages the senses more fully to create a holistic experiential environment. Architects sometimes write of haptic space, of coming to know the shape of space and the feelings this engenders through the sense of touch. Through living formations the visual, the auditory, the tactile, and perhaps the olfactory senses are all "touched" by the shape of things. The meaning of form and the form of meaning become inextricable.

The sequencing of formations, in keeping with premises of lineality, are at the experiential heart of the kinds of enactments that we have addressed. Indeed, as noted, they are intended to touch the heart of the little child, and so to impress upon his being lessons that otherwise may remain more exterior to his sense of self. In particular we have stressed certain themes that will be adumbrated for the child in numerous ways and contexts in the years to come: for example, the relationship between hierarchy and equality. The interior hierarchy of the family is supplanted and is subsumed by the superordination of the collectivity. The collectivity, the nation-state, is superior to each of its citizens; yet they compose it, and it exists only through their cooperative efforts. In relation to one another, as citizens, they largely are equals. So too, as children grow, they will succeed and replace their parents, both as heads of family and as citizens. These processes depend on the proper outcome of that of maturation: the parent should infuse the child with internal restraint and with a sense of responsibility towards the collectivity and its component units. In turn, all of the above seems to evoke elementary patterns of social boundedness, and of the categories and entities that these demarcate and define. Thus boundaries between people, as members of categories and as persons, between family and collectivity, and between the nation-state and whatever lies without are taken apart, constructed anew, and, in essence, shown to exist.

Such messages are essential to the reproduction of social order. In kindergarten celebrations they are communicated in ways that make them easy to grasp for the little child. Youngsters are full of feeling, but they have yet to develop the kind of critical attitudes that can buffer personal choice against the demands of group pressure and the inducements of collective sentiments. Socialization through celebration, as instruction books for kindergartens note, is first and foremost an appeal to the emotions of little children. Thus moods and feelings about collectivity, centricity, control, and cooperation are communicated early on to Israeli youngsters. These sentiments were crucial to the periods of the *yishuv* and the early state, years of self-defense for survival and growth. Yet one should inquire whether the emphasis today on these and related values survives primarily through inertia, and through the inability of the apparatus of education and polity to check the viability of its own involution. The further growth of the nation-state may depend as much on the teaching of critical perspectives and of personal choice as it does on values that continue to close the collective circle.

Notes

1. Both in the pre-state and post-state periods there is no especial distinction between nursery school and kindergarten. Youngsters may be in kindergarten at age 2, and at age 6 continue on to elementary school.

2. The Hebrew term for kindergarten teacher, in the feminine gender, is *gannenet*. Its meaning is literally that of "gardener." The connotations of the term, as in English, are those of one who is an active agent in the processes of growing, of cultivating, and of taming. The term likely is a translation of the German *kindergertnerin*, a gardener of children, and is distinguished clearly in Hebrew from "educator" (fem. *m'khanekhet*) and "teacher" (fem. *mora*). The Hebrew term for kindergarten, *gan yeladim*, again is a translation from the German.

3. Our usage is analogous to that of "hidden curriculum" (Gearing and Tindall 1973:103), although we stress more the contested relationship between parents and state that is implicit in the maturation of youngsters, from offspring to citizens.

4. These comments hold as well for social science in Israel. The major exceptions are the study of kindergarten birthday parties by Doleve-Gandelman (1982) and the unpublished work of Shalva Weil on this topic. These occasions emphasize more the development of the child as a certain kind of social person. The ceremonials of our essay relate more to the implicit prefiguration of a statist view of social order. Therefore birthday parties are excluded from our discussion.

5. Descriptions of daily life and of ceremonial occasions in kindergartens were collected during the course of a seminar on these subjects, in urban Israel, conducted by Lea Shamagar-Handelman at the Hebrew University. The ethnographers were supervisors employed by the Ministry of Education. They observed kindergartens that they themselves supervised, and so with which they were conversant. Their observations and responses, and those of the teachers that they reported on, convinced us that the distinction between explicit and implicit agendas of ceremonials, discussed in the text, was a valid one. These educators quite consistently understood such events in terms of the obvious

occasions that they celebrated; and in terms of that which they perceived as the cooperation between teacher and parent in the attainment of a consensus on the education of the child. They did not acknowledge that the form and substance of celebratory enactments in the kindergarten implicitly communicated a statist perspective. However they did agree that the task of the teacher was to educate, not only the child, but also the parents. This is discussed in the following section of the text.

All the kindergartens observed belonged to the state secular stream of education in Israel. All their classes consisted both of boys and girls; although, for the sake of convenience, we use the masculine gender to refer to the child in general terms. These kindergartens operated six days a week, four to five hours a day.

6. We do not discuss an example of holy days, the Days of Rest, like Passover and the weekly Welcome of the Sabbath (*kabbalat shabbat*). These occasions are celebrated primarily within the family; while, within the kindergarten these, and others of the same category, are observed as rehearsals for family celebrations rather than as enactments. Their performance in earnest is permitted only on the correct ritual date and time, and in accordance with procedures laid down in texts of sacred standing. Their format of rehearsal in the kindergarten also is largely in line with such textual directives. Therefore the extent of implicit symbolic manipulation is more restricted; and so these kinds of occasion are of less concern to this paper.

7. On each of the four sides of the Hannukah top is inscribed the first letter of each of the Hebrew words, "Ness Gadol Haya Po" (There was a great miracle here). Spinning the top is a popular children's game. Regardless of which side remains uppermost when the top topples, its letter signifies the integrity and unity of the whole message, as does the top in its circular spinning.

8. In order to avoid confusion it should be noted that the *hannukiah* is distinguished from the *menorah* (the candalabrum) that appears as the official emblem of the state of Israel. The hannukiah has 8 candles (excluding the shamash) to commemorate the eight days for which the miracle of Hannukah supplied oil for the 6 candles of the menorah of the Temple on Mount Moriah.

9. In modern Israel the circle dance became a popular form through which to express egalitarianism and the dynamism of enduring bonds between persons who, through their cooperative efforts, forged the embracing collectivity of which they were a part.

10. The age to which, tradition has it, Moses lived; and a customary greeting of well-wishing.

11. We should mention that other such celebrations did not ignore the family, but involved it in the scenario. In some cases, fathers were invited to reminisce about their experiences as soldiers fighting for Jerusalem; while in others parents were asked to tell about life in Jerusalem under siege during the War of Independence. In these instances the stress was on the obligation, transferred from parents to children, to serve the country under any circumstances.

References

Ben-Yosef, Yitzhak. 1976. "Ha'khag k'besis ha'khinukh" (The Holiday as a Basis of Education). In *Sefer Hayovel Shel Histadrut Hamorim (Book of the Fiftieth Anniversary of the Teachers' Union)*. Tel Aviv: Histadrut Hamorim B'Eretz Yisrael. pp. 305-8.

Bernstein, Basil, H.L. Elvin, and R.S. Peters. 1966. "Ritual in Education." *Philosophical Transactions of the Royal Society of London* 251 (772):429-36, Series B.

Burnett, J.H. 1969. "Ceremony, Rites and Economy in the Student System of an American High School." *Human Organization* 28:1-10.

Doleve-Gandelman, Tzili. 1982. "Identité Sociale et Cérémonie d'Anniversaire dans les Jardins d'Enfants Israéliens." Unpublished Ph.D. Thesis. Paris: Ecole des Hautes Etudes en Sciences Sociales.

Durkheim, Emile. 1956. *Sociology and Education*. Glencoe: Free Press.

Fayence-Glick, S. 1948. "Khanuka B'gan Ha'yeladim" (Hannukah in the Kindergarten). *Oshiot* 2:28-39.

_____. 1957. "Gan Ha'yeladim B'Eretz Yisrael" (Kindergartens in Eretz Yisrael). In *Sefer Hayovel Shel Histadrut Hamorim (Book of the Fiftieth Anniversary of the Teachers' Union)*. Tel Aviv: Histadrut Hamorim B'Eretz Yisrael. pp. 132-44.

Fuchs, E. 1969. *Teachers Talk*. New York: Doubleday.

Gearing, F.O., and B. Alan Tindall. 1973. "Anthropological Studies of the Educational Process." *Annual Review of Anthropology* 2:95-105.

Geertz, Clifford. 1972. "Notes on the Balinese Cockfight." *Daedalus* 101:1-37.

Gracy, Harry L. 1975. "Learning the Student Role: Kindergarten as Academic Boot Camp." In *Lifestyles: Diversion in American Society*, 2nd ed. Ed. S.D. Feldman and Gerald W. Thielbor. Boston: Little, Brown. pp. 437-42.

Handelman, Don. 1978. "Bureaucratic Interpretation: The Perception of Child Abuse in Urban Newfoundland." In *Bureaucracy and World View: Studies in the Logic of Official Interpretation*. Ed. Don Handelman and Elliott Leyton. St. John's: Memorial University of Newfoundland.

_____. 1980. "The Ritual Clown: Attributes and Affinities." *Anthropos* 76:321-70.

_____. 1982. "Reflexivity in Festival and Other Cultural Events." In *Essays in the Sociology of Perception*. Ed. Mary Douglas. London: Routledge & Kegan Paul. pp. 162-90.

_____. 1983. "The Madonna and the Mare: Symbolic Organization in the Palio of Siena." In *Spectacle—An Anthropological Inquiry*. Ed. Victor Turner and Masao Yamaguchi. Tokyo: Sanseido. pp. 153-84.

_____. 1984. "Inside-Out, Outside-In: Concealment and Revelation in Newfoundland Christmas Mumming." In *Text, Play, and Story* (1983 Proceedings of the American Ethnological Society). Ed. Edward Bruner. St. Paul: West Publishing.

Heffernan, Helen, and Vivian E. Todd. 1960. *The Kindergarten Teacher*. Boston: D.C. Heath.

Jones, N. Blurton. 1969. "An Ethological Study of Some Aspects of Social Behavior of Children in Nursery School." In *Primate Ethology*. Ed. D. Morris. New York: Doubleday. pp. 437-63.

Kapferer, Judith L. 1981. "Socialization and the Symbolic Order of the School." *Anthropology and Education Quarterly* 12:258-74.

Katerbursky, Zivya. 1962. *B'netivot Hagan (The Ways of the Garden)*. Tel Aviv: Otsar Hamoreh.

Langer, Susanne. 1953. *Feeling and Form*. London: Routledge & Kegan Paul.

Lee, Dorothy. 1959. "Codifications of Reality: Lineal and Nonlineal." In *Freedom and Culture*. Englewood Cliffs, N.J.: Prentice-Hall. pp. 105-20.

Manning, Frank E., ed. 1983. *The Celebration of Society*. Bowling Green: Bowling Green University Popular Press.

Ministry of Education and Culture. 1967. *Hannukah, Khag Ha'urim (Hannukah, Feast of Lights)*. Jerusalem: Ministry of Education and Culture.

Moore, Sally Falk, and Barbara Myerhoff, eds. 1977. *Secular Ritual*. Assen: Van Gorcum.

Moore, Elenora Haegele. 1959. *Fives at School*. New York: Putnam's.

Naftali, Nitza, and Nekhama Nir-Yaniv, eds. 1974. *Pirkei Hadrakha: Me'onot Yom (Subjects of Instructions: Day-Care Centers)*. Jerusalem: Ministry of Education and Culture.

Rabinowitz, Esther. 1958a. "Hakhag B'gan Ha'yeladim" (The Holiday in the Kindergarten). In *Khagim U'moadim Bakhinukh (Holidays and Times in Education)*. Ed. Esther Rabinowitz. Tel Aviv: Urim. pp. 39-44.

_____. 1958b. "Hakhag, Mashmauto V'erko Bakhinukh" (The Holiday, its Meaning and Value in Education). In *Khagim U'moadim Bakhinukh*, pp. 9-57.

_____. 1958c. "The Place of the Holiday in the Kindergarten." In *Khagim U'moadim Bakhinukh*, pp. 141-46.

Scholem, Gershom. 1971. "The Star of David: History of a Symbol." In *The Messianic Idea in Judaism*. New York: Schocken. pp. 257-81.

Shamgar-Handelman, Lea. 1981. "Administering to War Widows in Israel." *Social Analysis* 9:24-47.

Shemer, Aliza, ed. 1966. *Darkei Avoda B'ganei Yeladim (Ways of Work in Kindergartens)*. Tel Aviv: Tarbout V'khinukh.

Shulz, Jeffrey, and Susan Florio. 1979. "Stop and Freeze: Social and Physical Space in a Kindergarten/First Grade Classroom." *Anthropology and Education Quarterly* 10:166-81.

Shure, M. 1963. "Psychological Ecology of a Nursery School." *Child Development* 34:979-92.

State of Israel. 1983. *Statistical Abstract of Israel* (no. 34). Jerusalem: Central Bureau of Statistics.

Turner, Victor W. 1974. *Dramas, Fields and Metaphors*. Ithaca: Cornell University Press.

Turner, Victor W., ed. 1982. *Celebration: Studies in Festivity and Ritual*. Washington, D.C.: Smithsonian Institution Press.

Waller, Willard. 1932. *The Sociology of Teaching*. New York: Wiley.

Weiss, M.S., and P.H. Weiss. 1976. "A Public School Ritual Ceremony." *Journal of Research and Development in Education* 9:22-28.

Willeford, William. 1969. *The Fool and His Sceptre*. London: Edward Arnold.

Zanbank-Wilf, Aliza. 1958. "Hagan K'markiv B'yetzirat Avirat Khag Babayit" (The Kindergarten as a Component in Creating a Holiday Atmosphere at Home). In *Khagim U'moadim Bakinukh*, pp. 57-59.

4

Establishing Authority: The Memorialization of Jabotinsky and the Burial of the Bar-Kochba Bones in Israel under the Likud

Myron J. Aronoff

The romance of politics was best used to numb and quell the fears of the uninformed.
—Goethe, *Aus Meinen Leben*

The Likud came to power in 1977 after an extended period of Labor dominance of the political system which had begun during its formative period in Palestine two decades before Israel won independence. To gain power, Herut, the dominant party in the Likud alignment, had to overcome the pariah image that characterized it in the early years of statehood (as did Herut's parent, the Revisionist Movement in the earlier period). During the Likud's reign (1977–1984), it attempted to eliminate the last vestiges of ideological legitimacy which Labor retained and to establish its own ideological hegemony (Aronoff 1984a, 1984b). It systematically utilized the state agencies to propagate the Likud's heroes, myths, interpretations of both history and of present realities, and to incorporate them into the framework of the national political culture.

In this essay I analyze some of the ways in which this was done by focusing on selected decisions and activities of the Ministerial Committee on Symbols and Ceremonies (MCSC). From the records of twenty years of MCSC activities (April 1962–April 1983), I have selected two cases which illustrate the process through which the Likud's leaders, building on decisions and practices of previous Labor governments, attempted to shape political culture according to their unique interpretation of reality.

In the first case I analyze the memorialization (and near deification) of Vladimir Zeev Jabotinsky, the ideological guru of the Revisionist Movement and of Herut. Jabotinsky died and was buried in the United States in 1940. His remains were reinterred on Mount Herzl in Jerusalem at the decision of Prime Minister Levi Eshkol (Labor) in 1963. The process whereby Jabotinsky was elevated to the status of one of the nation's greats was continued to an elaborate extent under the governments headed by his disciple, Menachem Begin. I analyze the symbolic and political implications of the unprecedented festivities and events marking Jabotinsky's 100th birthday and related memorialization activities.

In the second case, I explore the implications of the elaborate state funeral that the Likud government gave for the reputed remains of the fighters and followers of Shimon Bar-Kochba, leader of the last Jewish revolt against the Romans. Although David Ben-Gurion (Israel's first prime minister) had initially agreed (with reservations) to the reinterment of these remains, neither he nor any of his Labor successors actually arranged to do so. These cases illustrate how the symbolic and ceremonial presentation of selected historic events and figures is manipulated to provide explanations of current political realities that support government policies. Such tactics increased the legitimacy of the Likud government but failed to establish its ideological dominance.

Background

A dramatic increase in the scope and volume of subjects covered in the MCSC occurred after the Likud came to power. Although over the years that Labor dominated the government, the number of meetings of the MCSC and the decisions made by it increased considerably, both grew substantially during the Likud dominated governments. As Table 4.1 shows, during fifteen years of Labor rule the MCSC met 134 times and made 429 decisions compared with 87 meetings and 615 decisions during the five year period of Likud rule analyzed. Leaving out the term of the committee in which the Likud took over from Labor, and comparing the last five full terms of the committee under Labor with five almost complete terms under the Likud, we find that the Labor MCSC met 52 times and made 174 decisions while the Likud MCSC met 82 times and came to 595 decisions. Labor averaged 10.4 meetings and 34.8 decisions per term while the Likud averaged 16.4 meetings and 119 decisions per term.[1] The Likud MCSC made almost three and a half times as many decisions as did the Labor MCSC. The difference is even greater than appears, because the Likud MCSC adopted the technique of approving *en bloc* decisions on entire series of stamps for the year, whereas many of the decisions during the Labor period included approval of individual series or even individual

TABLE 4.1
Comparison of the Number of Meetings Held and Decisions Taken by the Ministerial Committee on Symbols and Ceremonies during Labor- and Likud-led Governments

Labor-Led Governments (1962-1977)

	Term of Committee	Meetings	Decisions
1)	4/ 3/62— 6/18/62	2	9
2)	3/18/63— 5/ 6/63	2	7
3)	10/28/63— 5/ 5/64	5	14
4)	10/26/64—12/27/65	6	20
5)	3/ 8/66— 6/20/66	4	11
6)	11/ 9/66— 8/21/67	7	29
7)	11/ 6/67— 6/16/68	11	37
8)	10/27/68— 8/18/69	12	40
9)	10/ 5/69— 9/27/70	17	44
10)	1/ 3/71— 8/16/71	6	23
11)	9/26/71— 7/17/72	15	51
12)	10/ 8/72— 8/12/73	12	35
13)	11/14/73— 9/ 8/74	8	27
14)	11/19/74— 8/20/75	10	40
15)	10/19/75— 8/23/76	7	21
16)	9/29/76— 7/14/77	10	21
Total		134	429
Average		8.375	26.81
Labor	9/26/71— 8/23/76	52	174
Labor Average per term		10.4	34.8

Likud-Led Governments (1977-1983)

	Term of Committee	Meetings	Decisions
17)	7/26/77— 9/ 4/77	5	20
18)	9/20/77— 9/19/78	18	129
19)	10/31/78— 8/27/79	19	120
20)	10/15/79— 9/ 8/80	10	68
21)	10/12/80— 6/14/81	9	70
22)	10/14/81— 4/13/83	26	208
Total		87	615
Average		14.5	102.5
Likud	9/20/77— 4/13/83	82	595
Likud Average per term		16.4	119

stamps. Therefore the actual proportion of decisions made by the Likud MCSC is even greater than the figure indicates.

There are a number of reasons why the MCSC under the Likud-led government was considerably more active than it was under Labor governments. The two movements and their leaders had strikingly different philosophical attitudes toward symbols and ceremonies. Whereas Labor resorted to ceremonials, it denigrated their importance. Within the labor movement there was an element of exaggerated opposition to appearance and formality. For example, members of the Palmach (an elite military unit affiliated with the Labor-dominated Haganah defense organization before independence) neither wore insignia of rank nor saluted.

In contrast, the historic leadership of the Herut component of the Likud greatly valued the importance of the symbolic dimension of politics. Liebman and Don-Yehiya (1983:77) claim that, "despite their failure to create their own integrated symbol system, the revisionists regarded symbols with even greater seriousness than did the Zionist-socialists." Quoting Jabotinsky's statement, Remba (1964:159) writes, "Almost three-fourths of true culture is made up of ritual and ceremony. Political law and freedom rise and fall through parliamentary ritual and procedure, and the life of social groups would sink into darkness without the primeval ceremonies of culture and custom." Jabotinsky claimed that Jews have a special need to be educated to ceremonials. His disciple and successor, Menachem Begin, exhibited a similar orientation. He was from 1967 to 1969 an active member of the MCSC while he served in the National Unity Governments led by Levi Eshkol and by Golda Meir. During his tenure as Prime Minister, Begin not only took an interest in the decisions of the MCSC but directly intervened on several critical occasions to initiate and/or influence decisions. (Table 4.2 lists the responsibilities of the MCSC.)

The last Labor chairman of the MCSC, Shlomo Hillel, felt strongly that there were too many state ceremonials, and that their number needed to be reduced in order to maintain their value. The chairman of the MCSC during the tenure of Likud governments under discussion, Yitzhak Moda'i, agreed in principle with this position. However, he was an extremely dynamic and ambitious politician who was attempting to establish his leadership of the Liberal Party and a prominent position at the top of the Likud leadership. He served as a Minister without portfolio and as Minister of Energy at different times during this period. Moda'i utilized his MCSC chairmanship to improve his position in his party, in the Likud bloc, and in the cabinet as well as to gain greater public recognition. Therefore, against his own judgement, he gave in to Begin's pressures in the cases discussed below. As a former top business executive he used his considerable administrative skills to further rationalize and institutionalize the pro-

TABLE 4.2
Spheres of Responsibility of the MCSC

Protocol
The determination of priority lists of categories of officials invited to state events
The establishment of procedures for state funerals
State visits of foreign dignitaries and heads of state
The display of the flag and the playing of the national anthem
The official status of Jerusalem and its role as the capital of the state

State recognition and honor
The awarding of military citations by the state and granting permission to Israelis to
    receive citations from foreign countries
Memorialization through the naming of places, the holding of state ceremonies, or
    the creation of monuments
The issuance of stamps, currency, or medals
The authorization of all state memorial days and holidays, e.g., Holocaust and
    Heroism Remembrance Day, Memorial Day, Independence Day, and Re-
    unification of Jerusalem Day

Anniversaries of historic events
Balfour Declaration Day (November 2, 1917)
The anniversary of the United Nations resolution which led to Israeli independence
    (November 29, 1947)
Tel Hai Day (11th of Adar-discussed below) [established by Labor]
The Peace Treaty with Egypt (March 26, 1979) [established by the Likud]

The death anniversaries of national figures
The first three presidents (Chaim Weizmann, Izhak Ben-Zvi, and Zalman Shazar)
The first four prime ministers (David Ben-Gurion, Moshe Sharett, Levi Eshkol, and
    Golda Meir)
The father of modern political Zionism who was founder and first president of the
    World Zionist Organization, Theodore Herzl
The founder of Revisionist Zionism, Ze'ev (Vladimir) Jabotinsky

cedures of the MCSC. (After the 1984 election led to a grand coalition of Labor and the Likud, Moda'i, who had gained leadership of the Liberals, became Finance Minister.)

The government's positive orientation toward the symbolic dimension of politics and its recognition of the importance of symbols and ceremonies, combined with the more efficiently run MCSC headed by its ambitious chairman, created an environment in which requests by individual citizens and various groups were given prompt and frequently positive attention. This greater responsiveness of the MCSC, especially to the interests of groups close to it or which it courted, in turn encouraged more groups to turn to it with their requests, thereby increasing the volume of decisions handled by the committee.

Since the ascendance of the Likud to power ended nearly fifty years of Labor dominance of the political system, the new regime was faced with a particularly acute need to create a solid base of legitimacy for its rule. The MCSC became one of the principal (although certainly not the exclusive) means of establishing, extending, and consolidating the legitimacy of the Likud leadership of the nation. The increased number of meetings and decisions of the MCSC resulted in a much larger number of ceremonials having been held during the rule of the Likud than during any comparable period of Labor tenure in office.[2]

The Memorialization of Jabotinsky

When the Likud came to power, Moda'i proposed a single day to memorialize all of the "greats of the nation," however, this idea was opposed by Prime Minister Begin. The initial decision of the MCSC to the request by the Board of Trustees for the Memorialization of Jabotinsky for state memorial ceremony to be held within the framework of the celebration of Israel's thirtieth year of independence was that it should be held within the framework of the Jewish Agency as were the memorial ceremonies for Herzl and Weizmann. Upon Begin's insistence, nevertheless, the MCSC decided that the memorials for the three would henceforth be state ceremonies.

Begin was not content with honoring his former mentor through the framework of the Jewish Agency, but insisted on the honor which had been accorded to David Ben-Gurion—a state ceremony. He was sensitive to the symbolic implications in the difference between the two types of ceremonies, and by associating the decision with one involving memorials for Herzl and Weizmann, Jabotinsky was symbolically accorded equal position with the founder of Zionism, and his successor, the first president of the state. The political implications for the legitimization of Jabotinsky's disciple, Begin, and his followers are most significant. This symbolic act was an important step in the process through which the former pariah movement acquired legitimacy as an integral part of the Zionist enterprise, and through which its leaders attempted to establish their heroes, myths, and symbols as central to, if not dominant forces in, the political culture of the state.

In his efforts to normalize relations with the opposition (and perhaps to establish his independence from his mentor, Ben-Gurion), Levi Eshkol aided the Herut in several ways—most particularly by reburying the remains of Jabotinsky on Mt. Herzl in a state ceremony.[3] Other decisions by the MCSC during the same period contributed to the same process. For example, they stressed that representatives of all Knesset factions, including the opposition, must be invited to all state ceremonies. Since the MCSC stressed that it was the responsibility of the Foreign Office to enforce this decision and that it would check to make sure that the decision was being implemented, it is logical to assume that this practice had not always been scrupulously followed.[4]

The process of legitimization of the Likud was immeasurably strengthened when Gahal (the alignment between Herut and the Liberal Party) was coopted into the Government of National Unity on the eve of the 1967 War (see Levite and Tarrow 1983). Menachem Begin joined the MCSC for the first time on August 21, 1967, and served on it through the meeting on October 5, 1969. Begin's active participation on the committee further facilitated symbolic acts of legitimization of the movement he led. For example, during his tenure on the committee it included the members of the Irgun Zvai Leumi (IZL), which Begin commanded, and the Lehi undergrounds for eligibility for citations for Fighters for the Establishment of the State.[5] This act gave symbolic recognition to the important role these organizations played in creating the state. Their role had previously been downplayed, ignored, or delegitimized by emphasizing their dissident character and the terrorist tactics they employed.[6] The decision to issue a stamp bearing the picture of Jabotinsky during the period in which Labor was in power was another example of such a legitimating act.

Jabotinsky's 100th Birthday Celebrations

The memorial days for the great leaders of the Zionist movement and the State of Israel were set according to Jewish tradition on the anniversary of their deaths (based on the Jewish calendar). An unprecedented decision was taken by the MCSC at the strong urging of Prime Minister Begin to hold elaborate national celebrations in honor of the 100th birthday of Jabotinsky.[7] After the MCSC responded favorably to Begin's initiative and suggested the appropriate agencies to direct the ceremonies, the committee yielded to the Prime Minister's request that his office be placed in charge of the events.

The events were scheduled to take place between Jabotinsky's birthday and the anniversary of his death based on the Hebrew calendar. The activities which were held between October 22, 1980 and July 22, 1981 were unprecedented in scope. When compared with the most elaborate equivalent series of events conducted during Labor's rule, those which memorialized the first anniversary of the death of David Ben-Gurion (who died on December 1, 1973), the Likud's efforts, while following a basic pattern established by previous Labor governments, were far more extensive.[8] It is as if the Likud attempted to outdo Labor, by honoring their ideological mentor and leader far more elaborately than Labor had honored Ben-Gurion. The major activities are summarized in Table 4.3.

TABLE 4.3

Major Activities of the Jabotinsky 100th Birthday Celebrations

1)	Symposia in all universities and dissertation prize
2)	Pamphlets, guide to teachers, special programs in schools
3)	Audio-visual programs in schools (movie, educational T.V. programs)
4)	Special conferences for teachers, youth movement leaders, and students
5)	Jabotinsky essays assigned in schools with prizes for best ones
6)	World Zionist Organization produced materials (including collections of his writings) in foreign languages for Diaspora schools
7)	Pamphlet prepared by Jabotinsky Institute and poster published and widely distributed by the Government Information Office
8)	Biographical film, special television, and radio programs commissioned
9)	Ministry of Defense published book and held seminars in army units led by personnel specially trained at the Jabotinsky Institute
10)	Sound & Light shows held in ten major cities
11)	Settlement, neighborhoods, housing projects, schools named Jabotinsky
12)	Special recordings of Jabotinsky's poems issued
13)	100 shekel note bearing Jabotinsky's picture, coins, medallions, and stamps with a special cancellation issued
14)	A special celebration symbol including Jabotinsky's image commissioned
15)	Special tours, lectures, seminars, lectures, and conventions held throughout the country

The MCSC received reports confirming the implementation of all of its decisions regarding the events for the 100th anniversary of Jabotinsky's birth.[9] Whereas the MCSC authorized the expenditure of 320,000 shekels on July 30, 1980 and 800,000 shekels on September 8, 1980, it specified that each agency and institution engaged in the activities, e.g. the universities and the Ministry of Defense, would pay their share of the expenses from their regular budgets. Also a considerable amount of expenses came from special funds in the Prime Minister's Office (which may be one of the reasons why the Prime Minister insisted that his office should have direct responsibility). Therefore, the cost of these activities is extremely difficult to estimate. It is obvious that the actual expenses far exceeded the nominal working budget authorized by the MCSC. Referring to the aforementioned procedures whereby the events were financed, the chairman of the MCSC told me, "The practice should be forbidden."[10]

Notes on a Jabotinsky Memorial Ceremony

Most of the memorial activities were aimed at the wider public, although actual participation in some ceremonies involved primarily the already converted. To illustrate such an example I relate the following brief summary of the memorial service held for Jabotinsky on July 10, 1983 (taken from my field notes). Buses rented by Herut branches brought people from all over the country to Mount Herzl. Overseas Betar (Herut's youth movement) youths, looking more militaristic in their uniforms than the more casually clad Israeli Betar youngsters, dashed about as veterans of the "fighting family" (as members of the dissident undergrounds are called) greeted one another with hugs and kisses. A woman complained to a friend that only one of her grandchildren had joined Betar, and having found it boring, joined Maccabee (the youth movement associated with the liberal wing of the Likud). She disapprovingly said it was not the same as Betar, and her friend commiserated with her about losing the youth. Members of the honor guard took their places around Jabotinsky's tomb.

As various ministers, deputy ministers, members of the Knesset, present and former ranking party leaders arrived and took their reserved places on chairs arranged around the grave, people in the crowd called out their names. One could gauge the status and popularity of individuals by where they were seated, who greeted them, and the extent of applause they received from the crowd. For example, Ariel "Arik" Sharon, who timed his arrival after everyone was seated and just before the announced entrances of the Speaker of the House (who was greeted by silence), the prime minister, and President Herzog, was as warmly received by the crowd as was Begin himself.

The ceremony was formally opened by Eitan Livne, a senior member of the movement. The banner of Betar was raised (with a bugle salute) followed by the national flag and the singing of the national anthem. The memorial torch was lit by two of Jabotinsky's adult grandchildren as taps was sounded. Jabotinsky's writings were recited stressing the uniqueness and purity of the Land of Israel, the glory of the generation of the revolt, and the right of the Jewish people to all of Eretz Yisrael which should never be given up. The traditional mourner's prayer was led by the chief rabbi of Zahal and the chief cantor of Zahal chanted "*El maleh rahamim*" (God is full of mercy). (A young Betar honor guard fainted.) Wreaths were laid by the president, the Speaker of the Knesset, the prime minister (who looked aged, sad, and feeble), by representatives of the World Zionist Organization and the Jewish Agency, Zahal, the Israeli police, the foreign diplomatic corps in Israel, and Jabotinsky's Movement. The ceremony was concluded with the singing of the Betar hymn which I noted was sung with considerably greater enthusiasm and participation than the national anthem had been sung. (Yitzhak Navon, the former president, had objected to the singing of the partisan song during the state ceremony, and had requested that it be sung after the conclusion of the official ceremony so that he could leave prior to its being sung.) The dignitaries filed by the grave to pay their respects in order of rank followed by the others. At the conclusion of the ceremony the people were invited to go up to Herzl's grave, but I did not see anyone do so.

As people were leaving, I heard a grandfather ask his grandson, "It was impressive wasn't it?" When the boy failed to respond he continued, "Did I tell you about the time the Foreign Minister came to me at 2:30 a.m.?" Without waiting for a reply he continued to relate a tale (which he had likely told many times previously) about Yitzhak Shamir and a gun.

Analysis

Jabotinsky is the central mythical figure in a cult of personality established around him by his disciples and their followers. The 100th birthday celebrations of Jabotinsky were unprecedented in several respects. First, the celebration of the birthday, rather than death anniversary, of a deceased public figure was not within the terms of reference of the authority of the MCSC, and had never previously taken place. The decision to celebrate the birthday of their movement's hero was probably a pragmatic one to take advantage of the opportunity of the 100th birthday to launch such a series of celebrations while the party was still in power,. However, the celebration of a birthday, rather than a death anniversary, is suffused with symbolic significance and resonates with meanings—even if not consciously intended by those who made the decision.

The celebrations of Jabotinsky's birthday symbolized the rebirth of Revisionism through Herut's dominance in the Likud-led government after the symbolic death of its unusually extended period in the political wilderness. Don Handelman (in a personal communication) points out the parallel between these celebrations, which began on Jabotinsky's birthday and ended on his death anniversary, and the Christian celebration of the birth and death of Christ. Following this line of interpretation, the ceremonial deification of Jabotinsky also announces the resurrection of Revisionism through the rise to power of Jabotinsky's disciple, Begin. Given his image as the first truly Jewish (i.e., relatively religious) Israeli prime minister, Begin could not utilize the metaphor of resurrection as effectively as did the Reverend Jesse Jackson, who, during the Democratic primary in New York which was held on the anniversary of the assassination of the Reverend Dr. Martin Luther King, Jr., dramatically proclaimed, "Today a stone has been rolled away!"

Whereas Labor had memorialized leading Zionist figures including Ben-Gurion, there had never been celebrations of such an extensive scope for them. The unprecedented scope of the events which memorialized Jabotinsky, and the conspicuous manner in which they were carried out, were necessary because they elevated to the universal mythical plane of one of the greats of the nation a previously partisan figure, who had been consid-

ered by many—including leading intellectuals and key figures in the media—to have been a pariah in the Zionist movement.

Colonel Uziel, head of the unit in Zahal which is in charge of symbols
and ceremonies, suggested in a conversation that "Jabotinsky and Ben-
Gurion are not necessarily national leaders since not everyone identifies
with them."[11] Such an evaluation is an unusual one regarding the status of
Ben-Gurion, but not for Jabotinsky. Ben-Gurion has long been regarded by
most Israelis as the father of his country (a view fostered by Labor during
its years in power). Although he was a most controversial figure who not
only clashed with his political rivals and the leading intellectuals of the
country but also with leading figures in his own party, he is almost univer-
sally considered to have been one of the greatest, if not the greatest figure in
contemporary Israeli history.[12] Even some of his most bitter political enemies whom I interviewed referred to him with great respect and even
affection.

As much as Jabotinsky was revered by his disciples he was reviled by his
enemies. To be sure the passing of time and the death of the main pro-
tagonists had tempered attitudes. Jabotinsky had yet to approach the degree of universal acceptance in the pantheon of Israel's great heroes that
Ben-Gurion had acquired. The celebration of his 100th birthday was designed to rectify this situation which was viewed by the Prime Minister as a
grave historic injustice. Similarly, the elaborate measures taken to enshrine
the heroes and martyrs of the dissident underground movements were
aimed at correcting the injustice of their having been ignored or even
maligned by the former Labor establishment. For example, the special
series of stamps and first day cover with special cancellation, issued in
honor of the "martyrs of the struggle for Israel's Independence" (proposed
by Begin), prominently featured members of IZL and Lehi among the
nineteen men and one woman who were martyred—through hanging,
shooting by firing squad, or suicide (to cheat the executioner).

The extent to which partisan political bodies and perspectives were presented as nonpartisan national institutions and views in particularly sensitive areas such as the schools and Zahal is noteworthy. For example, the
Jabotinsky Institute (an unquestionably partisan institution) trained lec-
turers to lead discussions of Jabotinsky in army units. The same institution
prepared pamphlets and guides for teachers which were published by the
government and distributed in all Israeli schools. Whereas such things
undoubtedly occurred in previous years under Labor governments, both
the magnitude and the self-consciously planned nature of this particular
campaign by the Likud government were unprecedented.

To a certain extent every government attempts to make its own partisan
perspectives accepted as national ones. Politicians may be either sincere or

cynical (i.e., as a conscious political strategy to gain greater legitimacy) in so doing. Obviously the two are not mutually exclusive. Usually both factors are operative, as they undoubtedly were in this case. Prime Minister Begin was particularly sensitive since he had been the object of Ben-Gurion's strategy of projecting Jabotinsky and Begin, Revisionism and Herut, IZL and Lechi, as pariahs beyond the pale of legitimate Zionism. That he was committed to rectifying what he perceived to have been a grave injustice is clear. One's evaluation of whether he (and his government) either merely corrected an historic wrong, or went well beyond that by rewriting Zionist history and giving an exaggerated importance to the contributions of their leaders, ideology, and underground movements depends on one's values and understanding of history and the contemporary political situation. For example, labor leaders strongly protested that the sound and light pageant that opened the Zionist Congress in 1982 "was a falsification of Zionist history" which exaggerated the role of Jabotinsky and undervalued the contributions of Ben-Gurion.[13]

Moshe Shahal, the parliamentary whip of the Labor Alignment Knesset faction, suggested that when Begin looked out from the Knesset podium onto the seats of the Labor Knesset members he didn't see them, but instead saw Ben-Gurion. Shahal claimed that Begin sought revenge. "He knows he can't erase Ben-Gurion, but wants to chip away at his image."[14] When asked, Likud leaders emphatically denied such charges. Whether or not Begin was engaged in seeking revenge by delegitimizing Labor and its myths, he was unquestionably engaged in a concerted and even passionate campaign to establish his personal, his movement's, and his government's legitimacy through the resocialization of the Israeli public to gain a new and wider appreciation of Jabotinsky and all that Jabotinsky symbolized. He condemned those who refused to accept this new interpretation of reality, particularly intellectuals and the media.

The acceptance of a movement's heroes is a first step in accepting its values. One of the means by which the Likud government attempted to accomplish this was through the use of ceremony in commemorating historical figures whose heroic acts could be utilized to provide meaningful guides to understanding current problems and dilemmas.

The State Funeral for the Remains of Bar-Kochba's Fighters and People

In March 1960, the noted archaeologist Yigal Yadin discovered, in a cave in the Judaean desert, bones and artifacts from the period of the second Jewish revolt against Rome led by Shimon Bar-Kochba in A.D. 132-135. This discovery set off a lengthy chain of events which eventually led to an elaborate state funeral on May 11, 1982, in which the remains were reinterred in a place near their discovery. I shall briefly outline the main events as they relate to the discussion of the role of the MCSC in the efforts to extend the Likud's legitimacy and to impose its interpretation of reality.

Different issues complicated this case from the beginning. First of all, the determination of the probability that the remains were Jews brought pressure from religious figures, led by Colonel Shlomo Goren (who was at the time the chief rabbi of Zahal), to rebury them. It was first suggested that they be buried in a military cemetery in Jerusalem. Secondly, the Attorney General claimed that given the age of the bones, the Department of Antiquities had authority over them which created a jurisdictional dispute.[15] To complicate matters further, Professor Yadin informed the Director General of the Ministry of Religious Affairs, Dr. Kahana, that it could not be certain that the bones were those of Jews rather than Romans.[16]

Prime Minister David Ben-Gurion appointed a committee headed by Rabbi Goren to investigate the situation. The committee determined that the bones, which included those of women and children, were the remains of Jewish refugee families from the Bar-Kochba period since they were found with Jewish artifacts and there were indications that they had been buried according to Jewish custom. The committee determined that they should be reburied according to *Halacha* (Jewish law), and considered several possible sites including Mt. Herzl. It finally recommended a site near the cave where they had been discovered and suggested that a monument be constructed expressing the heroism of the uprising of the people and the connection between the heroism of that period and the present. Ben-Gurion wrote in a memo, "I authorize the recommendation of the committee to establish a memorial (*yad*) for the slain of Bar-Kochba. *I have some doubts regarding the recommendations . . .* I would like to know the opinion of Yigal Yadin" [emphasis added].[17]

Rabbi Goren told me he knew nothing of any reservations expressed by Ben-Gurion regarding the committee's recommendations (contained in the aforementioned memo). When asked to account for the fact that the committee's recommendations were never implemented, he responded that "Ben-Gurion became busy with other matters and Yadin and the [other] archaeologists stole the bones."[18] I was unsuccessful in verifying the nature of Ben-Gurion's reservations regarding the committee's recommendations, although I offer a possible explanation below. Clearly, he had more important priorities.

Since Ben-Gurion expressed a desire to discuss the matter with Yigal Yadin, it is noteworthy that Yadin refused to attend the state funeral in 1982. He publicly declared that he could not vouch for the Jewishness of the nineteen skeletons he discovered, and expressed political, ecological, and professional objections to the ceremonies that were held (cited below).

Rabbi Goren, by then chief Ashkenazic rabbi of Israel, had become embroiled in a conflict with the nation's archaeologists when he sided with ultraorthodox Jews who violently protested the excavations taking place in David's city, along the external perimeter of the walled part of Jerusalem, because they claimed the archaeologists were desecrating an ancient Jewish cemetery (a charge which the archaeologists vehemently denied). Rabbi Goren explained to me that after keeping quiet all these years, the controversy over the excavations in David's City gave him the opportunity to reopen the issue of the reburial of the bones discovered by Yadin and others twenty-three years earlier.

When Rabbi Goren approached Minister Moda'i with his request for a state funeral for the Bar-Kochba remains, Moda'i refused his request because he opposed state ceremonies for such historic cases. He feared there would be no end to such requests if the precedent were to be established. Goren then approached Prime Minister Begin who enthusiastically agreed and, overriding Moda'i's objections, obtained MCSC decision 17 on November 10, 1981 to hold a state funeral ceremony for "Bar-Kochba's fighters and people."

In this decision and two subsequent ones (54 on March 31, 1982 and 60 on April 25, 1982), the following policies pertaining to the ceremony were established. The Ministry of Defense and the Ministry of Education and Culture were instructed to hold informational and educational activities on the period of Bar-Kochba's revolt stressing the tradition of heroism. This complemented the decision to make the theme for the celebrations of Israel's 35th year of independence the "Year of Heroism." The MCSC delegated authority for all final decisions relating to the ceremony to the Prime Minister (including the location for the ceremonies), and delegated responsibility for the implementation of the ceremonies to Rabbi Goren and Zahal. In decision 60 on April 25, 1980, they approved the final plans which were carried out to the letter.

The funeral took place on May 11, 1982 at 10 a.m. at Nahal Chavare in the Judaean desert 500 meters from the camp from which the cave had been sieged by the Romans. The remains of the fighters (men), women, and children were buried in three separate identical wood caskets brought from Tel Hashomer cemetery by honor guard in helicopters to the burial site. Military chaplains acted as poll bearers. Prayers were recited by the chief military chaplain, including one especially composed for the occasion which berated the "evil" Romans. Psalms (*perek t'hilim*) were recited by the chief Sephardic rabbi. The chief Ashkenazic rabbi recited the traditional mourner's prayer (*kadish*). The prime minister gave the eulogies. The chief cantor of Zahal chanted "*El maleh rachamim*," and the head of the Zahal Chaplaincy for burials recited "*bakashat mechila*" (request for forgiveness). State wreaths were placed and the honor guard fired three volleys. The full ceremonies were covered by Israel's only television channel as well as by radio broadcasts, thereby reaching a wide section of the population.

One hundred fifty official guests were brought by helicopter. The guest list included: the president, the prime minister, speaker of the Knesset, president of the Supreme Court, the two chief rabbis, Cabinet ministers, chairman of the Jewish Agency, deputy ministers, attorney general, state controller, governor of the Bank of Israel, chief of staff of Zahal, commander of the police, secretary of the Cabinet, former presidents, heads of the Knesset party factions, deputy Knesset speakers, Knesset committee chairman, former ministers, a limited number of Zahal generals, limited number of police commanders, the president's and the prime minister's military secretaries and the sargeant of arms of the Knesset, the prime minister's security personnel, and the archaeologists who excavated the site (who boycotted the ceremony).

The budget for the ceremonies was 7,158,000 shekels, which came from a special fund for state funerals in the Prime Minister's Office. An additional 450,000 shekels was allocated for a tombstone which was authorized in decision 120 of the MCSC on November 17, 1982. The press estimated that actual costs were in the vicinity of $250,000, which included the cost of bulldozing helicopter landing pads, bringing protests from the Nature Reserve Authority because the government failed to follow the legal procedures for obtaining the proper permits and because the delicate desert ecology was extensively damaged.

In fact, protests against the ceremonies were expressed in different ways and for different reasons. Professor Yadin expressed a preference for burial on Mount Herzl, saying, "There are political implications here. And secondly, the landscape is too beautiful and it's a shame to ruin it. But the main problem is that in the end they utilized this event as a means of demonstrating against the archaeologists. And it had a somewhat overly nationalistic flavor to it."[19] Other leading archaeologists who did not attend the event evidently agreed with Yadin, that the ceremonies were being used by Rabbi Goren as a symbolic attack on the archaeologists. From my conversation with Rabbi Goren, I had the distinct impression that this was one of several motivations. I discuss others which were equally if not more important below.

A group of twenty-four protesters wearing Roman-style togas and helmets and carrying spears chanted, "You're making a laughing stock out of history." They sang a Hannukah song about chasing darkness from the land as Rabbi Goren emerged from a helicopter. Police and soldiers destroyed their protest signs and removed them from the area.[20] Shlomo

Hillel, former Labor chairman of the MCSC, called the ceremony "crazy" and *avoda zara* (the worship of false gods).[21] Rabbi Menachem HaCohen, a Labor Knesset member (who is a personal friend of Rabbi Goren), claimed that the cermony perverted and carried to "grotesque extremes" the meaning of the custom of the reburial of bones in Jewish tradition.[22] Obviously opponents of the government and its settlement policies opposed the political implications of the ceremony, but there were also members of the government who were less than enthusiastic about the event. For example, one senior cabinet member (who asked not to be quoted by name) said he did not attend the ceremonies because he thought the whole affair was a farce. He noted that it had appealed particularly to the Prime Minister, and elliptically concluded that the exaggerated emphasis on Bar-Kochba "can be very dangerous." Moda'i criticized the failure "to distinguish between state ceremonials and the personal feelings of leaders. They wanted to emphasize the historic connection with the hills of Judaea. In my opinion this was not the correct instrument."[23] Statements by Rabbi Goren confirmed Moda'i's interpretation. When Goren descended on a cable from a helicopter while looking for a suitable burial site, he candidly admitted that he was "seeking a new symbol of national heroism."[24] He expressed the hope that the new focus on the area precipitated by the funeral would lead to "the creation in the area of Jewish settlements."[25]

Analysis

To understand the controversial nature of this event, several aspects of the ceremony must be examined in greater detail. It was decided that the ceremonies would take place on the traditional holiday of *Lag Ba'omer*, the 33rd day of the counting of the *Omer* (a period of 49 days between Passover and *Shavu'ot*. This day is characterized by bonfires, weddings, and a mass pilgrimage to the north village of Meron, near Safed, to the tomb of Rabbi Shimon Bar-Yohai. Significantly, it is also an occasion in which children engage in games of acting out Bar-Kochba fighting the Romans.

By way of sharp contrast the committee appointed by Ben-Gurion had chosen the 16th of the month of Av which, according to Talmudic tradition, is the appropriate day for the burial and mourning of those who died fighting with Bar-Kochba. This day is preceded by the 9th of Av (*Tish'ah Be'av*), the most important fast and day of mourning for the destruction of both the first (586 B.C.) and the second (A.D. 70) Temples of Jerusalem. The day became a symbol for all the persecutions and misfortunes that befell the Jewish people throughout history. Since Rabbi Goren had chaired the earlier comittee, and he, with the prime minister, played the dominant role in planning and implementing the latter ceremonies, why was the more appropriate day in the month of Av not chosen? They probably wished to disassociate the acts of heroism, which they clearly wished to emphasize, from both the destruction of the Second Temple in Jerusalem during the Great Revolt and from the later consequences of Bar-Kochba's revolt, i.e., the loss of Jewish independence and the beginning of two thousand years of the Diaspora.

There are deep seated Jewish ambivalences and conflicting interpretations of the political consequences of this major catastrophe in Jewish history. The several revolts against Rome varied considerably in their consequences, including the physical destruction they wrought. Whereas the Great Revolt led to the destruction of the Temple, Bar-Kochba's revolt against Hadrian eighty-two years later, according to the Roman historian, Dio Cassius, led to the death of approximately 600,000 Jewish soldiers, the destruction of more than 900 villages, the banishment of the Jews from Jerusalem, the selling of many thousands of Jews into slavery and prostitution, and the beginning of the two-thousand-year dispersal of the Jewish people from its ancient homeland. Shlomo Aronson suggests that the conflicting interpretations of the political implications of the revolts are reflected in the contrasting emotions evoked by the two Jewish holidays identified with it, *Tish'ah Be'av,* the day of mourning and fasting for atonement for the loss of the Temple, and *Lag Ba'omer,* in which the ritual games played by children symbolize Jewish power, self-confidence, and heroism.[26]

Aronson claims that Ben-Gurion, as chairman of the executive of the Jewish Agency in the 1940s, was obsessed with the meaning of Masada, which he understood as the inevitable culmination of senseless decisions by a reluctant Jewish settlement compelled by religious terrorists to launch a suicidal rebellion. He argues that this understanding motivated Ben-Gurion's policies against the Jewish dissidents whom he felt made a political solution impossible; and that a contradictory lesson drawn from the same historic events convinced Menachem Begin, as commander of the Irgun, that a political solution was insufficient to regain the self-respect the Jews had lost through the exile and the Holocaust.[27]

This latter perspective was clearly reflected in the eulogy for the reinterred, in which Prime Minister Begin frequently referred to the liberation and unity of Jerusalem, and emphasized the link between the Bar-Kochba revolt and the rise and expansion of the Third Jewish Commonwealth. He reminded his audience that it had been the Roman emperor Publius Aelius Hadrianus who had given Judaea the name Palestine, "a name that still haunts us."[28] He declared, "Our glorious fathers, we have a message for you: We have returned to the place from whence we came. The people of Israel lives, and will live in its homeland of Eretz Israel for generations upon generations. Glorious fathers, we are back and we will not budge from here."[29]

The obvious political implications of Begin's eulogy for contemporary policies, and other aspects of the symbolism of the ceremony, added to the ceremony's controversiality. Even foreign journalists noted the Israeli obsession with the story of Bar-Kochba. The national debate over whether Bar-Kochba's rebellion was justified kindled passions because it is "a metaphor for Israel's contemporary quandary" (Friedman 1982:22E). One example of the interest generated over the subject was a conference on Bar-Kochba sponsored by the Van Leer Institute of Jerusalem in January 1982, which was attended by hundreds of Israelis. It was noted that whereas the Talmud and traditional sources referred to Bar-Kochba as a cruel, imperious leader and as a false messiah, one stream of contemporary Zionism viewed him as an heroic freedom fighter. That particular stream of Zionism, having attained power in the state, was now trying to impose its interpretation of history and contemporary reality on the entire nation.

The leading critic of the use of Bar-Kochba as a mythical hero is Professor Yehoshafat Harkabi, former head of military intelligence and currently a professor of international relations. Harkabi (1982, 1983) argues that Bar-Kochba waged an unrealistic policy which directly led to the decimation of the Jewish people. He suggests that "the problem is not how Bar-Kochba erred, but how we came to admire his error and how this influences the manner of our national thinking. By admiring the Bar-Kochba revolt, we are forced into the position of admiring our destruction and rejoicing over a deed amounting to national suicide."[30] Harkabi charges that current Israeli policy relating to the settlement of occupied territories and their de facto annexation including over a million Palestinian Arabs is unrealistic and could lead to disastrous consequences.

On one hand the debate over the burial of the bones, based on contradictory interpretations of the lessons drawn from Bar-Kochba's revolt, reveals the existence of highly polarized versions of the Zionist vision. On the other hand, the fact that secular scholars like Harkabi and Yadin (both played major military roles in earlier periods) engage in public debate with the prime minister and the chief Ashkenazic rabbi over the consequences and implications of events which took place two thousand years previously implies that they share an underlying Zionist/Israeli world view which makes the debate over such a root cultural paradigm both possible and significant.

Conclusions

To fully explain the implications of these cases it is necessary to clarify the relationship between the main values and symbols of the dominant element of the government and the ceremonial activities discussed in the chapter. Israeli political culture is generally characterized by the utilization of both history and mythology in the interpretation of contemporary political situations and events.[31] While this is true for laborites as well as previously mentioned academics, it applies particularly to the followers of Jabotinsky and to the religious ultranationalists who strongly emphasize the understanding of contemporary events through historic analogies and the understanding of the present as a phase in a historic process.[32] For example, they call the present state the Third Commonwealth, thereby stressing historical continuity with the previous two periods of independent Jewish national existence. Jewish statehood, poetically expressed through the biblical term *malkhut Yisrael* (Kingdom of Israel), was (and is) the supreme and sacred value to the revisionists. Jabotinsky coined the term *monism* to express his opposition to the adulteration of Zionism by adding on to it other ideologies, and to emphasize the supremacy of Zionist nationalism above all other values.

Heroism, especially self-sacrifice through military fighting spirit, is practically worshipped in the movement. In its extreme form the exaggerated adulation of military might led to the cultivation of a cult of power by Brit Habiryonim (named after the zealots who fought the Romans) in the early *yishuv*, by Lehi in a later period, and by their contemporary descendants among the extreme ultranationalists. The name of the youth movement— Betar—refers to and merges two symbols of heroism: the site of Bar-Kochba's last stand and the heroic image of Joseph Trumpeldor, a leader of the Jewish self-defense during the period of Ottoman rule over Palestine.[33]

Heroism is expressed in many symbolic forms, especially in the poems, songs, and stories of the underground. Those who went to the British gallows, or who blew themselves up with a grenade prior to their hanging, are revered as sacred martyrs. Their former prisons have been turned into permanent exhibitions testifying to their heroism, and at annual memorial ceremonies the feats of their heroism are retold. Among the mythical heroes selected from Jewish history the Zealots, who were the most radical and controversial activists in the Jewish revolt against Rome, are particular favorites of the revisionists. Similarly, the sites of heroic battles are important shrines for pilgrimage and memorial ceremonies. Among the more important are Tel Hai (where Trumpeldor died), Masada (where the Zealot defenders committed communal suicide rather than fall prisoner to the Romans), Betar (where Bar-Kochba fell), and Yodfat (another stronghold of the Bar-Kochba rebels). Significantly, the theme for Israel's 35th year of independence celebrations was declared to be the "Year of Heroism" by the MCSC.

Since the period of the British Mandate, revisionism preached activism and adventurism as opposed to restraint and self-defense practiced by the labor movement, which to the revisionists resembled too closely the passivity of the Diaspora Jew. Because this activist adventurism led to actions which were opposed by the main Zionist authorities as well as considered illegal by the British Mandatory government, conspiracy was a hallmark of the dissident underground movements. This left an indelible stamp on the character of the movement and its adherents for many years thereafter. Suspicion of outsiders, defined as all who disagree with the movement, is passed on from generation to generation.[34]

The youth are taught the revisionist interpretation of the Biblical reference to Israel as "a nation that dwells alone," that "all the world is against us." The general tendency of Israelis (and Jews in general) to be sensitive to anti-Semitism reaches paranoiac proportions among the more militant supporters of revisionism and Herut (as well as among those of Gush Emunim and other ultranationalist parties). Given the level of insecurity and sense of isolation expressed in this worldview, it is not surprising that such strong emphasis is given to military heroism. Although even paranoics may have real enemies, the more militant go as far as to charge those who disagree with their policies as being either anti-Semites (if non-Jewish), self-hating Jews (if Jewish, particularly in the Diaspora), or traitors (generally reserved for Israeli opponents).[35] Brit Habiryonim "portrayed labor Zionists as traitors to the national cause" (Liebman and Don-Yehiya 1983:64), and the contemporary descendants of the former call the descendants of the latter a "knife in the heart of the nation," and various other epithets (Aronoff 1984b).

The sacred right of the Jewish people to the entire Land of Israel (*Eretz Yisrael*) has been a central and consistently maintained ideological principle, and the Bible is invoked to give legitimacy to this claim. Liebman and Don-Yehiya (1983:66–70) suggest a number of other factors which drew revisionism close to traditional Judaism. The principle of monism precluded drawing from alternative symbol systems. The revisionists, rejecting the universalistic humanism of labor which they condemned as a foreign ideology, relied on the more particularistic interpretation of Jewish tradition (reflected in the aforementioned stress on "a nation that dwells alone"). They attracted many religious Jews whom they accommodated by adapting a more favorable attitude toward tradition. The militant anti-socialism of the ideology and the religious traditionalism of several top leaders were also influential. Finally, European romantic nationalism, particularly Polish nationalism, which lauded religion as an authentic expression of national spirit, influenced the appreciation of the contribution of religion to nationalism.

"Jabotinsky's intense regard for ceremony found expression in the concept *hadar* [literally: splendor, majesty, glory, beauty] which was used to describe the pattern of behavior appropriate to the members of Betar" (Liebman and Don-Yehiya 1983:77). He stressed noble and princely manners, in the image of the European gentleman. Samson was the ideal man according to Jabotinsky (who devoted a novel to the biblical figure). He represented Jewish adventurism, activism, and love of *Eretz Yisrael*. He was a hero who fought Israel's enemy and sacrificed his life for his people. He personified the beauty of body and mind expressed in *hadar*. He was handsome, wise, esteemed and respected. In short, Samson represented the opposite of Jabotinsky's image of the Diaspora Jew.

Shochat found a strongly mystical element in revisionist writings and ceremonies. Repeated themes were expressed in symbols of blood, death, redemption, renaissance, and rebirth linked to messianism.[36] Jabotinsky was a poet, and he expressed his ideological world view in highly poetic terminology and imagery. Jabotinsky deliberately emphasized nonrational elements in an attempt to create a revisionist man whose character and world view was largely instinctive, and dependent upon feelings. He felt that Zionism should be instinctive. In his first speech at the Zionist Congress Jabotinsky emphasized the importance of symbols and ceremony for teaching the values of a world view. Jabotinsky's disciples learned their mentor's lesson well, and applied them when they finally gained positions of national power.

Political positions are repeatedly posed in such terms as "our holy historic rights," "our holy graves," "our precious inheritance," and "the holy blood of our soldiers." Shochat suggests that the concept *tagar* in the Betar hymn written by Jabotinsky represents a call to activism as a character trait and a way of life rather than a solution to concrete political problems. Widespread manifestations of such an orientation, particularly in the form of government policies and actions, has led Robert Paine (1983) to suggest that a form of totemism—nonrational eschatological politics—has become the most influential political world view in contemporary Israel.

The mystical orientation toward nonrational symbolism and ceremonials both discouraged ideological innovation and change in Jabotinsky's movement and compensated for the lack of the same. With the death of Jabotinsky and his subsequent near deification by his disciples, his recorded words became like holy writ and, therefore, were not subjected to challenge or change. The one innovation that took place was the subtle dropping of the emphasis on both sides of the Jordan, and the focusing of Zionist activism and adventurism on the settlement activities in the territories, referred to by them by the biblical names of Yehuda and Shomron. The shared mystical and messianic orientation and preoccupation (almost to the point of obsession) with settlement of the historic *Eretz Yisrael* led the disciples of Jabotinsky who dominated the government and the disciples of Rabbi Kook who formed the militant leadership of Gush Emunim into an alliance (which is explored in Aronoff 1984a).

The state funeral for the reputed remains of Bar-Kochba's fighters and followers symbolically incorporated all of the aforementioned key ideological elements. The burial of the bones has deep resonance for religious Jews because it is necessary for the conservation of souls for the day of judgment. The burial site linked historic biblical rights to present political claims. The ritual associated mythical heroes to present leaders. It asserted historical continuity and justified present policies in terms of one interpretation of ancient history.

Begin utilized the MCSC in an unprecedented campaign to elevate revisionism's venerated leader to the pantheon of Israel's greatest mythical heroes.[37] Through an elaborate state funeral ceremony he attempted to impose a partisan definition of contemporary reality through the invocation and dramatization of a controversial mythical interpretation of history. Begin built upon past practice, but he carried the deliberate manipulation of political culture to extremes. Some scholars have argued that the Likud has succeeded in establishing its new Zionism or Civil Religion as the dominant one in Israel today. I disagree.

The majority of the nation's educational and cultural elite and leading figures in the media are among the substantial number of Israelis who do not share the cultural definition of political reality staged by the Likud in such ceremonies. In addition the blatant nature of such manipulation also helps account for the failure of the Likud to establish ideological hegemony (exemplified by the results of the 1984 election). The very obviousness of such manipulations called attention to the socially constructed and artificial symbolic edifice being built (Aronoff 1982, 1983).

Such examples of the invention of tradition are not uncommon. This kind of cultural manipulation is particularly characteristic of new nations, although by no means exclusive to them. Hobsbawm (1983:14) points out the paradox that "modern nations and all their impedimenta generally claim to be the opposite of novel, namely rooted in the remotest antiquity, and the opposite of constructed, namely human communities so 'natural' as to require no definition other than self-assertion." The heavy-handed, exaggerated, overuse of ceremonials and symbolic politics detracts from their effectiveness, and undermines the frail fabric of authority.

Notes

I am grateful to the Joint Committee on the Near and Middle East of the American Council of Learned Societies and the Social Science Research Council for a grant from funds provided by the National Endowment for the Humanities and the Ford

Foundation, and to Rutgers University which awarded me a Faculty Academic Study Program leave and grant that enabled me to conduct research in Israel during 1982-83. I wish to sincerely thank the hundreds of politicians, civil servants, educators, religious leaders, cultural figures, members of the media, and Israelis from every walk of life and political persuasion who generously gave their time in conversations with me. For lack of space, I only list by name those whom I quote in this essay. I am particularly indebted to Rita Aronoff, Yoram Bilu, Jerrold Green, Don Handelman, Aaron Klieman, and Arnold Lewis for their helpful comments on an earlier draft of this article.

1. The terms, which varied in actual length of time, are based on the system used by the Government which presumably corresponds with the terms of the Knesset.
2. This was attested to by Yaacov Shatz, Director of the Government Information Office (*Merkaz Hasbara*), the body which implements most of the decisions of the MCSC dealing with ceremonies and other forms of symbolic activities, in an interview on December 28, 1982.
3. When Arie "Lyova" Eliav informed Menachem Begin of Levi Eshkol's decision, Begin broke into tears and hugged Eliav with joy. Reported by Eliav in an interview on May 20, 1983.
4. The informants interviewed gave conflicting accounts on this topic. For example Dr. Bader, Herut's former top economic expert in the Knesset, claims (in an interview on June 3, 1983), to have been invited to more state occasions when Labor was in power than since the Likud came to power; while others claimed that Begin was excluded from some functions. It seems likely that leaders of the opposition who were on friendly personal terms with the leaders of Labor were invited, while others who were on less amicable terms with them were sometimes excluded from such invitations.
5. The proposal, made by the director of the Government Information Office, was supported by the Labor Chairman of the MCSC, Shlomo Hillel.
6. Rael Jean Isaac (1981:47), a scholar with obvious sympathies for the Likud, has gone so far as to argue, "It was the underground organizations that developed from the Revisionist perspective which made the most substantial contribution to winning the independence." Such historical revisionism is very much in the spirit of the ceremonies discussed in this chapter.
7. Interviews with Yitzhak Moda'i on January 12, 1983 and with Aharon Lishanksy (Secretary of the MCSC) on July 26, 1983 confirmed that the decision to hold the events was Begin's idea. Moda'i said the committee agreed to Begin's request that his office be in charge of the events in recognition of Begin's strong personal interest (*kirva nafsheet*—literally "spiritual closeness").
8. The details of the plans for the Ben-Gurion memorial were outlined in MCSC decision 23 on August 12, 1974. Details of the Jabotinsky memorial appear in the Government decision 350 on January 13, 1980, and in MCSC decisions 9 (December 17, 1979), 24 (February 24, 1980), 53 (June 22, 1980), 58 (July 30, 1980), and 68 (September 8, 1980). The aforementioned decisions deal only with those events officially connected with the celebrations, and does not include such items as the request by the Likud youth to name the new government circle in Sheik Jarah (East Jerusalem) after Jabotinsky.
9. Confirmed in an interview with Aharon Lishansky on July 11, 1983.
10. Interview with Yitzhak Moda'i on January 12, 1983.
11. Interview with Colonel Uziel on December 29, 1982.

12. Michael Keren (1983) analyzes the fascinating relationship between *Ben-Gurion and the Intellectuals*.
13. "It's Jabotinsky versus Ben-Gurion at the pageant," *The Jerusalem Post*, December 8, 1982, p. 2.
14. Interview with Moshe Shahal on December 7, 1982.
15. Document dated July 7, 1960 from Rabbi Goren's file.
16. Document dated November 24, 1963 from Rabbi Goren's file.
17. Documents dated July 7, 1960, November 17, 1960, March 29, 1961, April 25, 1961, and September 21, 1961 from the files of Rabbi Goren.
18. Interview with Rabbi Goren on July 26, 1983.
19. David K. Shipler, "Israel Buries Bones of Ancient Warriors," The *New York Times*, May 12, 1982:A3.
20. Ibid.
21. Interview with Shlomo Hillel on May 3, 1983.
22. Interview with Rabbi Menachem HaCohen on June 7, 1983.
23. Interview with Yitzhak Moda'i on January 12, 1983.
24. Jane Friedman,"For Israelis, Bar Kochba Isn't Ancient History," The *New York Times*, January 31, 1982:22E. Yadin speculated that the need to find a new symbol of heroism was because the old symbol, Masada, was religiously tarnished by its suicidal image.
25. *The Jerusalem Post*, May 9, 1982.
26. Shlomo Aronson, "Responses to Questions for I.S.C.S.C. Catastrophe and Political Consciousness Colloquiums," May 28, 1982, Pittsburgh, Pa. Unpublished written notes, p. 13.
27. Aronson, pp. 14-15.
28. *The Jerusalem Post*, May 12, 1982.
29. Shipler, "Israel Buries Bones."
30. Friedman quotes from *Facing Reality: Lessons from Jeremiah, The Destruction of the Second Temple and Bar Kochba's Rebellion*. Similar views can be found in *The Bar Kochba Syndrome: Risk and Realism in International Politics*. For example, p. 105.
31. For an interesting discussion of the distinction and the relation between myth and history see Karin R. Andriolo, "Myth and History: A General Model and Its Application to the Bible," *American Anthropologist* 83 (2), June 1981.
32. Among the several sources utilized in this discussion, I found particularly useful the unpublished graduate seminar report of one of my former students, Orit Schochat, on "Symbolism and Ritual in the Herut Movement." This report was based on her extensive fieldwork on the Betar youth movement (both the national leadership and local branches), and on the Arieh Ben-Eliezer National Seminar (*midrasha*) which involved participant observation and interviewing. She also conducted a content analysis of two years of the periodicals *HaUma* and *Maoz*, relevant literature by members of and about the movement. Chapter 3, "Revisionist Zionism As a Civil Religion," in Liebman and Don-Yehiya (1983) also contains a most useful discussion of similar material and themes.
33. They even changed the spelling of Trumpeldor's name, replacing the Hebrew letter tet with a taf, thereby making Betar an acronym for Brit (covenant) Trumpledor.
34. Shochat gives several examples which illustrate the continuation of a conspiratorial character. Her informants refused to discuss their relations with Gush

Emunim. Their plans for demonstrations, settlement activities, and prayer on the Temple Mount were carried out with the greatest of secrecy. I found a certain degree of suspicion of outsiders in the Labor Party (Aronoff 1977:acknowledgements and page 58). For example, almost all Labor politicians carefully shred the notes they pass to one another after reading them. However, I found far more suspiciousness among Herut politicians. Even among individuals with whom I established cordial personal relationships, such as with a former student, there was a level of distance and suspicion of outsiders which was more pronounced than I found with politicians from any other Israeli political party, including Herut's Liberal partners in the Likud.

35. See Amos Oz (1983:87-100) for an extreme example of this type.
36. When militant followers of Jabotinsky broke away from Begin's party in protest against the signing of the peace treaty with Egypt and the evacuation from the Sinai, they named their party HaTechiya which means the renaissance or rebirth.
37. Following the precedent established by its predecessor, the present government is preparing extensive celebrations for the 100th anniversary of the birth of David Ben-Gurion.

References

Andriolo, Karin R. 1981. "Myth and History: A General Model and Its Application to the Bible." *American Anthropologist* 83 (2), June.

Aronoff, Myron J. 1977. *Power and Ritual in the Israel Labor Party*. Amsterdam/Assen: Van Gorcum.

_____ . 1980. "Ideology and Interest: The Dialectics of Politics." In *Ideology and Politics: The Dialectics of Politics, Political Anthropology, Vol. 1.* Ed. Myron J. Aronoff. New Brunswick, N.J.:Transaction.

_____ . 1982. "Conceptualizing the Role of Culture in Political Change." In *Culture and Political Change, Political Anthropology, Vol. 2.* Ed. Myron J. Aronoff. New Brunswick, N.J.:Transaction.

_____ . 1984a. "Gush Emunim: The Institutionalization of a Charismatic, Messianic, Religious-Political Revitalization Movement in Israel." In *Religion and Politics, Political Anthropology, Vol. 3.* Ed. Myron J. Aronoff. New Brunswick, N.J.: Transaction.

_____ . 1984b. "Political Polarization: Contradictory Interpretations of Israeli Reality." In *Cross-Currents in Israeli Culture and Politics, Political Anthropology, Vol. 4.* Ed. Myron J. Aronoff. New Brunswick, N.J.: Transaction.

Aronson, Shlomo. "Responses to Questions for I.S.C.S.C. Catastrophe and Political Consciousness Colloquium," May 28, 1982, Pittsburgh, Pa. Unpublished notes.

Friedman, Jane. 1982. "For Israelis, Bar-Kochba Isn't Ancient History." The *New York Times,* January 31: 22E.

Harkabi, Yehoshafat. 1982. *The Bar Kochba Syndrome.* New York: Rossel Books.

_____ . 1983. *Facing Reality: Lessons from Jeremiah, The Destruction of the Second Temple and Bar-Kochba's Rebellion.* Jerusalem: Van Leer Institute (Hebrew).

Hobsbawm, Eric, and Terence Ranger, eds. 1983. *The Invention of Tradition.* Cambridge: Cambridge University Press.

Isaac, Rael Jean. 1981. *Party and Politics in Israel*. New York: Longman.

Jerusalem Post, The. 1982. May 9, May 12, and December 8.

Keren, Michael. 1983. *Ben-Gurion and the Intellectuals*. Dekalb: Northern Illinois University Press.

Levite, Ariel, and Sidney Tarrow. 1983. "The Legitimation of Excluded Parties in Dominant Party Systems: A Comparison of Israel and Italy." *Comparative Politics* 15:295-397.

Liebman, Charles S., and Eliezer Don-Yehiya. 1983. *Civil Religion in Israel*. Berkeley: University of California Press.

Oz, Amos. 1983. *In the Land of Israel*. Trans. Maurice Goldberg-Bartura. New York: Harcourt Brace Jovanovich.

Paine, Robert. 1983. "Israel and Totemic Time?" *Royal Anthropological Institute News* (December).

Remba, Isaac. 1964. "Religion and Tradition in His Life and Thought." *Haumah*, 3 (June).

Shipler, David K. 1982. "Israel Buries Bones of Ancient Warriors." The *New York Times*, May 12:193.

Shochat, Orit. "Symbolism and Ritual in the Herut Movement." Unpublished seminar paper submitted at Tel Aviv University.

5

The Poetics of Politics:
An Allegory of Bedouin Identity

Smadar Lavie

No Egyptian, Israeli, American, or Soviet political leader has ever asked the Mzeina Bedouin of the southern Sinai peninsula their opinions about decisions like starting wars, signing peace agreements, occupying lands, or returning them to their former rulers. But during the last century the Bedouin of the Sinai have been governed by the Ottoman Turks, the British, the Egyptians, and the Israelis. During the last thirty-five years the government of the southern Sinai changed hands at least five times: From the 1940s until 1952 the Sinai was governed by the Egyptian King Fārouq and patrolled by British army units. Between 1952 and 1965 it was under independent Egyptian control. In 1956 it was occupied by Israel, backed by France and Britain. Between 1956 and 1967 it was returned to Egypt, aided by the Soviets. Between 1967 and 1975 it was occupied again by Israel. Between 1975 and 1982 Israel withdrew from the Sinai in five stages in order to return it to Egypt once again.

Nobody has ever asked the Bedouin whether they prefer to make so-called progress and undergo a period of development initiated by Egyptian or Israeli agencies. No one has ever inquired how they feel when military patrols of their occupiers or armed peace patrols of the United Nations forces occasionally visit their encampments. And no governor has ever bothered to find out whether the Sinai Bedouin are interested in retaining the image the West has of them as "sons of the desert" for the purpose of marketing this image for mass tourism.

For all these external governments and agencies the southern Sinai is only a bargaining chip during negotiations over territories and borders—a cheap one because of its relative inaccessibility to motorized armed forces. The southern Sinai inhabitants are conceived by outsiders as another exotic component of the motionless, pristine, and scenic landscape, another tourist attraction like the rare corals, colorful sandstone canyons, red gra-

131

nite cliffs, and palm trees in the middle of "nowhere"—a human component without wills, desires, hopes, frustrations, angers, even without opinions about the political situation in which they find themselves.

International peace agreements and development policies for the southern Sinai have always been expressions of the national and global interests of Egypt and Israel. The Sinai Bedouin are perceived as both obstacles and resources for the implementation of these policies and agreements. Unfortunately, the cleft and arid southern Sinai peninsula cannot carry a pastoral economy. Hence, the Mzeina people are forced to acquiesce in the occupation of their land by either Egypt or Israel because of their dependence on the occupiers' economic hinterlands (Lavie and Young 1984; Marx 1977, 1980).

Describing the different work he had done during his life, one of the oldest living Mezeinis [Mzeina tribespersons] told me that during the Ottoman and British occupations of the Sinai he picked oranges in Jaffa. When the Egyptians controlled the Sinai he occasionally worked in the shipyards of Alexandria and in the Yugoslavian manganese mines on the coast of the Suez Gulf. During the period of Israeli occupation he washed dishes and cleaned toilets in an Israeli motel near his winter encampment, posed for tourists who wanted to take home a photograph of a "real" Bedouin, participated as an extra in films such as *The Life of Brian* and *Ashanti*, and guided some of the Club Med's Desert Safari tours.

This example shows how the Sinai Bedouin during this century have been forced to depend on wage labor provided by external agencies. However, because the Sinai labor market has been disrupted so often by changes in administration during the last thirty-five years, the Bedouin also stockpile basic food staples such as flour, sugar, oil, tea, and rice in amounts sufficient for a year of subsistence. They try to save the little extra cash left from their earnings by converting it to "safe" foreign currencies. In spite of a negative margin of profit from farming, many Bedouin families also maintain a small orchard, raise a few goats and sheep, and own a camel. All these, together with the food they have bought and stored, sustain them during periods when jobs are unavailable because the Sinai is changing hands.

Many of the mundane dialogues of Mzeinis can be seen as representations of the inconsistent, insecure living conditions which are imposed on the tribe because of the alternate occupations by Egypt and Israel. I have tried to bring into this anthropological text the polyphony of voices (Bakhtin 1981; Clifford 1983) with which Mzeinis express their opinions and feelings about the way international political processes interfere with every aspect of their lives.

When the Mzeinis try to figure out how to relate to Israeli or Egyptian soldiers, military governors, civil administrators, and settlers, and the influx of tourists from many nations, one of the themes that repeatedly emerges is hospitality. Hospitality is a pillar of Bedouin tradition. Mzeinis view the tradition of hospitality (*qarwat aḍ-ḍief*) as a sacred commitment of each tribal member to the honor of his or her community and tribe and the honor of the tribal alliance to which the Mzeina belongs. Hospitality embraces as well the human spheres beyond the tribe. By being hospitable to any member of the community of Muslim believers (*al-umma al-Islāmī-yya*), or even to anyone living in the universe (*ahl ad-dunya*) who visits the southern Sinai, a Mzeini brings honor to himself.

The duty of hospitality involves both the tribal structure and its many organizational modes. Traditionally, every stranger who comes to the Sinai is considered a guest. If a guest is not known to the host from previous meetings, he or she introduce themselves by name, and give a three- to five-generation genealogy of their agnatic blood group (*khamsa*), their clan and phratry affiliations, and the tribe they are members of. Since descent and territoriality do not exactly correspond among the Mzeina, the guest also mentions the name of the regional alliance to which she or he belongs. Then, before turning to talk on other matters, the host and guest gossip about the overlapping parts of their kinship and friendship networks.

Of course, the current sorts of strangers who visit the Sinai for various periods of time are incapable of introducing themselves to their Bedouin hosts according to the rigid customary etiquette described above. As a matter of fact, most of them totally ignore the Bedouin tradition of hospitality. Do these strangers need to be respected anyway by Mzeinis because of their membership in the Muslim community or the human world? Or are they simply temporary nuisances to be borne by tribal members?

Many of the Bedouin dialogues on the nature of hospitality turn into bitter arguments during which the participants' value of honor, derived from being Bedouin hosts, is confronted by the indeterminacy characterizing their mundane life as voiceless pawns tossed about by their uninvited guests. Many of these arguments end abruptly and inconclusively. But at times, the collision between the many voices of the present and a mono-logic voice that recites the inheritance of a common tribal past causes a crack in the taken-for-granted construction of Mzeinis' mundane reality (Berger and Luckman 1966). During these fragile interstitial moments, existential paradoxes that emanate from the geopolitical situation surface into the level of the Mzeinis' everyday discourse.

At these moments, a person who has theatrical and rhetorical talents may spontaneously speak up. He or she may playfully allegorize an event from everyday life into a story told in the Mzeinis' tradition monologic storytelling style. In so doing the teller will transcend both personal and communal experiences and thus incorporate them into the tribal tradition.

I refer to these tellers as playing out "allegorical types." As a category, they are my anthropological constructs. But since cultures also pay tribute to creative personae, some of "my" types are the central characters in traditional stories (ḥikayāt) and poems or rhymed epics (qaṣīd) recited by many Mzeinis as well.

Once, during one of these liminal moments, the tradition of hospitality was called into question. I, an Israeli anthropologist of half Yemenite descent, found myself acting as an allegorical type. Through a narrated allegory of my most humiliating experience among the tribe, I was able to bridge the gap between the Mzeina's tradition of hospitality and the inconsistencies of their current lives. As guest and yet the most marginal tribesperson, I spontaneously staged an allegory that enabled my audience and me to reconstruct both the reality and structure of the tradition of hospitality. So I was able to momentarily resolve the paradoxes that both the Mzeina and I faced in our relations to Western culture and politics.

On September 24, 1978, Anwar Sadat, Menachem Begin, and Jimmy Carter signed the framework for the Egyptian-Israeli peace treaty in Camp David, near Washington D.C. I was in 'Ein al-Akhḍar at that time, a small oasis in the central part of the southern Sinai peninsula. Only seven furrowed elders were there, spending their days in the men's club,[1] playing shīza (a complicated form of checkers) while they tore the forthcoming peace agreement to shreds. For them it meant separation of families during the gradual return of the Sinai to Egypt, which was to take place between 1979 and 1982; obtaining licenses to visit relatives on both sides of the temporary border; and shrinking possibilities of migrant work with Egyptians or Israelis. Two days later I was sent by the local fool[2] to a deserted well and spent a memorable night alone on an empty stomach in the middle of nowhere. The next morning I luckily ran into a woman who shared her food with me and took me to her encampment, where I was received with the traditional, generous Bedouin welcome for guests.

After a month I returned to Dahab, a sedentarized Mzeina community on the shore of the 'Aqaba Gulf. There lived a family who offered me tribal protection as an adopted daughter. I was told I could take the fool and his agnatic group to the customary tribal court for having sent me off into the wilderness. But as an Israeli I felt I barely had the right to stay with the Mzeina, let alone sue them.

Dahab, 30 October 1978, 8:45 p.m.

Flattened cartons and wooden boxes supported by dry palm branches make up Ghānma and Mūsa's hut. In the inner yard, Ghānma, Abu-Mūsa, or Mūsa's old father, who makes his living from fishing, and Omm-Mūsa, or Mūsa's mother, sit in a circle around the transistor radio, which is lighted by glowing embers. A teakettle bubbles on the red-hot coals. Mabsūṭa and Rāshda, two neighbors whose husbands are now at the Israeli army camp in Sharm ash-Shēikh, where they are employed as unskilled, underpaid but tenured workers, sit next to Ghānma. 'Id and Salīm, their elbows resting on their woolen body wraps, recline near Abu-Mūsa. 'Id is a neighbor who has been hired several times by the local Israeli ranger to clean up the heaps of trash left by the tourists. Salīm is married to Omm-Mūsa's brother's daughter. Salīm lives in the western peninsula, which will be returned to Egypt in the summer. He is about to go job hunting in Eilat (an Israeli town on the northern tip of the 'Aqaba Gulf). Smadar, an Israeli anthropologist, sits hidden in the corner, trying to write down every detail.

A mundane conversation glides from analyzing the last news broadcast to the consequences for the people present.[3]

Abu-Mūsa: Ya Salīm, soon we will need a passport and some licenses in order to visit you and your family, and your family is our family [Salīm is a member of Mūsa's lineage in addition to his being married to Omm-Mūsa's brother's daughter]. What do you think [a mischievous look in his eyes], will the Egyptians photograph my bald head in color, or black and white? [He laughs and the rest join.]

Salīm (with a raised voice): Folks, this is not the time for jokes! When the Egyptians find out that I drive a Russian jeep [which was left in 1967], you will probably need to apply for a license to visit the jail.

Mabsūṭa (calmly): Leave it. Long times have passed since then. They have forgotten . . . .

Salīm (louder): I swear to God, they haven't forgotten. [Slowly, emphasizing each word]: When they got back Ras as-Ṣadr [in 1976], they fined everyone who drove Russian vehicles. Those who could not afford to pay went to jail. I heard it from the ones who came [for visits to relatives] through the [Red] Cross.

(A pause.)

Omm-Mūsa (awakening): Yes, this is the time to start thinking where to hide what we "took" from the Egyptians, and start "collecting" things from the Jews [Jews is used here as a generic term for anyone who is not Bedouin and came to the Sinai during the Israeli occupation, including tourists from all over the world, even Palestinians] . . . .

Abu-Mūsa (playing with the prayer beads between his fingers, mutters to himself): It's tabooed (*ḥarām*)!

Mabsūṭa (confused): My husband says that he doesn't know what to do, to leave [his work] and start "collecting," or wait till the Israelis are about to leave and get his severance pay (*mkafā*), since he has worked with them since 1972.

Omm-Mūsa (firmly): If they'll give him his severance pay in dollars, let him wait. If in Israeli pounds, he should "collect" other things, since the Israeli money is but pieces of worthless paper, which will buy us nothing from the Egyptians. . . . This time, it does not look as if these people [the Israelis] will return for several years. . . .

Abu-Mūsa (stops playing with his prayer beads, firmly): Ya wife, the Bedouin don't work with and steal from the hand greeting them in peace, whether it is Egyptian, Israeli, or Greek. Our God is one, and all of us wish to live in honor and peace. Enough of this ugly talk! Israelis, Egyptians, and the rest of them are our guests in the Sinai, and our tradition of hospitality is well known and respected (*wa-garwat ad-ḍeif 'ind Mzeina ma'arūfa*)!

Ghānma (angry): Ya Abu-Mūsa, guests don't give you ID cards and licenses and tell you where to go and where not to. Guests don't employ you or give you severance pay. Guests don't write you medications or take your blood samples to Tel Aviv. Guests don't govern and punish you. What sort of guests are you talking about?

(A pause.)

Rāshda: And what about the huts in al-Billij? [Al-Billij is the fake Bedouin village built by Dahab entrepreneurs for the many tourists wishing to spend a vacation in an "authentic" Bedouin atmosphere.] We have four huts. Now we have there a couple from near Tel Aviv, a German couple, three girls from some *moshav* [Israeli agricultural co-op], and a peculiar guy with a long beard—*yuk*—who does not lie naked on the beach. Always, when the tourists come, they buy clothes like ours, and my son prepares flat bread and tea for them. Sometimes, some generous suckers give him some of their food because they think he's hungry, and afterwards they also pay for what he prepares for them. And this sort, they want to be like us. Sometimes, when I see them from afar, dressed in our men's robes, I am not so sure who they are. . . .

'Id (shouts): So who are the Bedouin and who are the guests? Our kids run around in Eilat and Sharm ash-Shēikh in pants and shirts, and not only during worktime. Very soon, men will start showing up in pants at the men's club!

Abu-Mūsa (shaking his head with worry and sorrow, to himself): And us, where shall we go? These days, even the tradition of hospitality is missing. We do not know who is a Bedouin and who is a guest. We don't know whether our guests respect us (*yakramūna*) and how should we respect them. And the honor has left us and disappeared (*wa-ash-sharāf qāoṭar wakhalanā*).

Silence prevails. When honor is mentioned silence always prevails. Honor is holy.

But this evening, Abu-Mūsa's penetrating question shakes me. I want to tell the people present that in spite of the impingement of foreign agencies into their daily life, ideas like tribal structure and organization and rituals of tradition are still alive and well.

"I swear to God, ya Abu-Mūsa," I say, "among the Mzeina, a guest is still a guest, and hospitality *is* hospitality. If one has an agnatic blood group or is offered protection by such a group, if that person or the ones who have offered protection have only one karat of dates (every date tree contains 24 karats, which are 24 parts of shared ownership), then it becomes very clear when one is a guest and when one is a host." In this way I repeat to them what they once told me about tribal membership and hospitality.

All looks are focused on me. "You probably heard how Shgēṭef-the-Fool fooled me."

"A deed which should not be done among us," some murmur to themselves.

As I start narrating I remind myself: Smadar, now narrate your personal experience in Bedouin storytelling style. Do not be emotional. It is not allowed.

After I spent the night alone I woke up the next morning and decided to go down to the next encampment. . . . Suddenly, I saw a woman, two toddlers, and a donkey climbing toward the well. Upon noticing me, the woman veiled, took her kids, and started fleeing away to the hills around. . . . She probably thought I was from some tourist group because of the way I dress. . . . Since my adopted father told me that one can never simultaneously have his self and be another (*mā fī wāḥad illi yākhodh zamāno wazamān gheiro*), I wear long pants and a shirt.

"Good morning, a morning of roses and jasmine to you, the mother of children," I called. . . . Suddenly, the woman stopped running in order to listen carefully. . . .

"I am from the people of Dahab, under protection of Khnēibish, son of 'Aūda, son of Ṣabāḥ, from [the agnatic blood group of] the Children of Salīm, of the [clan] Ghseināt, from [the phratry named] the Children of 'Ali," I said in the way you taught me to introduce myself.

"Are you the one people call 'the one who writes us?' (*dī illi tuk-tubna*)?" the woman shouted toward me, removing her veil both so that I could hear her more clearly and to connote that I was no longer a stranger. . . .

"Yes, it's me. . . ."

She returned to her donkey. . . . and I approached her. Her toddlers noticed my clothes and started crying. Meanwhile, we greeted each other . . . in the exact manner you taught me to greet women. . . .

"Shut up, naughty kids! This is a woman from the people of Dahab, on the coast. That's the way our people there learned from strangers how to dress," she soothed her kids and winked at me.

Then she said formally, "I am Fṭāima, daughter of 'Abdallh, son of Maḥmūd, from the Rawāḥla [clan]. Our people camp in Umm Ba'atheirān, near here."

"You must be the sister of Faṭṭūm, son of 'Abdallh, son of Maḥmūd. I met him with the rest of the Shadhdhādhna [the phratry to which the Rawāḥla clan belongs] last week, during the pilgrimage to Farānje [Mzeina's ancestral tomb]," I said trying to find mutual friends and relatives.

Suddenly, we established eye contact. Fṭāima held my arms and said, "You, what's wrong with you?" . . . I shortly told Fṭāima the events of the previous night.

"The Fool is a fool," she said angrily. Immediately, she searched the pocket sewn to the bottom of her headdress and got out of there a mash of dates. "Eat, my child," she said softly.

I ate . . . and said, "God will bring peace to the mother of children. . . ."

Arriving back at the well, Fṭāima seated me and her kids in the shade and started kneading dough, from which she baked the bread offered to guests. . . .

Just before dusk, we walked back to Fṭāima's encampment. She took me then to the men's club. She introduced me and my whole descent line to the men and told them my story. . . . One went aside and took from a box a long, narrow rug, reserved for guests. . . .

"The duty of hospitality is with us tonight," announced Fṭāima's husband. . . . We started in cycles of drinking bitter coffee followed by sweet tea, as hosts and guests do.

After the sunset prayer (*maghreb*), Fṭāima's eldest son brought a tray packed with rice and dried fish. [Rice and dried fish are luxury foods for the highlands Bedouin, and are served on special occasions or to guests.] We blessed, ate, blessed again, and washed our hands. Afterwards, the men prayed the after-dinner prayer (*'asha*). Then, we talked about things, the situation, and the world (*hajāt wakhāl wadunya*). . . .

Three evenings I spent with the men, and wrote about summer migrations and date tree ownerships and conflicts and trials and foreign currencies and the job market, and the Israeli and Egyptian governments, and the Camp David agreement, and war and peace.

Three days I spent with the women and wrote about marriages and divorces and births and illness and amulets and herds, on the Camp David agreement, and war and peace.

Afterwards I rented a camel and joined some riders who came from 'Ein al-Akhḍar, and we went down to the orchards of Tarfat al-Qdeirāin. And here I told you about Mzeina's tradition of hospitality, and this is the end of my story, and this is your peace (*wasalamatkum*). [This is a common ending to stories of rhymed epics.]

"And this is your peace," everyone answers me in unison. (This is the customary reply from the audience to someone who has finished telling a story or reciting a poem or rhymed epic.)

The looks are gradually shifting from my corner. After several moments of silence Abu-Mūsa repeats, "And this is Mzeina's tradition of hospitality." After more moments of silence Ghānma says, "This is it. Ah, I forgot, anyone for tea?" And once again, Salīm turns on the transistor radio, and we gallop to Cairo, Monte Carlo, Damascus, Jerusalem, Amman, listening to elusive voices that tell us bits of the late night news.

During the winter I told my story of the 'Ein al-Akhḍar experience five more times to groups of Mzeinis. The context which led to it was always some unsolvable argument about the Mzeina tradition of hospitality. Among the "guests" who arrived in the Sinai that winter were high army officers of Egypt, Israel, the United States, and the United Nations, various developers who were making preliminary surveys for the Egyptian government, and thousands of tourists who felt that this would be their last chance to catch a glimpse of the "real" wilderness of the southern Sinai peninsula before it lost its pristine charm for good.

I spent the spring in Jerusalem. I was puzzled as to whether my story reconstructed Mzeina members' image of themselves or of myself. I also was not sure whether my role as an anthropologist included telling the people I studied stories about themselves. I also felt embarrassed asking what were the meanings behind the contradictory actions of the Fool and Fṭāima, and what meanings my story generated.

Ramaḍān, in August 1979, was the last month of my fieldwork. Arriving at Dahab I said to myself that this was my last chance to decode the mystery.

During the long, hot days of the daytime fast, everyone but the children napped between the daily prayers. In the shade of date trees on the outskirts of the settlement men lay on the beach. The women rested in the huts. During the short nights, men gathered in their club and women in one of the huts, both spending their time eating slowly, reciting long traditional poems and epics, or discussing human relations.

Dahab, 20 August 1979, 11:00 a.m.

I notice Abu-Mūsa and 'Id stretching after waking from naps caught after the morning prayer. In preparation for the noon prayer they go down to the tidal zone and wash their arms, legs, and faces in the sea. On this dry, hot day the three of us are captivated by the wet caress of the breeze as we wait for the muezzin's cry.

As if talking to myself, I hesitantly say, "Ever since last summer, I have been perplexed by why the Fool sent me with my equipment to the deserted well."

A long moment passes till 'Id says, "You are an Israeli. Now that all the kinds and sorts of Jews are about to leave, we don't owe you anything. . . . Not that we want the Egyptians over here, but your peace has left us no choice."

"If so, why did Fṭāima respect me with all the tradition of hospitality?" I ask with less hesitation.

Abu-Mūsa answers, "Because you are one of us. You are the one who writes us. . . . And the stories in your notebooks on our lives and words serve us and one day they'll serve our children."

At this moment I hit the paradox and say, "Once you taught me that one can never simultaneously have his self and be an other."

Abu-Mūsa and 'Id spontaneously rhyme their answer, "But the one who writes us has taken both selves." And then we laugh.

Dahab, 22 August 1979, 5:00 p.m.

The last day of the Ramaḍān fast. In Ghānma's hut, Ghānma, Omm-Mūsa, and I have just finished cooking the meal which will break the fast.

We try to keep talking in order to forget our hunger and the creeping time. I take a deep breath and dare to ask it: "So, what do I mean to you?"

Omm-Mūsa answers decisively: "You are the one who writes us. Once we argued which type of phony Bedouin we are, and you had your notebook opened and read us one of the stories about our roots (*asālna*)."

"OK, but . . . other Israelis also write about your life," I argue.

Omm-Mūsa thinks for a moment and says, "True, but when they come here, they live in the settlements of the Jews."

It is my turn to talk now, but I am searching for words. "The roots of those Israelis are in Europe. But my roots are mixed. One of my halves is from Yemen. (Thankfully, right now it is hard to notice when I blush.) In Israel we are called Arab Jews." I stop without finishing what I intended to say. I suddenly connect my Israeli label with Mzeina vernacular. In the southern Sinai dialect of Arabic, only Bedouin are referred to as Arabs. The rest are labeled farmers (*fallahīn*) or city dwellers (*mudunīyyah*), who may be Egyptians, Syrians, Lebanese, or natives of other Middle Eastern countries. For the Mzeina, an Arab Jew is a Bedouin Jew.

"Oh, yeah. . . . We know you, ya Smadar," says Ghānma. "Only you and Mister Marri, the English Bedouin, lived with us," continues Omm-Mūsa. (G. F. Murray lived with the Sinai Bedouin during the 1920s and wrote a travelogue entitled *Sons of Ishmael*.) "You came here to update and correct his book. . . . Both of you always told us how beautiful it is to climb to the top of mountains in order to see the rest of the mountains. My greatuncle taught Mister Marri to fish, and my husband taught you to fish. Old people like me can connect the past to the present (*illi kān lilmakān*),"[4] says Omm-Mūsa, and I wonder whether we are still in the same story or maybe have started narrating another one.

An allegory is a story of the present, which at the same time reflects the stories of the past. I see it as a story about a story about a story, which, at the same time is a story within a story within a story. And all these stories have clear cosmological, religious, and political overtones (Clifford 1984).

Unlike epics, allegories are always calling attention to themselves as both cultural texts and the literary criticisms of those texts (Quilligan 1979). Therefore, allegories voice at the same time subjective and objective representations of both the text and its many meanings. In the allegorical text the particular characters, which as a rule are created ad hoc, serve as examples of a general whole (Fletcher 1964). Telling or listening to allegories evokes the feeling of being in a hall full of mirrors. Mirrors, as allegories, attempt at capturing the inclusiveness of timespans and the completeness of spaces (Wimsatt 1970). And allegories mirror onto the past the richness of details captured at the present and reflect onto the present ideals and archetypes from the past.

Both Egypt and Israel have attempted to redirect Bedouin labor and residence patterns by offering paid employment and public services. Force and negotiation have been used to win the acquiescence of the Sinai Bedouin (Lavie and Young 1984). Torn betwixt and between economic and cultural survival, one of the few avenues for protests which is still open to Mzeinis is transmuting their experience into ongoing allegories rooted in tradition.

During my four years of fieldwork among the Mzeina I recorded many mundane, after-prayer conversations which developed into loud and painful arguments. Some of these arguments were open-ended, abruptly discontinued, and never resolved. Others ended in a communal agreement accompanied by a feeling of communitas (Turner 1969).

In my third year I wrote in my field diary that the latter kind of debate reminded me of a sonata form. Just like the first movement of a sonata, these conversations/debates consisted of an exposition of a theme, a development phase which explored and exhausted the many variations of that theme, and then a grandiose finale, in which the original theme was recapitulated. The Mzeina's after-prayer arguments, however, did not match the sonata's rules of vocality: while the exposition of the argument's theme and its many explorations were multivocal, the recapitulation of the theme was performed by a solo voice. But to my amazement, although the voice was single, it had the persuasive power to tie all ends of the debate together, and thus it brought the argument to a harmonious end.

Tracing the sources of these powerful solos, I discovered a handful of people who have the theatrical talent to play on the fact that though Mzeina's tradition is marginal to everyday life circumstances, it still defines the identity of each tribesperson. When these individuals chose to rise up and participate in the discussion, they changed the abrupt openendedness of the argument by recapitulating its major theme. I call these creative individuals "allegorical types." Gifted with the dramatic power to persuade, they summated the arguments by improvising on the traditional tribal forms and poetically "adjusted" them to the lived experience of the present (Lavie 1983, 1984).

Among the Mzeina members who may act as allegorical types I found the Symbolic War Coordinator, the Administrator, the Fool, the Madwoman, the Old Woman, the Ḥajj (pilgrim to Mecca) who is a Fisherman, the Ḥajj who is a Smuggler, and finally, the Anthropologist, or "The One Who Writes Us." I recorded traditional stories and poems about most of these characters. The poems and stories made me realize that the life of allegorical types extends beyond the lifespan of individuals. Therefore, allegorical types are also creative personae.

When individuals act as allegorical types they improvise on their own life experiences and recapitulate them as stylized stories. Thus they communicate not only a message about themselves as particular types, but also a metamessage about the historical context of Mzeina's general social structures and cultural action (Bateson 1972; Turner 1982). But all these creative personae are also ordinary persons. Hence, the question to be asked is what in the social context allows these persons to move into and out of their allegorical selves?

In the midst of their ad hoc routines (Garfinkel 1967), conversations of Mzeinis may drift from matters of their daily life into arguments in which the participants try to find the essence of their being in the world as members of a Bedouin tribe (Husserl 1913; Levi-Strauss 1967). Reflecting about themselves in such a reductionist fashion, Mzeinis' routine typifications of reality temporarily become discrete, contradictory, anomalous, and paradoxical (Schutz 1967; Grathoff 1970). Imbued with liminal qualities, the paradoxes characteristic of ritual transformations gradually surface into both the context and text of everyday dialogues, until the participants in the situation are no longer able to define the situation (McHugh 1968).

At that moment, a creative person may become a persona and act as an allegorical type. By entering into the inconsistent social situation with an allegorized experience, he or she reconstructs the thematic meaning of the social context. In this manner the person/persona is able to eliminate open-ended discontinuity and transmute the paradoxes of Mzeina taken-for-granted, precarious reality into an allegory of temporary make-believe linked to the immortality of tradition (Handelman and Kapferer 1980; Handelman 1981; Fernandez 1981).

The allegorical type transforms all the participants in a mundane situation into partakers in the nonnegotiable frame of ritual/play (Handelman 1977; Schechner 1977). The ritual/play is constructed according to the unambiguous messages of the person about herself or himself as a type. Hence, the social selves (Mead 1962) of others become irrelevant during the type's performance. Nevertheless, the allegory demonstrates some identity which the participants have sensed in themselves before the artistic instrusion of the type into their everyday life. This reservoir of types, who are at the same time the main characters of traditional stories and the tellers of allegories of current experience, may help the Mzeina to construct their identity as an "ideal type" of a Bedouin tribe (Weber 1949).

In sum, allegorical types are theatrical figures, appearing in solo performances on the societal stage in phases of transition, when Mzeina members ask themselves whether their tribe exists, and on what level of organization it does so. Narrating personal experience, the types bridge the geopolitical paradoxes of the present and the traditional forms and figures of the past. In this manner they provide sets of specific answers to existential and organizational dilemmas which arise in the course of everyday life for the Mzeina.

As an Arab Jew, I noted that no Israeli leader ever bothered to find out whether I was interested in retaining the image that Western Jews had of me as an exotic and semi-civilized component of their society. No anthropologist asked the question either. During my graduate studies, when going back to classifying and analyzing my fieldnotes, I noticed that the theme of two exotic and voiceless "others" emerged (Fabian 1983). Somehow, my life experience in Israel was mirrored in the life experience of the Mzeinis, and theirs in mine.

And as an anthropologist, once I reached the Sinai I was fully dependent on the Mzeina's hospitality. When the tradition of hospitality was called into question, I spontaneously felt the urge to rise up and allegorize my Shgētef-the-Fool and Ftāima-and-her-two-toddlers experience. In spite of being a stranger dressed in baggy jeans and a T-shirt, I was taught how to introduce myself to my hosts. Whenever I introduced myself to my Bedouin hosts I momentarily became a live representation of their traditional tribal structure and organization. I was adopted by the tribe, and so I was shown the path of Mister Marri. Three years and a year I lived in the Sinai, and then I moved to the University of California at Berkeley. And here I have told you my story, and this is your peace.

Notes

This essay is based on 27 months of fieldwork conducted between October 1975 and August 1979 in the southern Sinai peninsula. In 1978 my research was sponsored by the Ford Foundation. During the rest of the time I funded the research by guiding tours for the Israeli Society for Nature Protection. I also spent August 1981 in the Sinai in order to update the research, with the generous help of the Lowie Fund of the Anthropology Department, University of California, Berkeley. The issues presented are discussed in greater detail in my dissertation in progress. I am also grateful to the MaBelle McLeod Lewis Fund and the Hebrew Free Loan Association for their support during the writing stage. An early version of this essay was presented at the American Anthropological Association in November 1984. I wish to thank Grace Buzaljko, Jim Clifford, Marko Fong, Emanuel Marx, Kirin Narayan, and my spouse, Forest Rouse, for their valuable comments. I am deeply obliged to the Mzeinis for their hospitality.

1. The men's club, or *maq'ad rejjāl*, in a semi-permanent settlement such as 'Ein al-Akhdar is a structure of one or two parallel stone walls, supported by wooden pillars, and roofed by sheet metal. The club is at the spacious center of the

settlement. The men's club in a summer encampment is a stretched sheet of woven goat hair, providing shade and halting the wind. A summer encampment's men's club such as that at Umm Ba'atheirāan is located at the outskirts of the tents' cluster, so that the men and their guests are set apart from the camp's hustle and bustle, and also do not invade the privacy of the women and children. In the middle of the club's designated space is a circle of stones marking the stove area, in which there are some burning coals. In the corner are two to three storage boxes, where coffee beans, tea, sugar, and flour are stored, together with a pestle and a mortar, a roasting pan for the beans, a copper coffeepot, and an aluminum teakettle, special cups for tea and coffee, and sometimes a round piece of sheet metal on which flat bread is baked. Long, narrow handwoven rugs, the best of which is reserved for guests, are used for sitting or reclining in a circle around the embers.
2. Many communities of the Mzeina have a male character called The Fool, or al-Ahabal. This person has the social license to violate many of the tribal codes of conduct. Thus he is able to serve as a legitimate device for criticism of both tribal ideology and everyday life (Lavie 1984).
3. The following transcribed text has been generously pruned.
4. *Kān ya-makān*, or "Once upon a time, there was a place," is one of the sentences used to mark an opening of a story.

References

Bakhtin, Mikhail. 1981. *The Dialogic Imagination*. Ed. M. Holquist. Austin, University of Texas Press.

Bateson, Gregory. 1972. "A Theory of Play and Fantasy." In *Steps to an Ecology of Mind*. New York: Ballantine Books. pp. 177-93.

Berger, Peter L., and Thomas Luckman. 1966. *The Social Construction of Reality*. Garden City, New York: Doubleday.

Clifford, James. 1983. "On Ethnographic Authority." *Representation* 1(2):118-46.

———. In Press. "On Ethnographic Allegory." In *The Making of Ethnographic Texts*. Ed. J. Clifford and G. Marcus. Berkeley: University of California Press.

Fabian, Johannes. 1983. *Time and the Other: How Anthropology Makes Its Object*. New York: Columbia University Press.

Fernandez, James. 1981. "Moving Up in the World." A paper given at the Center for Art and Symbolic Studies, University of Pennsylvania.

Fletcher, Angus. 1964. *Allegory: The Theory of a Symbolic Mode*. Ithaca, N.Y.: Cornell University Press.

Garfinkel, Harold. 1967. *Studies in Ethnomethodology*. Englewood Cliffs, N.J.: Prentice-Hall.

Grathoff, Richard. 1970. *The Structure of Social Inconsistencies: A Contribution to a Unified Theory of Play, Game, and Social Action*. The Hague: Martinus Nijhoff.

Handelman, Don. 1977. "Play and Ritual: Complementary Frames of Metacommunication." In *It's a Funny Thing, Humor*. Ed. A.J. Chapman and H. Foot. Oxford: Pergamon. pp. 185-92.

———. 1981. "The Ritual Clown: Attributes and Affinities." *Anthropos* 76(1/2):321-70.

Handelman, Don and Bruce Kapferer. 1980. "Symbolic Types, Mediation, and the Transformation of Ritual Context: Sinhalese Demons and Tewa Clowns." *Semiotica* 30(1/2):41-71.

Husserl, Edmund. 1913. Ideas: *General Introduction to Pure Phenomenology.* Trans. W.C. Boyce Gibson (1962). New York: Collier.

Lavie, Smadar. 1983. "The Madwoman: Spontaneous Theatre and Social Inconsistencies Among the Mzeina Bedouin of Sinai." A paper presented at the 1983 meeting of the American Ethnological Society, Baton Rouge, La.

_____. 1984. "The Fool and The Hippies: Ritual/Play and Social Inconsistencies Among the Mzeina Bedouin of the Sinai." In *The Masks of Play.* Ed. B. Sutton-Smith and D. Kelly-Byrne. New York: Leisure Press. pp. 63-70.

Lavie, Smadar, and William C. Young. 1984. "Bedouin in Limbo: Egyptian and Israeli Development Policies in the Southern Sinai." *Antipode* 16(2):33-44.

Levi-Strauss, Claude. 1967. *Structural Anthropology.* Garden City, N.Y.: Anchor Books.

McHugh, Peter. 1968. *Defining the Situation: The Organization of Meaning in Social Interaction.* New York: Bobbs-Merrill.

Marx, Emanuel. 1977. "Communal and Individual Pilgrimage: The Region of Saints' Tombs in the South Sinai." In *Regional Cults.* Ed. R.P. Werbner. London: Academic Press. pp. 29-51.

_____. 1980. "Wage Labor and Tribal Economy of the Bedouin in South Sinai. In *When Nomads Settle.* Ed. P.C. Salzman. New York: Praeger.

Mead, George H. 1962. *Mind, Self, and Society.* Chicago, Ill.: Chicago University Press.

Quilligan, Maureen. 1979. *The Language of Allegory.* Ithaca, N.Y.: Cornell University Press.

Schechner, Richard. 1977. *Ritual, Play and Performance.* New York: Seabury Press.

Schutz, Alfred. 1967. *Collected Papers, I.* The Hague: Martinus Nijoff.

Turner, Victor. 1969. *The Ritual Process.* Chicago: Aldine.

_____. 1982. *From Ritual to Theatre.* New York: Performing Arts Journal Publications.

Weber, Max. 1949. "The Ideal Type and Generalized Analytical Theory." In *The Structure of Social Action.* Ed. T. Parsons. Glencoe, Ill.: Free Press. pp. 601-10.

Wimsatt, James I. 1970. *Allegory and Mirror: Tradition and Structure in Middle English Literature.* New York: Pegasus.

6

Popular Music of the Clash:
A Radical Challenge to Authority

Douglas B. Emery

In this essay I examine the efforts by the punk-rock band, the Clash, to create radical, social change through the mass media. The Clash and the punk movement constitute an important area for study by social scientists for the following reasons. First, the punk movement provided a point of reference for youth rebellion in Great Britain, Western Europe, and the United States between 1977 and 1983. Punk played a role in such diverse political activities as Carnivals Against the Nazis (*New Society* 1977:576), the riots that swept through cities in Great Britain, Zurich, and Berlin in 1982 (Marcus 1981:271-72), and the European Nuclear Disarmament Campaign.[1] The Clash was the leader of the punk movement from the Sex Pistol's demise in 1978 throught the early 1980s (Gilmore 1979:8).

Second, the efforts of the Clash to use popular music and the mass media to create social change constituted a new type of political praxis that exploded onto the world scene in the late 1970s. Jamaican reggae (Troyna 1977:491-92), New York's Zulu Nation (*Newsweek*, July 2, 1984:47-48), and Victor Jara and New Song in Chile (Voorhees 1979) all attempted to use music to create social change. The Clash accepted as a matter of fact that the days of using small journals, as Lenin and Marx had done, to communicate radical messages were over.

Third, the Clash are important as participants in a general cultural form that exerted a large cultural influence on Western society in the late 1970s. The cultural significance of punk is evinced by the movement's coverage, for example in the United States, by such diverse magazines and newspapers as *The Wall Street Journal, The National Review, Teen, Horizon, Penthouse, Rolling Stone, People, The New Republic,* and *Saturday Review.*

My specific concern in this study is limited to the nature of the Clash's communication itself. What precisely was the relationship between the

FIGURE 6.1
The Research Project

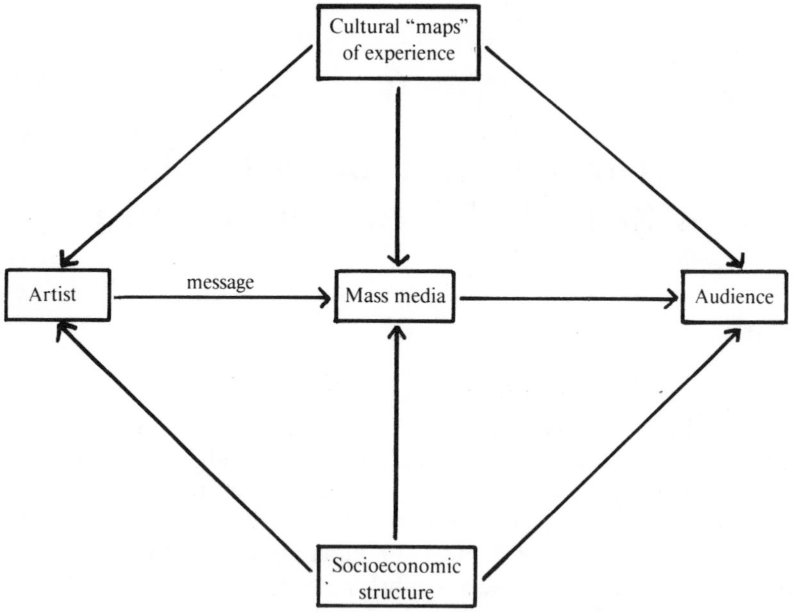

Clash *qua* artists, the mass media through which the political vision was communicated, and the audience who interpreted this message? In answering this question I will adopt some of the analytic approaches of political anthropology and will consider the specific interconnections between cultural forms and socioeconomic processes (Aronoff 1983). Figure 6.1 diagrams the research topic.

This study suggests that during periods of rapid socioeconomic change the status quo's hold over the reigning cultural symbols in a society may become highly precarious. Radical groups may be able to enlist dominant cultural myths during such periods of time to the end of social change. However, the very manner in which these symbols can actually be coopted in everyday life means that the new message is likely to be increasingly misunderstood as it is communicated to a wider audience.

The Artist

What is involved in the attempts by political actors to both create and communicate a political vision through the mass media? To begin with, one must consider the personal resources available to the politician-as-artist. In the case of the members of the Clash—Joe Strummer, Mick Jones, Paul Simonon, and Topper Headon—this means a consideration of both their concrete life experiences and the artistic influences that shaped their work. It was the particular conjunction of these two dimensions that gave power and meaning to the Clash's message.

In "Dole Queue Rock," Peter Marsh has stressed the extent to which punk was an indigenously arising movement rooted in the social experiences of poor working-class youth. He predicted that punk would not survive if it moved out of this milieu, lamenting that "you can't play dole-queue rock and eat well at the same time" (Marsh 1977:114). Simon Firth took issue with Marsh's thesis, suggesting that punk was not a product of folk experience but rather that it occupied a "firm place in the history of British art . . . punk was and is a bohemian culture." He suggested that "while bohemians can certainly be found in the dole queue their lives are not defined by it" (Firth 1978:536). Both of these views are overly simplistic. It is precisely in the relationship between the dole-queue and the art school that the Clash's activity becomes intelligible, and one cannot ignore either of these factors.

The Clash's *weltanschauung* as communicated in the band's lyrics was a product both of the group's experiences on the streets of Brixton and their exposure to certain strands of radical art.

Life on the Streets of Brixton

The personal experience that is overwhelmingly communicated in the Clash's lyrics is that of social marginality. This is hardly surprising since all of the members of the band had direct experience with the Brixton ghetto. The themes contained in their lyrics reflect this influence in several ways. In identifying these influences, I have drawn on David Dodd's "Police and Thieves on the Streets of Brixton" (1978) and Melanie Phillip's article "Brixton and Crime" (1976).

First, intergenerational conflict was the rule in Brixton and homelessness and broken families were widespread. Economic marginality was particularly severe (Phillips 1976:66; Dodd 1978:599). These types of experiences were found in all of the Clash members' biographies, albeit they were not always directly attributable to the Brixton environment. None of the band members had ever held decent jobs (Hall 1982a:20). Simonon, Jones, and Strummer had all squatted in abandoned buildings in the Notting Hill area (Henke 1980:39). Family dislocation was a common experience of the band members. Strummer had been abandoned to boarding school at an early age and had called his father a bastard (Coon 1977:62). Simonon and Jones, who both grew up in Brixton, watched their families break up at the age of eight (Coon 1977:62; Henke 1980:39).

These experiences of social marginality are found in songs like "City of the Dead," in which the helplessness of their situation is conveyed (Clash 1980a), "Career Opportunities" (Clash 1980b), in which the lack of jobs is lamented, and "Working for the Clampdown" (Clash 1979) in which the Clash rejects their parents' factory lives. "Up in Heaven Not Only Here" forcefully conveys the chaos of the Brixton-type experience: "The wives hate their husbands and the husbands don't care/. . . the children dub slogans to prove they live there/. . . you can't live in a house which should not have been built/. . . Fear is just another commodity here" (Clash 1980b).

Second, police-youth conflict was widespread in Brixton. The occupation of criminal became a central facet of an emerging Brixton identity among youth (Dodd 1978:600; Phillips 1976:65-66). The criminal persona is central in the Clash's own identity and message.

Both Strummer and Simonon participated in the Notting Hill Carnival riots; Strummer has taken credit for spray painting the title of one of the band's songs, "White Riot," on Capitol Radio's offices (Coon 1977:68); Simonon and Headon have been criminally charged for shooting expensive racing pigeons; Jones has been criminally charged for cocaine possession (Gilmore 1979:22); and Headon was arrested in 1982 for heroin possession (Hall 1982b:27). Strummer has publicly stated that while he is opposed to violent crime he sees nothing wrong with pickpocketing and thieving (Hall 1982a:25), the two dominant criminal activities of Brixton youth (Phillips 1976:65-66).

In "Bank Robbers Dub," the band sings "her Daddy was a bankrobber but he never hurt nobody. . ./some are rich and some is poor . . ./But I don't believe in lying back/Saying how bad your luck is" (Clash 1980a). Drug addiction is the topic of "Koka Kola," "The Right Profile," "Hateful" (Clash 1979) and "Ghetto Defendent" (Clash 1982). In no song is the Clash's attitude to the police better conveyed than in the "Guns of Brixton": "When they kick at your front door/How you gonna go. . ./When the law breaks in. . ./You see he feels like Ivan/Born under the Brixton sun. . ./ You can crush us/You can bruise us/You even shoot us/But oh—the guns of Brixton" (Clash 1979). "White Riot" (Clash 1977), "Police on My Back" (Clash 1980b), and "Jimmy Jazz" (Clash 1979) repeat this theme of resistance to the police.

Third, a central element of the Brixton experience is dependency on the welfare state and the adoption of strategies for playing the governmental system (Dodd 1978:600). All four members of the band were living on the dole when the band was formed (Coon 1977:64). In fact, Mick Jones first saw Joe Strummer, with whom he wrote the majority of the Clash's songs, while standing in the dole line (Henke 1980:39). In songs like "Cheat"

(1980) and "Death or Glory" (1979), the necessity of playing the system is asserted.

Fourth, in the Brixton experience is found the source of what might be described as the overwhelming maleness of the Clash's message. As Dodd points out, the subculture in areas like Brixton is "structured around the activities available to men who spend . . . much of their time away from home either on the street or in many public facilities which serve as [the streets] functional extension." In those contexts "males . . . engage in 'character contests' to acquire a reputation and secure an identity" (Dodd 1978:600).

While women were always given equal access to the punk identity, this identity in the Clash's lyrics reflected the male dominated experience on the streets of Brixton. The character contest is a theme in their work. As the Clash sing out in "I'm Not Down," "on my own I faced a crowd of jeering. . . /I did not run. I was not done/So you rock around and think that you're the toughest. . ./But you're streets away from where it gets roughest/You ain't been there" (Clash 1979).

From the streets of Brixton, the Clash acquired a series of powerfully felt experiences that would bestow upon its music a sense of authenticity. More importantly, perhaps, during this exposure the Clash received intimations of their own future political role. The black youth of Brixton, as an under-class, was more quickly hit by the economic dislocation that would snow-ball in Great Britain as the decade proceeded. A musical movement, reggae, came to provide marginal black youth with a new identity to cope with this social strain (Troyna 1977:491-92). As working-class white youth became increasingly marginalized in the British economy, the Clash real-ized that they could perform a comparable service for this audience (Hall 1982a:23). As Mick Jones noted, punk is "the only music which is about young white kids. Black kids have got it all sewn up, they have their own cultural music, reggae" (Coon 1977:63).

As white youth familiar with the Brixton experience, the Clash could borrow from reggae's apocalyptic imagery (Marcus 1980:454) while at the same time drawing on an entirely different cultural tradition from reggae—the bohemian art school movements.

The Art School Connection

The art school connection is easily established. The principal song-writers of the group, Jones and Strummer, both attended art school before dropping out of established society. Simonon also attended art school (Coon 1977:62, 76). In this milieu, they were undoubtedly exposed to the currents of Dada and Surrealism. Examining the visions of these earlier art school movements, especially Berlin Dada, certain potential influences upon the Clash become apparent. The conception of anarchist communities of, for example, Richter, Hausmann, or Huelsenback bear certain rough similarities to the Clash's view of the punk community (Sheppard 1979:50, 54, 56). The emphasis on the revolutionary potential of irrational desires found in the works of such figures as Baader and Jung (Sheppard 1979:57-58) is mirrored in the Clash's own tactics. Greil Marcus (1981) in "Liliput at the Cabaret Voltaire" has suggested certain general similarities between the Dadaist negation and the negations of punk.

While these connections between Dada and Surrealism and punk remain circumstantial, those of the Clash to the Situationist International (*SI*) are more direct. The *SI* was a neo-Marxist, avant-garde art school movement that mixed play and politics, art and revolution. It believed that the legacy of modern capitalism was boredom and that bourgeois society could only be toppled at the level of culture (Marcus 1982:17). The spectacle of consumption, it argued, had become the modern religion that maintained the existing status quo (Marcus 1982:18). Consequently, the locus of social change had shifted from the sphere of political institutions to the realm of everyday life (*SI* 1981:68-75). In the 1950s the *SI* assaulted both consumer society and Stalinism (*SI* 1981:74) and was a force in Paris, May 1968 through their followers the Enrages (*SI* 1981:241-46). In 1972, the *SI* officially broke up (*SI* 1981:ix).

The Clash in all likelihood became exposed to the SI through their manager, Bernard Rhodes, who helped to define the band's original identity (Coon 1977:89; Hall 1982:26). Rhodes was the associate and confidant of Malcolm McLaren who was the founder of the punk movement. McLaren created the first punk band, the Sex Pistols, in 1976. McLaren was an ex-hippy, art school graduate who had been involved in May 1968 and was a follower of the *SI* (Coon 1977:80; Firth 1978:535). In originating the punk movement, McLaren had made extensive use of his knowledge of the *SI*, saying at one point: "It's wonderful to use it in rock and roll" (*SI* 1981:391-92; Firth 1978:535).

The perspective of the *SI* would have been highly appealing to the Clash. First, the *SI* had a particular interest in life on the street. One of the earliest of Situationist activities, the "derive," consisted of a journey through the city's streets exploring the life of neighborhoods (*SI* 1981:50-54). Second, the *SI* suggested that institutional politics, which the Clash had no access to, was a meaningless avenue for creating social change and that the realm of culture, which the Clash did have access to, was the center of revolutionary praxis (*SI* 1981:68-75). Third, the criminal, the hoodlum, who was a central defining element of Brixton life occupied a central place in the *SI* perspective. Debord had suggested that the next revolution would begin in a "criminal guise" among youth (Debord 1977:115). That is, the Clash members stood in the center of the SI's perspective and the SI imparted meaning to their marginality.

The Clash's political *weltanschauung* was, for all extents and purposes, that of the SI and this lends strong support for the connection of the band to the SI:

1. The Situationists believed the spectacle of consumption had destroyed all self integration (Debord 1977:ch. 1); the Clash (1979) says precisely this in songs like "I'm So Lost in the Supermarket."
2. The Situationists were dedicated to the destruction of idols (*SI* 1981:371); the Clash in songs like "The Right Profile" destroys media idols, and they even attack their own status as stars (Clash 1979).
3. The Situationists called for self-starting worker councils of direct democracy and a general strike (*SI* 1981:283-89); the Clash (1980b) in "the Equaliser" calls for the same, crying out: "We don't need no gang-boss" and "go home, paint strike on the door."
4. The Situationists suggested that the origins of the Vietnam War were rooted in the dominant myths of American society (*SI* 1981:57, 194-204); the Clash (1982) repeats this theme in songs such as "Charlie Don't Surf" and "Straight to Hell."
5. The Situationists attacked the imperialism of all the superpowers (*SI* 1981:148-52); the Clash (1980b) in songs like "Sandinista" does the same.

The Clash's artistic message combined the map of the world of the *SI* with the concrete imagery of the street found in Brixton. It was the combination of these two elements that shaped the group's own self definition and gave power to their lyrics. But, of course, the revolutionary identity that followed from this synthesis had to be translated into an artistic form that could be readily communicated to the audience through the mass media.

Mass Media

The Clash had a revolutionary identity, but how could they successfully communicate this identity through the mass media? Fortunately for the Clash, the dominant myth in popular music is that of "the outsider." B. Lee Cooper in "The Image of the Outsider in Contemporary Lyrics" has defined the substance of this myth in popular music. The outsider, as found in rock and roll music, tends to be an arrogant individualist who participates in such unconventional activities as sexual promiscuity, drug abuse, gambling, and criminal activity as a way of life. He is not afraid to use physical violence, rejects all authority, especially that of the police, and is an exhibitionist by nature (Cooper 1978:169-70). Guns, knives, outlaw bands, murder, cars, strange appearances, and drugs all prominently figure in the imagery of the outsider (Cooper:170-71). It is through the association of their identity with this myth that the Clash was able to communicate their message to their audience. Almost every single one of their songs has the image of the outsider as a central theme.

The Clash was able, therefore, to connect its experiences in Brixton to the dominant imagery of rock music. These experiences gave artistic depth and emotional vigor to the Clash's songs. The Clash did not simply traffic in cultural symbols. But what was the Clash to do with the other half of its identity? How was the group to communicate the political meaning they now attached to their marginal status as a result of their exposure to the views of the *SI* through their manager Rhodes. To answer this question it is necessary to examine the Clash's use of the SI's theory of detournement.

Detournement: Constructing a Revolutionary Identity

The idea of detournement was a central theme in Situationist writings. As the International *Situationist #5* suggests, detournement was "the signature of the Situationist movement: the sign of its presence and contestation in contemporary cultural reality" (*SI* 1981:55).

Detournement was to involve a struggle for political control of the dominant myths of society. The turning of the language of society in a new direction (*SI* 1981:170-71) leading to a reinterpretation of reality. The technique was simple enough: it involved the old Lautreamont notion of plagarism, of taking existing symbols and connecting them into a synthesis (*SI* 1981:8-14, 171) and the old Surrealist notion of creating an emotionally powerful experience through the linking together of seemingly contradictory symbols.

"The discoveries of modern poetry," the SI wrote, "regarding the analogical structures of images demonstrate that when two objects are brought together, no matter how far apart their original context may be, a relationship is always forced" (*SI* 1981:9). A successful detournement had to involve relatively nonsophisticated images "since the main force of detournement is directly related to the conscious or vague recollection of the original contexts of the elements." The intended audience had to be clearly defined; the appeal was nonrational. The more a rational reply was possible to the communication, the more the enterprise failed (*SI* 1981:10).

The SI often looked to the lumpenproletariat as a revolutionary class since this group was so alienated from the existing social world of consumption and work. (*SI* 1981:87, 126, 249). The criminal and marginal figures in society were unconscious revolutionaries in the same way that the Clash had been unconscious revolutionaries prior to their own political awakening. The Clash now sought to direct a message at a group of youth, if not themselves criminal, at least identifying through popular music with this image. How could this group be made revolutionary? A detournement presented itself: the image of the outsider in contemporary lyrics could be connected to the image of the revolutionary. This connection would be subtle yet powerful. A rebellion characterized by false consciousness would become a rebellion of conscious revolutionaries.

All of the Clash's songs involve just such a connection of images. Old images of revolution are connected to the dominant image of the outsider. A new myth is created.

The Concert Setting

The concert is perhaps the most transparent communication between the Clash and their audience, and it is in the context of such a nonmediated communication that the Clash's political efforts are most clearly seen. In the Spring of 1984, I attended a Clash concert at Rutgers University. The actions of the Clash at this concert might have appeared to an uninformed observer to be quite unintelligible, but in terms of the above discussion of the group's intention, its praxis made complete sense.

I will describe here only its use of video images. A series of large televisions were placed around the stage and played videotapes throughout the show. These videos, in classic detournement fashion, continually juxtaposed two kinds of images against one another. First, for example, Clint Eastwood would appear on the screen and then footage of the youth riots in Great Britain would appear. Back and forth from the image of the outsider to the image of the revolutionary, the video moved.

One concert reviewer was upset that Strummer, in concert, quite self-consciously affected the character of a tough Marlon Brando on stage, but on the basis of the above understanding of the group's intention, this made sense: Marlon Brando was singing about social injustice. The Clash, dressed like hoodlums, were decrying the lack of justice in the world, U.S. and Soviet imperialism, and police brutality.

The Record Industry

If the Clash were to have an audience for their revolutionary message they had to succeed in the music industry. The music industry is big business. In order to achieve artistic success, musical groups need to be backed by large record companies. I interviewed an independent record producer who detailed the problems in capturing an audience without big label backing. Not only is it all but impossible for independent labels to pay the hundreds of thousands of dollars needed for adequate record promotions, but most big record companies have privileged relationships with the radio stations due to the regularity and reliability of their products. While in the wake of punk, a host of small record companies came to life. The big names in the movement, such as the Sex Pistols and the Clash, were from the beginning connected to the big labels, and such a connection was a precondition for punk's success. How then did the Clash succeed in the music industry?

Bernard Rhodes, the group's manager, played a key role in the Clash's success. Rhodes quickly landed a $200,000 contract with CBS records for the group in February 1977 (Henke 1980:39). There is also circumstantial evidence that Rhodes helped the Clash to maintain the necessary balance between their revolutionary goals and ideology and their use of the image of the outsider. The one album produced during the absence of Rhodes, due to a dispute with the band, *Sandinista!*, involved more of a purely ideological appeal and a curbing of the Clash's sophisticated use of detournement. The record companies balked at promoting the album (Hall 1982b:26).

Rhodes's return to managing the band in 1981 saw a rebirth of a more sophisticated construction of images. Rhodes was able, almost immediately, to renegotiate the Clash's contract with CBS along more favorable lines (Hall 1982b:26). The example of the Clash suggests that musical groups attempting to create social change may need an intermediary figure like Rhodes to plot strategy for them (Hall 1982b:26). Implicit in the use of detournement is the walking of a tightrope in communicating one's political message. One can fail to differentiate one's perspective sufficiently from the dominant social myths to create a new myth for the audience, or one can break too fully with these dominant myths and lose one's audience (Marcus 1980:460).

The Clash succeeded in the record industry because of the tactical wisdom of their manager, Rhodes. Their revolutionary image remained camouflaged behind imagery the record companies were only too familiar with. An additional factor was that the record industries, hit by the recession of the early 1970s, may have been sympathetic to any new musical fad which seemed to offer the potential of increased record sales (Harron 1983:55).

The Audience

The Clash succeeded in communicating their message through the mass media and in capturing a large audience (e.g., their last album *Combat Rock* sold over a million records). But how was this message received by their audience? The communication of a message was due to the medium, even in a concert setting largely one directional. Hence, once the Clash communicated its message, the manner in which the audience interpreted the message was beyond its control.

Economic Dislocation

A sudden mass exodus of youth out of mainstream British society and into a socially marginal status began in 1974 as a result of economic dislocation. Between January 1974 and January 1977 the number of young people seeking employment with the British career office increased 2,000 percent and the ratio of all unemployed people to job vacancies increased five fold. By 1977, *The New Statesman* reported, the number of unemployed youths in urban centers had topped 25 percent (Mack 1977:117). This same year marked the time when punk music became a social force in great Britain.

During this period, there was a major increase in time youth spent without work out on the street. In 1971 this averaged less than five weeks a year for 18-19 year olds and only three weeks a year for those under 18. By 1976, the average time spent unemployed and out on the street had dramatically shifted to over three months a year for 18-19 year olds and more than two and one-half months a year for those under 18 (Mack 1977:117).

Under the stress of the this dislocation the number of youth suicides increased and so did criminal activity. Serious crimes committed by youth increased 21 percent in 1974 and 9 percent more in 1975. One commentator noted "the staggering increases in young offenders" (Forester 1976:266).

The Experience of Social Chaos

As a result of this sudden and rapid marginalization, youth came to experience the world as dangerous and chaotic. The usual avenues for establishing a social identity through work were foreclosed for many members of this youth cohort. The social order that had been largely taken for granted appeared suddenly to be in flux. Individual experience ceased to conform to the available dominant symbolic universes in British society. Nor did it conform to the available countercultural definition of reality of the hippies. Under these circumstances of rapid economic change, the legitimation of the institutional order was threatened with collapse. In the words of Berger and Luckman (1966:103): "All social reality is precarious. All societies are constructions in the face of chaos. The constant possibility of anomic terror is actualizated whenever the legitimations that obscure the precariousness are threatened."

If one were seeking a psychological description of the punk state of consciousness it would be overwhelmingly schizoid (Laing 1969:51), but without reference to the social context of this emotional state one would fail to understand the full depth of this experience. All of the informants I spoke to were angry at the time they were involved with punk and felt the world was disorderly and life threatening, but they were also all at least partially conscious of the social foundations of these emotions. Their response to feelings of chaos took place in a group setting.

Punk music offered an explanation for youth's experience of the world, as reggae had done for black youth. Punk performed two interrelated functions. First, it provided a language to understand the new experiences and social conditions in British society and to a lesser extent American society when the movement spread across the Atlantic. Punk gave a voice to marginalized youth (Marsh 1977:114; Harron 1983:54). This language presented reality to the punks but in a disguised manner. Yes, social reality was terrible and hideous, but this new experience was linked to the reigning myths of the outsider which made this reality less threatening. Second, as Cooper has suggested in his article on the outsider in contemporary lyrics, this mythology of the outsider allowed the emotional release of anger toward the system (1978:168, 175-77; See also Harron, 1983:55). Such an emotional catharsis could occur at an individual level whenever a Clash song was played. Ex-punks often continued to play the Clash's music when they were feeling depressed, angry, and confused. However, during the early years of punk in Great Britain, a punk community existed centered around the concert hall. An emotional catharsis occurred in a group context, through what have been called by anthropologists "rituals of rebellion."

Rituals of Rebellion in the Concert Setting

In *Order and Rebellion in Tribal Africa*, Max Gluckman (1963:110-36) used the term *rituals of rebellion* for the ceremonies of the South Eastern Bantu linked to the agricultural cycles. In these rituals, social tensions were openly expressed: "Women have to assert license and dominance as against the formal subordination to men, princes have to behave to the king as if they covet the throne, and subjects openly state their resentment of authority" (Gluckman 1963:112). In these rituals, underlying social tensions were given momentary cathartic release. In the case of the Zulu Nomkubulwana ceremony the strains associated with agnatic lineage on women were purged through female liscentiousness (Gluckman 1963:116), and in the Swazi incwala ceremony the social strains associated with the annual harvest were expurgated (Gluckman 1963:132). Just such a release of social tension occurred in the punk community in the concert setting.

Consider the following scene, reconstructed from informant interviews, of a Clash concert in London during the early years of the punk movement.

A large number of punks are jammed into the undersized dance club. They stand elbow to elbow on the large dance floor. They are dressed in the masks of the movement: spiked hair, razor blade necklaces, studded bracelets, designed to depict feelings of anger and power. Police, the symbol of authority, stand in the back of the hall sternly. The audience noisily calls for the Clash to appear.

The Clash appears suddenly and defiantly. Joe Strummer raises his hand and gives the crowd the finger. The Clash blasts out an extremely aggressive sound that has been labeled "Amphetamine rock." In songs like "Guns of Brixton" and "London Calling" (Clash 1979) they speak directly to their audience and against the political status quo. Strummer's hoarse voice and toothless mouth scream out the lyrics.

Youths begin to pogo up and down, a form of dancing appropriate to such a tightly packed space. Bodies violently bang into each other while a few people fall to the floor and do "the fly" squirming every which way. The release of aggression is controlled though. Everyone understands that no one is supposed to purposefully hurt anyone else, and everyone participates in this release of emotion.

People at the front of the hall begin to spit at the Clash. Perhaps a member of the band charges out into the audience or breaks his guitar against the floor. Suddenly the Clash launches into "Police on My Back," the song's lyrics blaring across the hall: "Well I'm running, police on my back/I've been hiding. Police on my back/There was a shooting. Police on my back. . ." (Clash 1980). The symbols of authority, the police remain fixed in the back of the hall. This scene is given further depth when one considers that outside the dance club lie Teddy Boys, a group of youths who assert the 1950s lifestyle, waiting to attack the punks after the show.

Underlying Social Tensions

A whole array of social tensions within the punk community and between the punk community and the larger society received momentary cathartic release in the above ritual of rebellion. I will only allude to three of the more significant social strains here. These social strains can be identified by the presence of contradiction: the inability of the punks to either fully accept or reject the social situation leading to these strains.

First, the core membership of the punk community was in a highly contradictory position in relationship to the larger society. On the one hand, the punks were asserting a new identity. On the other hand, this punk identity was continually threatened by other competing identities. Other musical movements such as the Teddy Boys and punk's fascistic cousin, the Skinheads, competed for youth allegiance. Many punks had only recently broken with their parents' own definitions of reality and the punk community as substitute family was continually threatened by alternative sources of social support. The earlier hippy culture of the 1960s continually called into question the nihilistic stance of punk by suggesting that the apocalypse was not inevitable and that love and fraternity could offer an alternative response to social fragmentation.

In the concert setting these strains were all given symbolic expression. The punk community came together and asserted its unity. A particular experience of the world was legitimated in a consensual event. With Teddy Boys waiting outside, with parents rejected but still close by, with the perceived failure of the 1960s calling into question the permanence of the punk identity, the punk community came together and asserted its social unity.

Second, punks were in an extremely stressful situation in relation to political authority. On the one hand, punk sought to transform society and the symbols of the political order; the government and the police were detested. On the other hand, the punks were extremely dependent on the state. They needed the protection of the police from groups like the Teddy Boys and they needed the dole-queue to survive. None of the punks I spoke to believed they could actually overthrow the system. The police were too strong. The punks waited for the apocalypse and they believed that when it came their identity would reign. In the meantime, the police in the back of the concert hall were there to stay and the punks were rebels, not revolutionaries.

Third, the Clash was in a highly ambivalent position. On the one hand they rejected capitalism and a consumer oriented society. On the other hand, they needed the mass media and the music industry to reach their audience. While the locus of the punk community was the concert setting, punk was dependent on media exposure to attract its initial audience and to maintain that audience (Hall 1982b:28; Marcus 1980:457). Hence the Clash was situated in the midst of the punk paradox and when the audience spit at the band this was a symbolic acknowledgement of this fact.

The Clash and punk as a whole made strong use of paradox and irony because of their ambivalent social position. Consider one music critic's description of Jones and Strummer in concert: "Strummer, his eyes alight and staring as he snarled . . . his message, looked like a man who'd just seen everything he loved destroyed—unsure whether to explode with rage or run for his life. But his extraordinary expressive face conveyed as much wit as passion; his anger often slipped over the line into a wonderfully comic display. Jones swaggering like a hussar was hardly less impressive. He cheerfully introduced 'Stay Free' as the wimpoid ballad of the night, then belied these works with a howling teeth bared vocal" (Carson 1979:84).

For the Clash, I suspect, this use of irony was a conscious product of their efforts to redefine the myth of the outsider. For the audience who reacted to the message of the Clash as a ritual of rebellion, however, the Clash may have been playing the role of court jester.

The Failure of Rituals of Rebellion

A ritual of rebellion was the central defining element of the punk community. As such, the Clash failed since it sought to create revolution not rebellion, to create a new revolutionary identity that would be acted upon. The tactic of detournement failed as the spectacle of popular music was not turned, as the SI would have hoped, into a situation that would be acted upon (Firth 1978:535). More importantly, even the basis for rituals of rebellion was undermined as the movement grew in popularity.

In Great Britain, as several informants noted, as punk gained increased media attention a whole series of "part-time punks" entered the scene. These were, by and large, middle-class youths who had secure jobs or lived at home and were punks only on the weekends when they'd go out to clubs with friends.[2] The settings in which rituals of rebellion occurred became inundated with youths who had a radically different stake in and understanding of these events. The new identity defined by the Clash in which the dominant cultural myth of the outsider was connected to a new myth of the revolutionary was not understood by this new audience. This new audience did not have to fully act upon this new definition of reality. In the early years of punk, to become a punk was to dress in a manner that excluded one from any job or place in established society. The experience of the concert was one's fundamental source of self-affirmation. As the part-time punks entered the scene, the punk look became more and more respectable, even stylish, and the concert lost its transcendental quality. The new participants failed to acknowledge the rules of the game and the meaning attached to the symbols of punk. (Marsh 1977; Goldberg 1982: 25; Harron 1983; Hall 1982a:22).[3]

This failure of understanding often became extreme. For example, in North Hollywood there grew up a "hardcore" movement that did not understand the parody in punk's sadomasochistic stance (Keating 1982:77-78, 156-8). Controlled pogoing in which no one was hurt gave way to brutal slam dancing.

Perhaps more significantly, the punk communities organized around rituals of rebellion were bound to fail due to the fact that participation in a subculture that would allow such rituals to take place required a continual state of immaturity. As a transient reaction to social stress, punk was highly successful, but as a lifetime identity it was impossible. The moment one considered getting a job in established society or raising a family, one was no longer a member of the core of the punk community by definition. Punk placed a burden on individual lives few could handle over time. Without the possibility of genuine revolution the punk identity became almost delusional, for it required one to give up all avenues for human growth and creativity save one, namely, the symbolic portrayal of social marginality and rebellion.

At a general level, then, this study of the Clash speaks to the fragility of reigning cultural myths and their susceptibility to such tactics as detournement. However, this case study also points to the residual strength of these myths in the long run. A small community may be able to sustain a new definition of reality concretized in a new personal identity. But as this movement spreads outward, these new definitions are likely to be misunderstood by an increasingly naive audience with a different stake in this mythology. In the long run the familiar aspects of cultural symbols are likely to win out over new interpretations. More importantly, unless a youth movement is able to somehow overcome this contradiction and change the overall definitions of reality of a society, life cycle maturation will create an irreconcilable tension between the needs of the youth community to safeguard its autonomy from the larger society and the needs of its members to create families in the midst of a larger work world.[4]

Conclusion

Figure 6.1 can now be filled in with some detail. A model emerges as to what is involved in attempting to use popular music to create social change. The artist must somehow unite his own experiences with a broader political vision and artistic stance. The identity which emerges must be translated into a form that can succeed in the mass media, and this requires an understanding of the dominant myths in popular music and the nature of the record industry. Finally, this message is likely to be used as a ritual of rebellion when a small subculture springs up, and to be misunderstood completely when a large audience is reached. This model is, of course, very sketchy and preliminary. On the basis of the above discussion, however, is it likely that popular music will ever play more than the role of opiate in society? (See Figure 6.2.)

Here, it seems to me, no definite conclusion can be reached. Are rituals of rebellion inevitable? Or if the Clash had seen how the audience would use its message and not concentrated so exclusively on myth, would it have been able to transform such a ritual into revolutionary praxis? Could an audience using a message as a ritual of rebellion be made conscious of this use? Aggression could then be creatively released in a group setting. The

FIGURE 6.2
The Clash's Communication and Social Change

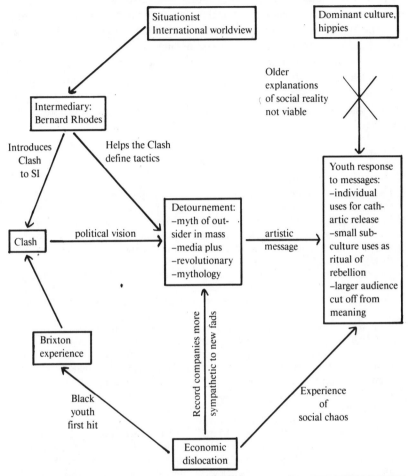

Zulu Nation in New York City used breakdancing partially in this manner as an alternative to gang violence.[5]

The line between rituals of rebellion and revolution is a thin one. If the punks believed they had the power to transform society as a whole, they probably would have acted. As it was, they simply remained trapped in a social situation they could neither fully accept nor change. The Clash could have seen the use of popular music as a first step in the organization of politcal groups and might have sought to give the punk community a more genuine understanding of its own potential power.

Until the full lessons of punk and the Clash are grappled with and acknowledged, any effort to use popular music to create social change amounts to simply a grasping in the dark at shadows. We certainly have not seen the last of efforts like that of the Clash to use popular music toward revolutionary ends. Greater self-consciousness by groups like the Clash might indeed lend credence to the words of Socrates in Plato's *The Republic* (1968:102): "For they must beware of a change to a strange form of music taking it to be a danger to the whole. For never are the ways of music moved without the greatest political laws being moved, as Damon says, and I am persuaded."

Notes

1. I was told by an informant that the Clash helped to put out a fundraising album for the European Nuclear Disarmament Campaign.
2. In the United States the problem of the "part-time punks" was particularly bad. As the Clash suggest, the music tended to be listened to by a white, middle-class audience as opposed to the kind of working-class audience punk had in Great Britain (Hall 1982a:22).
3. The difficulties involved in reaching a wider audience without losing the cohesiveness of the movement were frequently commented upon by the popular press, the Clash, and informants. None of these observers, I believe, adequately understood the problem. Since punk was frequently seen as "access music" (Marsh 1977:113) in which there was no distance between audience and group, it was suggested that the commercialization and expansion of punk music would undermine the transparent communication. As this essay has argued, however, there was a great deal of distance between the Clash and its audience even from the beginning of the movement. The Clash, it seems, sought to consciously manipulate its audience through the tactic of detournement, and the communication was one-directional. Observers make a second error in attributing the failure of the movement to the distortion of the Clash's message by the mass media. The Clash reached even its initial audience by distorting the dominant myths of popular music and using this symbolism for their own ends. Instead, the Clash's political failure needs to be attributed to its inability to recognize, let alone cope with, the use its message was being put to as a ritual of rebellion. In the early core punk community the message of the Clash and its symbolism was received and understood by the audience but used in a different manner than the Clash desired, as a ritual of rebellion. And as the movement spread to groups with a different stake in the status quo, without a need to expatiate anger against the system, the unintended use of the Clash's symbols by the core audience for catharsis was undermined in turn.
4. Marsh suggests that such a fate is a common one for musical movements that lose their audience as their fans grow up and get jobs and marry (1977:112).
5. A Newark, New Jersey, informant suggested that before breakdancing rivalries were always decided by fights (often gang fights), but after the advent of breakdancing dance-offs often decided authority relations instead.

References

Aronoff, Myron J. 1983. "Conceptualizing the Role of Culture in Political Change." In *Political Anthropology Yearbook*, vol. 2. Ed. Myron J. Aronoff. New Brunswick, N.J.: Transaction.

Berger, Peter L., and Luckman, Thomas. 1966. *The Social Construction of Reality.* Garden City, N.J.: Anchor Books.

Carson, Tom. 1979. "The Clash Conquer America." *Rolling Stone*, April 15.

Clash. 1977. *The Clash.* CBS.

———. 1979. *London Calling.* CBS.

———. 1980a. *Black Market Clash.* CBS.

———. 1980b. *Sandinista.* CBS.

———. 1982. *Combat Rock.* CBS.

Coon, Caroline. 1977. *The New Wave Punk Explosion.* London: Omnibus Press.

Cooper, B. Lee. 1978. "The Image of the Outsider in Contemporary Lyrics." *Journal of Popular Culture.* Summer.

Debord, Guy, 1977. *The Society of the Spectacle.* Detroit: Black & Red.

Dodd, David. 1978. "Police and Thieves on the Streets of Brixton." *New Society.* March 16.

Firth, Simon. 1978. *New Society.* March 9.

Forester, Tom. 1976. "The New Depression." *New Society.* February 5.

Gilmore, Mikal. 1979. "Clash: Anger on the Left." *Rolling Stone.* March 8.

Gluckman, Max. 1963. *Order and Rebellion in Tribal Africa.* London: Cohen & West.

Goldberg, Michael. 1982. "The Clash: Revolutionary Rock." *Down Beat.* December.

Hall, Peter. 1982a. "Revolution Rock: The Clash, Fight Back." *Mother Jones.* April.

———. 1982. "The Year of the Clash." *Rolling Stone.* August 19.

Harron, Mary. 1983. "Punk is Just Another Word For Nothing Left to Lose." *Village Voice.* March 28.

Henke, James. 1980. "There'll be Dancing in the Street." *Rolling Stone.* April 17.

Keating, Robert. 1982. "Slamdancing in a Fast City." *Penthouse.* February.

Laing, R.D. 1969. *Self and Others.* New York: Penguin.

Leepson, Marc. 1977. "Rock Music Business." *Editorial Research Reports.* June 10.

Mack, Joanna. 1977. "Youth Out of Work." *New Society.* April 21.

Marcus, Greil. 1980. "Anarchy in the U.K." *The Rolling Stone Illustrated History of Rock and Roll.* New York: Random House.

———. 1981. "Liliput at the Cabaret Voltaire." *Triquaterly.* Fall.

———. 1982. "The Long Walk of the Situationist International." *Village Voice Literary Supplement.* May 7.

Marsh, Peter. 1977. "Dole Queue Rock." *New Society.* January 20.

Phillips, Melanie. 1976. "Brixton and Crime." *New Society.* July 8.

Plato. 1968. *The Republic of Plato.* Trans. Allan Bloom. New York: Basic Books.

New Society. 1977. "Rock Politics." *New Society.* September 28, 1977.

Sheppard, Richard. 1979. "Dada and Politics." *Journal of European Studies* IX.

Situationist International. 1981. Situationist International Anthology. Ed. and trans. Ken Knabb. Berkeley: Bureau of Public Secrets.

Troyna, Barry. 1977. "The Reggae War." *New Society.* March 10.

Voorhees, Mark. 1979. "The Music of Blood and Violence." *The Progressive.* August.

7

Challenging Authority:
Calypso and Politics in the Caribbean

Frank E. Manning

The relationship between performance forms and political phenomena has long intrigued students of politics. In the past decade interest shifted from the functionalist axiom that performance "reflects" and typically stabilizes and legitimizes politics, to the semiotic notion that performance "interprets" politics and "comments" on it. More recently observers have argued that performance genres can play a dynamic role in the actual making of political phenomena. Performance has a life of its own, but it is also potentially an influential constituent of a society's political life. This view is espoused by MacAloon (1984) and Cohen (1982), both of whom ground their arguments in discussions of large-scale performances in contemporary societies.

In this essay I will explore the political significance of calypso performances in the Caribbean. A music that originated among ex-slaves in Trinidad a century and a half ago (Rohlehr 1972; Elder 1973), calypso has been closely associated with that country's famous carnival. As the carnival form has spread throughout the eastern Caribbean, calypso has become the region's principal festival music. I begin by commenting on the political role of calypso in Trinidad and then proceed to examine the music's impact on the politics of two neighboring countries, St. Vincent and Barbados. I will seek to demonstrate calypso's commensurate and at times decisive influence as a popular challenge to established political authority.

The Voice of the People

Calypso music is best known for its topical commentary. The singers or "calypsonians" are social observers who lyricize, usually in a mode of satirical humor, about the everyday world around them. The calypsonian lampoons established authority, inverts normative systems to expose their underlying absurdity and injustice, and reveals the comic underpinnings and possibilities of situations that are usually taken seriously. In Turner's (1969) vocabulary, the calypsonian is a liminal figure, a personal embodiment of social antistructure. He is also popularly understood as an authentic voice of the people, a spokesman capable of recognizing, and unafraid of reporting, the unvarnished truth. Trinidad's Mighty Sparrow, undoubtedly the best known calypsonian of all time, once certified his own infallibility: "If Sparrow say so, is so." While this type of claim exemplifies the playful braggadocio that is part of the calypsonian's routine, it also correctly suggests the authority and influence that calypso can carry.

Politics has long been part of the calypsonian's repertory. In 1898 Richard Coeur de Leon, who is generally credited as the first calypsonian to write lyrics in English rather than patois (Hill 1972:60), took aim at the British colonial government in Trinidad for threatening to abolish the Port-of-Spain City Council. His calypso became popular, marshalling enough support to force a reconsideration. A half century later another calypsonian, the famous Attila the Hun, was elected to that same legislative body. His position dramatized the political significance of calypso, and his material has often been cited in parliamentary speeches (Warner 1983:60).

When the decolonization movement developed in the early 1940s, calypso achieved a greater potential for political influence. Albert Gomes, an early leader of the movement, made the following observation in the mid-1940s:

> The calypso is the most effective political weapon in Trinidad. The singers—all of them—are men reared in poverty and oppression, and they sing of the life they know. Thus it is that even when cleverly camouflaged with wit and banter, the sharp tang of social criticism is evident in their songs. Moreover, people go to the calypso tents to be entertained. What politician, who must harangue from the rostrum, can boast of a better opportunity for influencing people's minds? The fact that the tents are so sedulously supervised by the police reveals the extent to which the calypso singers influence political thought (Gomes, quoted in Warner 1983:61)

Gomes knew, ironically, of what he spoke. He was defeated a decade later by Dr. Eric Williams in an election campaign which the Mighty Sparrow, then a strong Williams supporter, described as a contest between "Big Brain" (Williams, an Oxford-trained historian) and "Big Belly" (the portly Gomes):

> *I am sure you've heard the story*
> *about Big Brain and Big Belly*
> *Well, Sparrow ain't 'fraid to talk*
> *Who don't like it can take a walk*

Fight finish, no bruise, no cuts
But a man fall down on he guts.

Like Gomes, Williams appreciated the political power of calypso. He spoke of it in some of his historical writings (Williams 1964), sought to gain wider recognition for the music, and once delivered a three and one-half hour speech to the ruling party in which he quoted repeatedly from Black Stalin's calypso, "Caribbean Man" (Warner 1983:85).

While old and relatively obscure calypso traditions have been discerned in a number of West Indian islands (Quevado 1983:14-20), the music in what Elder (1973:31) calls its "modern" and "contemporary" forms (1920s onwards) was associated almost exclusively with Trinidad until the 1950s. Since then, however, the development of modified versions of the Trinidad Carnival in several eastern Caribbean countries has provided a stimulus and a context for the emergence of local calypso forms. Today the "small" islands claim some of the region's best calypsonians, along with a growing number of top arrangers, musicians, and producers.

I will examine the recent political role of calypso in two of these smaller Caribbean countries: St. Vincent and Barbados. In St. Vincent, calypso was a major factor in a startling electoral upset in 1984. In Barbados, a celebrated calypsonian has been engaged in lively controversy with the Prime Minister since 1982, and has emerged as the de facto leader of popular opposition to the incumbent government. Both cases reveal not only the ways that calypso impinges on politics, but also, and rather more importantly, the ways that calypso defines, shapes, and orients politics. Without calypso, Caribbean politics would be something quite different from what it has become.

Horn for Them

St. Vincent is a small southeast Caribbean island of 132 square miles and about 25,000 inhabitants. Like the other Windward Islands, it was alternately held by the British and the French during most of the late seventeenth and eighteenth centuries. Anglicization proceeded relatively rapidly after the final British takeover in 1783, but French creole influences remain in language, folklore, and some other areas of popular culture.

St. Vincent is poor and underdeveloped, even by Caribbean standards. Regional statistics place it near the bottom on most social and economic indicators (Brana-Shute 1983:11). The economy is based primarily on agriculture, mostly large-scale banana production and the peasant cultivation of arrowroot, cotton, tobacco, and various other crops raised for subsistence and for local markets. Tourism and fishing are marginal, although the former is often envisioned as having great promise.

St. Vincent began the process of political decolonization after World War II. In 1967 it was granted associated statehood, a status conferring internal autonomy. National independence was declared in 1979. Included in St. Vincent's political boundaries are several miniscule islands in the Grenadines, an archipelago stretching southwards.

St. Vincent held its first organized carnival in 1950. The festival proved popular and encouraged the emergence and steady improvement of local steel bands, masquerade designers and craftsmen, and calypso artistes. Eventually Carnival's political significance as a cultural property was realized by nationalist leaders, who succeeded in wresting control of it from business and service groups. In 1977 Carnival was rescheduled from pre-Lent to late June-early July, in order to avoid a time conflict with the Trinidad Carnival that was seen as restricting its appeal locally and diminishing its potential as a tourist attraction, chiefly for Vincentian emigres in North America and carnival enthusiasts in other parts of the Caribbean. The new schedule achieved its aims, and has also made it possible for the festival to attract top entertainers from Trinidad. Nevertheless, the St. Vincent Carnival is a distinctively Vincentianized celebration in which local performers and performance items are chauvinistically valued more highly than Trinidadian imports.

Calypso shows and contests have highlighted the St. Vincent Carnival from the beginning. In a recent carnival program a writer indicates that the local calypsonian quickly "blossomed into the historian, politician, social commentator, prophet, and 'commess'[1] man" (*Carnival: St. Vincent and the Grenadines* 1981:5). As in other Caribbean countries, there has been a picaresque conflict between political criticism in calypso and attempts to silence it. Some recorded songs are banned from air play, but it is more difficult to control what calypsonians sing in their tents[2] and at the competitive shows. In one competition that was broadcast on radio, there was an unexplained "technical failure" during an antigovernment song. On another occasion, a government supporter furtively unplugged a stage microphone, plugging it in again after a critical song was finished. To minimize such frustrations, calypsonians often wait until the final round of competition to sing a politically controversial song, hoping to surprise their potential censors.

St. Vincent's 1984 election was deliberately scheduled two weeks after Carnival, to catch the public in a jubilant mood.[3] The Labour Party of Prime Minister Milton Cato held ten of thirteen seats in Parliament, and appeared likely to retain, perhaps even increase, that majority. Cato also hoped to capitalize on his support for the 1983 military intervention in nearby Grenada, an episode that was locally popular and that had already served the reelection interests of several other Caribbean leaders.

But the calypsonian Becket, a supporter of James Mitchell's New Democratic Party, had other ideas. Late in the Carnival season he released a calypso entitled "Horn for Them." The term *horn*, a Caribbean colloquialism, means roughly the same as the English word *cuckold*. A creole dictionary offers this definition: "To horn someone. To connive with someone's loved one to win his or her love, usually with the someone being ignorant of the connivance" (Ottley 1971:15).

One of the primary tropes in calypso is the double entendre or, more appropriately, the multiple entendre. The song enhanced the popularity of a New Democratic Party candidate named John Horn, who was contesting a seat held by the deputy leader of the Labour Party, Hudson Tannis. Becket played artfully with the humorous potential of the situation, lyrically urging his audience to "Horn for Them; Horn for the Sheriff and the Deputy"—a reference (from another calypso) to a wife and a mistress, and a more specific reference to Cato and his deputy leader. The song was thus a public invitation to participate in a festive conspiracy against an unsuspecting government, taking away its resources and giving them to an opponent.

This scenario derives its popular appeal from the widespread view of West Indians that their governments are corrupt and deceptive. National governments, as Lowenthal observes, are seen as more extortionate than their colonial predecessors (1972:310). Such sentiment has been particularly rife in St. Vincent, where a decade ago the wife of a government minister, after being elected to parliament on the same party ticket as her husband, proceeded to cross the floor so that she could be appointed leader of the opposition! Political critics, Mitchell included, have succeeded in drawing public attention to bribery and victimization, describing St. Vincent as the "Tammany Hall" of the Caribbean (Brana-Shute 1983:11).

In this context the invitation to "Horn for Them" offered the electorate an opportunity for retribution. They had a chance to play collectively the role of Anansi, the celebrated trickster figure who wins against the odds through stealth and shrewdness. One of the lines in the song pointedly suggested this theme: "What goes around, comes around." The powerful will be beaten, and others will assume their place.

As the campaign intensified after the carnival, "Horn for Them" became the theme song of Mitchell's party. It was played incessantly at open-air rallies, on soundtrucks, and by live musical bands friendly to the party. T-shirts inscribed with the lyrics were seen throughout the country. One nightclub owner who supported Cato wanted to ban the song on his premises, but a large crowd let him know they wanted to hear it and would take their business elsewhere if he refused. The Labour Party tried belatedly to offset the song's appeal by introducing a counterslogan, "Horn for Horn"—a suggestion to deceive and defeat John Horn, not his opponent. That version, however, failed to catch on, as the other had already acquired the same infectious appeal as the calypso.

Becket released two other songs during the campaign, both of them more serious in tone than "Horn for Them." The first, "Oppression," catalogued government oppression in every Caribbean country except St. Vincent, which was subtly omitted from the litany. In calypso tradition it was left to the audience to fill in the blank, situating their personal grievances in a larger context. The second song, "Love is the Answer," extolled what the title suggests, but went further to associate that quality with Mitchell's party. Neither song had the general popularity of "Horn for Them," but both complemented its political influence.

When it became apparent that John Horn stood a good chance of beating the incumbent deputy leader, a bandwagon effect developed. On election day an impressive 89 percent of the voters went to the polls, and most of them heeded the advice of the season's favorite calypso. Mitchell's party won nine of the thirteen seats, while five of Cato's ministers went down to defeat. Among the successful candidates was John Horn.

Gabby and Tom

Lying 90 miles east of St. Vincent, Barbados differs from its neighbor in ways that richly illustrate the Caribbean's broad range of contrasts. A quarter million persons inhabit the island's 166 square miles, most of it low-lying, rolling countryside that served as an ecological base for Barbados' historic role as the Commonwealth Caribbean's foremost sugar plantation society. Significant diversification did not happen until the 1950s, when tourism started to be developed into what is now the economy's major employer and foreign exchange earner. Industrial development began in the 1960s when a variety of manufacturing plants were built, some of them off-shore branches of multinational corporations. Like tourism, manufacturing now eclipses sugar in economic importance.

Settled in 1627, Barbados was one of Britain's "mother colonies" in the Caribbean, a base from which the further colonization of the region was conducted in the latter seventeenth and eighteenth centuries. It was also the only Caribbean territory to remain without interruption in British hands throughout its colonial history. National independence was achieved in 1966, but the country clings tenaciously to traditions of classical education, conservative Protestantism, class deference, and many other symbols of its cherished identity as the Caribbean's "Little England."

The development of carnival in such a social climate is problematic. An attempt to introduce a pre-Lenten carnival a quarter century ago was unsuccessful and eventually abandoned. In the mid-1970s Government sought to create a summer holiday and tourist attraction by reviving Crop Over, an old Barbadian celebration marking the end of the sugar harvest. The new version of Crop Over became popular, evolving during the next decade into a festival that combined carnival performance items, chiefly calypso music and street masquerading, with a variety of Barbadian folk traditions.

The outstanding calypsonian to emerge in Barbados is the Mighty Gabby. His music synthesizes the ludic and licensed ethos of the calypso tradition with a Protestant and rather didactic emphasis on reform, retribution, judgment, justice, and accountability. His chief target is the government of Prime Minister Tom Adams, in power since 1976. The Gabby and Tom controversy is not only one of the best shows in the Caribbean but a political phenomenon that is at the very center of partisan conflict.

Gabby's big break as a calypsonian came with "Jack" in 1982. The song is aimed at the chairman of the Tourist Board, Jack Dear, who mooted recommendations to let hotels own private beaches and to have government restrict the activities of vendors at other beaches. Gabby's strident defiance of Dear, whom he maligned as a non-Barbadian of uncertain parentage, struck a responsive public chord. The song became a smash hit in tent shows, a big record seller, and the year's "Tune of the Crop."

The next year Gabby released his now classic "Boots," a frontal attack on the militarization policy which, at that time—the summer of 1983—was seen in the sizable growth of the Barbados Defense Force and its deployment a few years earlier in St. Vincent to quell an anti-Cato protest. Gabby builds the song on a series of rhetorical questions, a style reminiscent of both pulpit and classroom. The questions are answered by his chorus.

> *Can we afford to feed that army*
> *While so many children go naked and hungry?*
> *No, no, no, no (choral refrain)*
> *Can we afford to remain passive*
> *While that soldier army grow so massive?*
> *No, no, no, no (choral refrain)*
> *Well don't tell me, tell Tommy*
> *He giving them four square meals,*
> *Some of them so fat, they could hardly run*
> *And they shooting bulls eyes with automatic gun.*

Like "Jack" and several of Gabby's earlier (and later) songs, "Boots" was banned from air play on Barbados radio—a move, Gabby gleefully maintains, that fired public interest and spurred record sales. The song's major international publicity, however, was generated by the event which it fore-shadowed—the invasion of Grenada in fall 1983. Even *Time* magazine was led to take notice of Gabby—one of the few occasions when a calypsonian has enjoyed that dubious distinction![4]

Gabby's opposition to Prime Minister Tom Adams took on a more per-sonal tone in "Mr. T."[5] Skillfully presenting himself as the voice of the public, he opens by citing gullibility as the reason for his earlier support:

> *I was so dumb,*
> *When you come with rum,*
> *To steal my "X" from me*
> *You came with big tricks*
> *Corned beef and biscuits*
> *To rob my democracy.*

As the song continues, he gains political wisdom and pleads to be re-leased from Mr. T's fold:

> *Look I learn my lesson well*
> *You can't trick me again*
> *No more rice again*
> *Can turn my brain*
> *So "T", I dropping out and saying. . .*
> *"T", lemme go, don't hold me*
> *Lemme go, unfold me, lemme go*
> *"T", lemme go, don't hold me*
> *Lemme go, I aiming now to be free.*

Then he intensifies his opposition and vows to bring down his foe, first through public humiliation and finally at the ballot box—a fitting defeat in the one West Indian country where the "Westminster system" of politics has worked more-or-less consistent with British practice:

> *I goin' rip yuh pants*
> *I goin' make yuh dance*
> *You will know that I*
> *Is a nest of ants*
> *I goin'milk yuh goat*
> *I goin' sink yuh boat*
> *And next, I goin' get yuh with my "X."*

In several conversations I have had with him, Gabby has articulated a worldview based on revivalism and social reform—twin themes with deep roots in Barbadian history. "We have a situation in the Caribbean that is very disturbing," he once said. "We used to be a people who were so serene. Now, all of a sudden, we're breaking heads." Then he continued in rhyme: "We used to have visitors who came for the sun. Now we have visitors who come with the gun." With the zealous dedication of a crusader, he vows to set matters right—whatever the cost: "A calypsonian is a social commentator, and he has got to do that. . . . Me, Gabby, I cannot be bought. And nothing can stop me from saying what I have to say. I'll say it regardless. There's no way to stop me—except by physical death."

Gabby's biggest hits in 1984 were "One Day Coming Soon" and "Cadavers." The former predicts an imminent mass uprising against the politicians and the "ruling class." Millenial images are abundant. The wicked will be "running, stumbling . . . sliding, hiding . . . bawling, crawling." They will be "begging we . . . to ease the pain"; but it will be "too late."

"Cadavers" was a stinging attack on one of the controversial consequences of the Grenada invasion: the establishment in Barbados of a campus of the St. George's University Medical School. The medical profession in Barbados strongly opposed the move, and there were also persistent rumors that the venture was financed by underworld money. Gabby, dressed in a skeleton costume in his tent performances, focused on an issue that deeply stirred the public imagination—the school's practice of importing corpses for medical analysis:

> *Barbados is a big joke*
> *To them big boys, in their big tie and coat*
> *We barely got space to bury*
> *Anybody in we cemetery*
> *But just to put pressure on all of we*
> *Them fellas importing duppy*[6]
>
> *Just go to your butcher*
> *He will sell you a piece of cadaver*
> *Look under your cellar*
> *They hiding another cadaver*
> *I tell you, Ahhhhhhh, Them importing dracula.*
> *Ahhhhhhhhhhhhh! Them importing dracula.*
>
> *Who is this jackass, who is this fool*
> *That bring to Bimshire, St. George's Medical School?*
> *Who tell them we want in Barbados*
> *All them skeleton, obeah*[7] *bone, and duppy?*
> *Who tell them to bring in the Mafia money?*
> *I hope it is not that Tommy.*

Gabby's political stance has been echoed by other prominent calypsonians. Red Plastic Bag made a thoroughgoing criticism of the political status quo in "Bim," which also raises the cadavers theme: "Even if them Yankees bring in cadavers to frighten me/They can't move me, I ain't leaving this country." Grynner recorded "Stinging Bees," a song which identifies Adams and his cabinet—as well as several like-minded politicians elsewhere in the Caribbean—as "bees, stinging you and me." Young Blood sang "Sport Billie," a thoroughgoing attack on the minister of education replete with allusions to sexual perversion. Black Pawn shifted Gabby's apocalyptic theme into a Rastafarian context, predicting in his "Judgment Day" a millenium when "wickedness," "inequality," and "oppression" will be revealed and rectified.

Adams also has his supporters among calypsonians, although none have achieved the success or popularity of some of his detractors. The best known is Serenader, who praised Adams in a 1984 calypso, "Tom is de Man":

> *Who is the man with all the brain?*
> *I don't like to call no name*
> *Let me hear you loud and plain*
> *It is Tom (choral refrain)*
>
> *Who is the man we read about*
> *That make Coard[8] shut up he mout'?*
> *Let me hear you loud, and shout*
> *It is Tom (choral refrain).*

While calypso has yet to sway the outcome of an election in Barbados, its overall role in partisan politics is even greater than in the St. Vincent case. Gabby's tent, Battleground, is significantly located in the headquarters of the Democratic Labour Party, the official parliamentary opposition. Gabby has often been mooted as a political candidate, and Adams himself has frequently said that he expects Gabby to run against him. Gabby, however, denies interest in elective office, wryly observing that calypsonians have more power than politicians.

An interesting debate on calypso took place in the Barbados House of Assembly during the 1983 Crop Over season. The debate was instigated by the opposition, which questioned the censorship of Gabby's top calypsos. Adams's reply was masterful, if contradictory. It was not government which was under attack, he said, but tourists, soldiers, and other innocent people. Filled with hatred, calypso needlessly injured these people and caused resentment and hostility throughout society. Then, in a humorous vein, he advised calypsonians not to take themselves too seriously, and not to sing songs that politicians have written for them—a reference to his earlier contention that members of the Opposition were writing calypsos.

Gabby's response to the House of Assembly debate was to ridicule and reverse Adams's admonition to calypsonians about not taking themselves seriously. That statement, he told me, was a "joke."

> When the prime minister said that calypsonians should not take themselves seriously I thought it was one of the biggest jokes I have ever heard. . . . If the politicians don't take us seriously, we're going to cause them an awful lot of problems—not in terms of violence, but in terms of telling the people what we know.

The conflict between Adams and Gabby escalated the following year. Gabby's songs were again banned from air play, and were also—as a result of what one astute informant calls "executive action"—removed from the shelves of Barbadian record stores. In addition, Adams took personal legal action against Gabby for defamation, a charge tied specifically to "Cadavers." Finally, Adams instigated litigation against other parties involved in publicizing Gabby.

Performance and Politics

The performative character of Caribbean politics has long impressed sensitive observers. Politicians are master showmen, rendering in political discourse the flamboyant styles of pulpit, stage, and streetcorner (Manning 1980). A literary scholar (Clark 1984) has recently lighted on Geertz's (1980) concept of the "theater state" in nineteenth-century Bali, suggesting that the concept applies equally well to Haiti during the same period. It might also be extended to the cases discussed in this essay, but with qualification. Here it is not the type of classic theater discussed by Geertz and Clark that steps forward, but a popular theater of comedy, absurdity, and what West Indians call "pappyshow," a blend of foolishness and mockery.

Calypso plays a major role in creating this version of a theater state. If Caribbean politics is theatrical, it is in part because Caribbean performance is political. Genres like calypso shape politics to their form and style, inject themselves in myriad ways into the political arena, and at times decisively affect the direction and outcome of political processes. The tent shows, the competitions, the censorship controversies, the lampooning of incumbent politicians, the calypso debates in Parliament, the musical mobilization of mass movements—all are crucial ethnographic constituents of the cases discussed in this essay and, more generally, of contemporary Caribbean politics. Calypso's role in politics is integral, instrumental, and influential. It is a force before which even the most powerful forms of political authority are rendered potentially frail.

Notes

1. A commess man is a gossip, one who talks about other people's business (Abrahams 1983:93). This is the calypsonian's familiar role as "the people's newspaper."
2. A tent is any venue where a calypso show is held during the carnival season.
3. My account of the election campaign and calypso's role in it owes much to Adrian Fraser, a Vincentian student at the University of Western Ontario who went "home" for summer research in 1984 (See Fraser 1985).
4. For a different account of Gabby's political calypso, see Manning 1984.
5. Gabby wrote "Mr. T" for another calypsonian, Grynner, who recorded it, but the authorship was openly known, and it was generally considered Gabby's calypso.
6. A duppy is a general term for a ghost or spirit.
7. Obeah is a form of divinatory and manipulative magic with sinister connotations.
8. Bernard Coard, leader of the faction which ousted former Grenadian prime minister, Maurice Bishop, in 1983.

References

Abrahams, Roger. 1983. *The Man of Words in the West Indies.* Baltimore: John Hopkins University Press.

Brana-Shute, Gary. 1983. "Interviewing James F. 'Son' Mitchell." *Caribbean Review* 12:3, 10-13.

Carnival: St. Vincent and the Grenadines. 1981. Kingston, St. Vincent: NMM Associates.

Clark, Vèvè. 1984. "Haiti's Tragic Overture: Statecraft and Stagecraft in Plays by Glissant, Trouillot, and Cesaire." Unpublished paper read at the Caribbean Studies Association Meeting, St. Kitts.

Cohen, Abner. 1982. "A Polyethnic London Carnival as a Contested Cultural Performance." *Ethnic and Racial Studies* 5:1, 23-41.

Elder, Jacob. 1973. *The Calypso and its Morphology.* Port of Spain, Trinidad: National Cultural Council.

Geertz, Clifford. 1980. *Negara: The Theatre State in Nineteenth Century Bali.* Princeton: Princeton University Press.

Fraser, Adrian. 1985. "Horn for Them: The Role of Calypso in St. Vincent's 1984 Election." Unpublished paper read at the University of Western Ontario.

Hill, Errol. 1972. *The Trinidad Carnival: Mandate for a National Theatre.* Austin: University of Texas Press.

Lowenthal, David. 1972. *West Indian Societies.* New York: Oxford University Press.

MacAloon, John. 1984. "*La Pitada Olimpica*: Puerto Rico, International Sport, and the Constitution of Politics." In *Text, Play and Story: The Construction and Reconstruction of Self and Society.* Ed. Edward Bruner. Philadelphia: ISHI Press. pp. 315-55.

Manning, Frank E. 1980. "Go Down, Moses: Revivalist Politics in a Caribbean Mini-State." In *Ideology and Interest: The Dialectics of Politics*. Ed. Myron J. Aronoff. New Brunswick, N.J.: Transaction.

———. 1984. "The Performance of Politics: Caribbean Music and the Anthropology of Victor Turner." *Anthropologica* 26:1.

Ottley, C.R. 1971. *Creole Talk*. Port-of-Spain, Trinidad: Victory Printers.

Quevado, Raymond. 1983. *Attila's Kaiso: A Short History of Trinidad Calypso*. St. Augustine, Trinidad: University of the West Indies, Extra-Mural Studies Department.

Rohlehr, Gordon. 1972. "Forty Years of Calypso." *Tapia* 2:3-16.

Turner, Victor. 1969. *The Ritual Process: Structure and Anti-Structure*. Chicago: Aldine.

Warner, Keith. 1983. *The Trinidad Calypso*. London: Heinemann.

Williams, Eric. 1964. *History of the People of Trinidad and Tobago*. London: André Deutsch.

8

Royal Authority and Religious Legitimacy: Morocco's Elections, 1960-1984

Dale F. Eickelman

There is a Moroccan saying that the *Makhzan* (strongbox), the traditional name by which the government is still popularly known, has a thousand lives like a cat. In the turbulent years since the end of the French protectorate (1912-1956) in 1956, most of the major challenges to the monarchy have been internal. These include rural rebellions in 1958 and 1972; war with Algeria in 1963; aborted military coups or plots in 1971, 1972, and 1983; severely suppressed riots in Casablanca in 1965 and 1981; and, most recently, violent demonstrations in smaller towns throughout the interior at the time of the January 1984 Islamic summit conference in Casablanca.

Following the 1972 coup attempt, "knowledgable observers" (cited in "Periscope," *Newsweek*, August 28, 1972) predicted the imminent demise of Morocco's monarchy. Following this attempt, the monarchy briefly benefited from a combination of fortuitous economic and political circumstances. Worldwide the cost of energy escalated dramatically in the early 1970s; Morocco in turn was able to cope by raising prices for phosphates, its principal natural resource, of which it possesses 75 percent of the world's supply. Hasan II's enormously popular "Green March" in November 1975 forced Spain to cede the Sahara and united Morocco firmly behind its ruler. Yet by 1976, Morocco's fortunes again waned as the costs of the Saharan conflict mounted. By 1983 the conflict accounted for an estimated 40 to 45 percent of the national budget, excluding reported contributions from various states of the Arab peninsula (Ramonet 1984:8).

The conjuncture of a worldwide recession, a drastic drop in the demand for phosphates, diminished opportunities for work in Europe, European Economic Community restrictions on the importation of Moroccan agricultural produce, a serious drought beginning in 1980, the continuing Saharan conflict, and the presumed "halo effect" of the Iranian revolution led to renewed predictions by some foreign analysts that Hasan's days were numbered. The Saharan conflict continues to be a massive drain on the Moroccan budget, government austerity measures have provoked major demonstrations, and a military plot was aborted in 1983.[1] Nonetheless, predictions of Hasan's imminent downfall are decidedly out of fashion. Since the French Revolution, ruling monarchs have become an endangered species worldwide, yet general "trends" are poor predictors of specific developments.

An analysis of changes in the form and context of Morocco's elections since 1960, dismissed by many Moroccan and foreign observers because of barely concealed government intervention, provides a means of assessing long-term transformations in Moroccan politics. Indeed, the changing forms of government intervention themselves suggest that the monarch is more responsive to long-term changes than the leaders of the country's political parties or Islamic militant movements. The palace's sustained attention to long-term political shifts, and not just to immediate vicissitudes, suggests that the Makhzan has many lives to go.

A complementary goal is to suggest the value of incorporating an analysis of the supposedly silent majority, those persons or collectivities who do not actively participate in formal politics, into a discussion of long-term political change in countries such as Morocco. The term *silent majority* encompasses a range of attitudes and comportments. It includes those who do not participate in a political system because of indifference to the system or exclusion from it to the point of being disregarded by political actors. Many Moroccans regard formal political parties solely as vehicles for the self-interested objectives of their leaders. The term also designates persons who, although lacking explicitly formulated political objectives, support leaders who express their impatience with the conduct of politics and the state. For most Third World countries, the distinction between these types of silent majority becomes clear only in the case of popular insurrections. The Moroccan monarchy shows signs of greater pragmatic success in recent years than in the past in incorporating new voices into its political system. In other words, some of type one of the silent majority, the indifferent and the excluded, are being converted into type two.

The lack of a formally articulated ideology on the part of most Moroccans does not imply the lack of a pervasive political orientation (Mannheim 1971). Even when the conduct of the state appears firmly in the hands of a ruling elite, it is the supposedly silent majority which, when sufficiently pushed by violations of popularly accepted notions of social justice and authority, creates major ruptures with political givens and shows the limits to the effective use of force and repression (McWilliams 1971; Scott 1976:4, 182). The French reluctantly recognized the frailty of colonial authority after their deposition and exile of Muhammad V in 1953. They expected violent urban demonstrations, but failed to anticipate sustained resistance and hostility on the part of tribesmen, peasants, and small town merchants and notables, who had been written off as politically uninvolved. By deposing the monarch, the French attacked what was perceived as an Islamic institution. The monarch's deposition was the major, unanticipated factor in hastening the end of French rule. Ironically, it breathed new life into the monarchy by making it the symbol of independence and national integrity.

Even before Hasan II assumed the throne after the death of his father in 1961, he realized that the approximately 20,000 rural and small-town notables constituted a clientele more stable and loyal than the leaders of political parties. Largely to maintain the support of these "defenders of the throne," the sweeping programs of land and fiscal reform proposed after independence were never seriously implemented (Leveau 1976, 1977).

For foreigners and the Moroccan elite, Hassan II is an urbane, French-educated monarch, protected from direct criticism by the constitutional provision that the king is the state.[2] For a majority of Morocco's population, the constitutional stricture is redundant; the king is "God's deputy on earth" (*khalīfat Allāh fi-l-'arḍ*). This colloquial appellation, embarrassing to modernist Muslims, is much more pervasive in Morocco that the constitution's more formalistic "Commander of the Faithful (*amīr al-mu'minīn*). The monarch's name is invoked in Friday sermons in every mosque throughout Morocco, in special prayers for rain (*ṣalāt al-istisqā*), and other occasions. During Ramadan he appears nightly with the nation's official religious leaders and gives televised religious lessons himself. His command of formal Arabic, itself an important popular symbol of religious authority, is regarded as the best of any contemporary Arab leader, and his public image is constantly associated with the nation's religious and material welfare. On occasions such as the ban on the traditional sacrifice of sheep for the Feast of Abraham, which occurred on September 5, 1984 the monarch can alter basic religious obligations to emphasize the gravity of the country's economic crisis.[3]

The monarchy does not discount the voices and expectations of those who fail to participate in the formal political arena. Nor does it assume, as do some foreign-educated technocrats and the leaders of some political parties, that persons not directly participating in formal politics possess unchanging political and economic expectations. Implicit "offstage" political forms set limits to the monarch's ability to change the rules of the game of Moroccan politics, but in turn force changes upon the monarch himself.

Islamic Pluralism in Morocco

Through numerous recent actions, the monarch shows an acute awareness that popular expectations are not confined to the allocation of material resources alone. There is a growing expectation that a just government is an Islamic one, an expectation at odds with the practical scope of activities of both states and their rulers, despite intensified efforts to coopt religious leadership. The idea that Islam prescribes a code of conduct not only for individuals but for states, and can hold the state accountable for its deeds, has begun to capture the admiration of a small but significant minority for whom the Iranian revolution provides a practical exemplar. Unlike other Arab monarchies, the Moroccan one has been traditionally associated with religious authority. At the same time, Islam in Morocco can be characterized by a plurality of expression and interpretation, much of which has no direct tie with the monarchy or stands in implicit opposition to it (Eickelman 1976; Etienne and Tozy 1979).

Until the Iranian revolution, Islamic fundamentalist spokesmen in Morocco were cautiously tolerated, even when they questioned the legitimacy of the state, as has the former primary school inspector from Marrakesh, Abd as-Salam Yasin.[4] Since the January 1984 riots, the latitude for fundamentalist Islamic expression has been firmly curtailed. In a January 22 televised address to the nation, the monarch claimed that a "multifaceted conspiracy perpetrated by Marxist-Leninists, Zionist agents, and Khomeinists" was responsible for the riots. Nonetheless, the immediate rescinding of unpopular fiscal measures suggests a recognition that the state had crossed the threshold of basic understandings of social and economic justice.

For the first time in Moroccan history, mosques in some quarters of Casablanca and other large towns were closed outside of the hours of prayer. From the point of view of security officials, such closings may represent a more minimum response than the posting of uniformed or plainclothes police at mosques. Any form of intervention in religious activities is a serious matter for a ruler claiming religious legitimacy. Some student activists recall that Islamic groups in the mid-1970s were tolerated both among students and in popular quarters, possibly because they were seen by the state as a means to counter the growing influence of leftist groups. In the late 1970s, Islamic associations proliferated (Etienne and Tozy 1979). A study of the mid-1970s suggested that only 3 percent of university students were actively associated with fundamentalist groups ('Aqbib 1976). The very fact that students felt free to discuss their religious orientations with Moroccan interviewers indicates the openness of this earlier period.

Some Moroccans currently estimate the numbr of fundamentalist groups at over forty. Since these groups have been driven underground, they are of unknown strength. In February, seventy-one militants were arrested in connection with the January riots. Severe sentences, including thirteen death penalties, were subsequently imposed (*Arabia*, September 1984, p. 25). Foreign observers have commented upon the weak case presented by the prosecution, but there can be no doubt of the government's determination to discourage religious movements perceived as antithetical to the monarchy. Even if the spokesmen for these movements refrain from direct criticism of the monarch, they are perceived as potential detractors from his popular support.

Hasan is aware of both formal and popular understandings of religious legitimacy supporting his rule. He claims to have told the late Shah after his downfall that his first error "was not to have been able to appreciate the place of religion in social life. He wanted to reign as an emperor, but as a lay emperor. . . . [T]he Shah was the Shah of Iran by the will of the United States and England, and not by the will of his people" (cited in Markham 1980:121). On occasions such as a conference of men of learning (*'ulamā'*) in "Ujda in 1981, the monarch urged religious figures to concern themelves more with contemporary issues, and to renew their numbers. In February 1984, he went so far as to claim in a speech that fifty senior Ministry of the Interior officials had been equally trained in Islamic law and in administration, and that the numbers of such officials with dual training would increase (Hasan II 1984; Tozy 1984:146).

Religious studies are encouraged by the state for all children at the primary level, and at the advanced level for future religious scholars. In 1981, nine regional councils of 'ulama were added to five that previously existed. These councils were entrusted with carrying out programs of preaching and religious lectures and providing regular counsel to local authorities. These councils, together with less successful efforts to assume government control of mosque-schools—the cost is too high to assume direct control of all of them—appear intended to limit the potential for developing an oppositional Islam. As Leveau (1984:22-23) contends, it is not entirely out of the question that the monarch will manage to coopt the leaders of oppositional Islam just as he has coopted other political opposition in the past. In Morocco, unlike other Arab countries, the religious basis of the monarchy is accepted as a fact of existence by much of the population. The fact that religion has never been totally separated from politics can be used to the advantage of the monarchy.

The King as Patron

Soon after the French protectorate was established in Morocco, French perceptions of Moroccan politics settled into a "colonial vulgate," a set of conventional assumptions about the nature of political forms (Burke

1973). In a similar fashion, a postcolonial vulgate emerged in the decade after Morocco's independence.

The postcolonial vulgate holds that Moroccan politics is a zero-sum game centering upon the king as "great patron," rewarding loyal clients and discouraging others, but above all keeping all participants off balance. In the past, politics revolved around the pitting of tribes, merchants, officials, and religious leaders against one another. In today's Morocco, labor unions and political parties have taken over from the tribes, at least at the national level. Clients of the monarch in turn serve as patrons for others, in a "trickle effect" system encompassing all Moroccans. The political opposition acts as a shock absorber for the system. It alternately signals potential points of strain and takes the blame when things go wrong. In this view, rural rebellions are seen as a means by which clients in the periphery call attention to their situation, not as challenges to the system itself (Gellner 1973; Zartman in press). Corruption also works in the service of this system, since its implicit tolerance ensures the loyalty of key supporters and mutes possible moral objections to the conduct of the state (Waterbury 1970:5; 1976).

Seen from the periphery, the prevailing popular perception of politics remains a labyrinthine network of overlapping patron-client ties. A 1969 study found that local notables, persons of influence capable of mobilizing support and translating it into votes, or submission to established power, were perceived as more significant representatives of the state than the official state apparatus (Pascon and Bentahar 1969:223). Since the late 1960s, the number of provinces in Morocco has expanded from twelve to forty, and 1976 reforms devolved genuine local fiscal powers and responsibilities upon elected officials, creating new links between the government and local communities. Local councils in effect serve as proving grounds for a new generation of Moroccans to build up effective ties with state authorities independent of formal administrative channels.

Over the last decade, elections in Morocco have become an integral element in maintaining political legitimacy and accommodating political change at a level below the top. Hasan prides himself that elections in Morocco are conducted more skillfully than elsewhere in the Arab world. Just before the fall of the Shah, he sent one of his most trusted emissaries to Tehran with the offer of Moroccan technical assistance in conducting elections (Markham 1980:121). Indeed, they provide a key to discerning how Hasan has faced the classical problem of how "some men come to be credited with the right to rule over others" (Geertz 1973:317), and how he has accommodated shifting popular expectations of what is politically and religiously just throughout nearly a quarter century of rule.

Morocco'a political arena for the 1980s differs significantly from that of the 1960s. Between 1960 and 1984 its population has almost doubled from 11.5 to 21 million. Seventy percent of this population is under thirty years of age, and 42 percent is under the age of fifteen. For the majority of the population, the colonial period is not even a memory. Twenty-five percent of the population was urban in 1960; at least 45 percent were in 1984, with an additional 20 percent living on the periphery of sprawling urban centers such as Casablanca. The number of towns has grown since 1960 from 107 to roughly 200. Between 1971 and 1982, the number of students more than doubled, reaching 3.6 million. Education and health spending account for about one-third of government expenditures. The illiteracy rate has dropped from about 75 percent in 1971 to 65 percent in 1982. Schools cannot be built quickly enough to make more rapid progress. According to the 1982 census, 44 percent of the urban and 82 percent of the rural population remains illiterate. An estimated 2.5 million of the country's 3.1 million households live on less than $110 (MDH 900) monthly, below the World Bank's level of "absolute poverty." Official figures are unreliable, but unemployment is put at 11 percent of an active population of 6 million, up from 9 percent in 1971 (Escallier 1981:12-14; *Middle East Economic Digest*, April 13, 1984: 27; Morocco 1961:35; Ramonet 1984:7-11). In the 1960s, much agricultural land was still in the hands of foreigners. By 1973 these lands had been "recuperated," to be redistributed for the most part to the monarch and to his key loyal supporters. Agricultural production augmented, even if the number of rural Moroccans above the poverty line did not (Leveau 1984:8-11). Developments in Morocco's electoral system suggest recognition of these long-term transformations.

Elections in Morocco

The Moroccan election structure is a complicated one because some members of parliament are elected by the Chambers of Agriculture, Commerce, and Industry; this analysis is primarily concerned with direct elections for the country's municipal and communal councils and for parliament.[5] In 1957, when Hasan was still crown prince, he called upon his former teachers of public administration, Maurice Duverger and André de Laubadère, to devise an electoral system (Leveau 1976:40, 53).

Referring to the works of sociologist Maurice Duverger, Hasan stated early in his reign that "genuine liberties" such as those available in many European countries would be possible only "after a certain standard of living and educational level" were attained (in Vaucher 1962:70). Hassan intended Morocco's elections to symbolize Morocco's break with its colonial past. In this respect, they were an integral part of the technocratic elaboration of central planning and administrative reorganization that followed independence. The decree formally establishing rural communal councils (*jamā'as*) in 1960 was largely based upon French models.[6] The legislative intent behind these councils was to replace tribal units, tied to the colonial past in the eyes of Morocco's emerging technocrats, with "rational" local entities appropriate to a modern Morocco. After several delays, the first communal elections for some 10,000 local posts were finally held May 29, 1960. The next local elections were then repeatedly postponed—Morocco was under a state of emergency from 1965 to 1970—but finally held in 1969. Elections for the first parliament occurred in 1963. A renewed political liberalization followed the Green March in 1975. Municipal elections next took place in 1976 and parliamentary ones in 1977 (see López 1979:11-53). After several postponements, subsequent elections were held June 10,1983 for municipal posts, and on September 14, 1984 for parliament. The irregular intervals between elections leaves no doubt as to the source of ultimate authority. Moreover, since most senior participants in electoral politics have had the expreience of earlier parliaments and local government, they possess a keen sense of the implicit limits of electoral politics.

The experience of the 1984 parliamentary elections suggests that the image of the monarch as Great Patron is not to be dispelled at the global level of national politics. Since August, when campaigning was officially allowed, parties worked tirelessly to generate popular support and government public works activities noticably increased. Nonetheless, there was a discernable lack of popular enthusiasm, largely because of massive government intervention in the 1983 local elections. Political rallies attracted smaller audiences than those of 1977. Photographs of rallies were not infrequently doctored in party newspapers to show larger crowds than those actually present. When the Union Socialist des Forces Populaires (USFP) organized a rally in Rabat's Océan stadium in 1977, some 15,000 persons attended.[7] On September 12, 1984, only 1,500 showed up, at least one-third of whom were below the voting age of twenty-one (my estimate).

Campaign speeches were well within the implicit rules of the game. In their public appearances, including television for the first time, party leaders thanked the monarch for allowing elections, praised the armed forces, and confined their remarks to the discussion of general principles. Corruption and "the crisis in which we are living" were evoked by the left of center parties, but only in general terms unrelated to specific incidents or policies. At least for the foreign press, even the leader of the Constitutional Union (UC), a party widely believed to be the most recent incarnation of the monarch's wishes, was quoted as saying that he was reserving agreement to participate in a coalition government because "we don't know [yet] how many seats are going to be reserved for us" (*Le Monde,* February 21, 1984). The USFP leader echoed this perception of fixed elections when he commented that "the sharing of seats in advance is not real elections but perverts the voter's will" (cited in Marks 1984:12).

Le Monde (September 16-17, 1984:12) claimed apathy among voters. Turnout was officially put at 67.43 percent of the 7.5 million registered voters, who turned up at 20,000 polling places, including some overseas (Morocco 1984:6). This was less than the 82 percent turnout declared for the 1977 elections, but nonetheless a significant figure, especially if compared with turnouts of 20 percent for recent Egyptian elections (Balta 1984; Ansari, personal communication).

Moroccan cognoscenti spoke of a nuanced rigging of the elections. Of the 204 seats at issue in the general elections—prior to the elections Morocco's parliament had been enlarged from 264 seats to 306; the remaining 102 seats were determined by indirect elections—the first results announced on election night just after the close of the polls happened to include the seats of all twenty persons designated as "personalities" in a Ministry of the Interior press release. These included all the party leaders and the parliament's sole Jewish delegate, a member of the newly formed UC (*Le Matin du Sahara,* September 15, 1984:4).

Three hours after the close of the polls, televised election results began to be delivered to the Moroccan public with unprecedented flair, and continued through the early hours of the morning. A live telecast direct from the Ministry of the Interior treated viewers with lavish multicolored compputer displays of pie and bar graphs showing the number of voters and candidates, the age and educational background of the candidates, divided by region and political party, and an explanation of how results were reported and communicated to Ministry of Interior headquarters. The performance suggested an updated, televised adaptation of Rémy Leveau's *Le Fellah marocain* (1976), perhaps in no small part because a number of key interior officials were Leveau's former students. The results themselves were interspersed with lavishly produced musical videodiscs, one of the first of which was by a popular Egyptian singer, praising the monarch against the varying technicolor backdrop of Morocco's major cities. An otherwise apolitical Casablanca office worker commented that perhaps the long musical pauses were to allow further results to be "cooked."

In contrast to the crude tactics of the 1960s, the Moroccan government can now engage in the fine tuning of elections at every stage from initial registration and campaigning through balloting and the announcement of results. This fine tuning is a recognition of the changed contexts of internal politics. A brief evocation of practices reported in 1977, 1983, and 1984 suggests a sophistication that would be the envy of any Chicago precinct captain under Mayor Daly. In a town in southeast Morocco, for instance, a qaid reported his obligation during registration for the 1984 elections to meet daily with his subordinates (*shaykhs* and *mqaddams*) to ascertain how many persons had registered to vote and their probable party preferences. This information was telexed daily to the governor's office, and was also regularly forwarded on printed forms provided for the purpose (interview, November 10, 1984). In a major Moroccan city, the president of a polling place in 1983 recalled that just before the polls opened, an official handed him a stack of ballots to be placed in the election urn for a favored candidate. The president at first refused, but then relented when it was intimated that he would be disobeying Ministry of the Interior orders. He then refused a subsequent summons (*istidā'*) to serve in the same role the following year (interview, September 14, 1984). Reports of alleged instances of electoral abuse are routinely published in Moroccan newspapers and include such tactics as favored registration for some parties over others, the switching of colors of ballots (an important consideration in a country where the majority of voters are illiterate), the registration of fictitious voters and the casting of ballots for "absentees" (e.g., Ben Messaoud 1976; Berrada 1984; Lamghili 1976; *L'Opinion* 1984; Yazghi 1977).

The View from the Center

The remarkable success of the newly-formed UC in the 1983-84 elections (see Table 8.1) was aided by the perception that the party was fulfilling the explicit wish of the monarch. Nonetheless, the UC managed to attract a constituency of both young and old Moroccans, a mixture that other parties, including earlier royal creations, had failed to achieve. This fact is more significant than success at the polls itself, for it suggests that the UC organizers are more aware than the leaders of the other parties of basic changes in Moroccan society.

The UC's success reflects the growing skill of the palace in shaping domestic electoral politics. It culminates two decades of experimentation which began in 1963 with a coalition called the Democratic Front for Constitutional Institutions (FDIC), led by a close confidante of the monarch, Ahmad Reda Guedira. Only the intervention of a group of senior army officers kept this coalition from calling itself the Constitutional Monarchic Front, a transparent name that would have linked the party's successes and shortcomings too directly with the throne (Leveau 1976:78). Later efforts included the Independent Assembly (RI) for "neutral" candidates, formed in 1977 and also benefiting from official favor.

TABLE 8.1
Moroccan Election Results by Seats Won and Share
of Popular Vote, 1976-1984

Party and Date Founded	1976 Local	1977 Parliament	1983 Local	1984 Parliament
Constitutional Union (UC) (Jan. 1983) (Maati Bouabid)	NA	NA	2,731 (15.57%)	55 (24.79%)
National Assembly for Independents (RNI) (1978) (Ahmad Osman)	NA	141[1]	2,211 (13.58%)	38 (17.18%)
Union of Socialist Popular Forces (USFP) (1959, reorganized 1972) (Abderrahim Bouabid)	874 (8.53%)	16	538 (6.22%)	34 (12.39%)
Popular Movement (MP) (1957) Mahjoubi Aherdane)	1.045 (7.50%)	44	1,896 (11.63%)	31 (15.64%)
Istiqlal (PI) (1944) (Mhammed Boucetta)	2,184 (17.83%)	49	2,605 (17.98%)	23 (15.33%)
National Democratic Party (PND)	NA	NA	1,339 (11.59%)	15 (8.92%)
Progressive Socialist Party (PPS) (Ali Yata)	26 (0.94%)	1	19 (0.69%)	2 (2.30%)
Organization for Democratic and Popular Action (OADP) (1983) (Mohamed Bensaid)	NA	NA	NA	1 (0.74%)
Popular Democratic Constitutional Movement (MPDC) (Abderahman Khatib)	452 (3.58%)	3	94 (0.89%)	0 (1.57%)
Independent Democrats (PDI) (Arsalan Eljadidi)	NA	NA	46 (0.61%)	0 (0.45%)

[1]The RNI was not officially in existence at the time of these elections. This figure represents the number of seats accorded to its informal predecessor.
Note: The above tabulation excludes some small parties that won no seats in the 1984 elections. For the 1976 local elections, it omits the "independent" candidates, who won 8607 seats and 59.07 percent of the vote.
NA = Not applicable.
Sources: Daoud 1976; Marks 1984; *Le Monde*, September 18, 1984:4.

The UC emerged in part from regional associations of former students (Associations des Anciens Elèves) that sprang up throughout Morocco in the first months of 1983. These ostensibly apolitical associations managed to attract educated younger Moroccans outside of the major cities. After announcement of the UC, many of its regional organizers turned out to have been active in constituting the associations of former students.

Formation of the UC was officially announced only six weeks prior to the June 1983 municipal elections. Maati Bouabid, until then the prime minister, announced that the monarch allowed him to step down in order to lead the party. Even prior to his resignation there were persistent accounts of directives sent from his office to the heads of various government services which facilitated the party's creation (interview, Casablanca, September 13, 1984).

As one retired official (cited in Kahn 1984:45) stated, all political parties represent Hasan II. Nonetheless, the UC currently seems to represent him more than the other parties. Unlike Reda Guedira, seen by many Moroccans as the king's shadow, the UC leader, Maati Bouabid, represents a different style of educated Moroccan. A former leftist union activist and subsequently a Minister of Labor (1958-1960), he represents the "greening" of an entire generation of Moroccans because he has also played forceful roles outside the government. More so than other political leaders, he has managed to speak convincingly across the lines of class, education, politics, and region, and yet remain at home in Morocco's sole corridor of power.

Because of the party's implicit official sanction, the UC attracted widespread support from an older group of notables anxious to rally around to the presumed will of the monarch and a younger generation increasingly disenchanted with traditional partisan politics. Much of its voting strength, especially apparent in municipal elections where results by precinct are available, appears to have been at the expense of the USFP. At the same time, the earlier coalitions of older "independents" continue. No party has an absolute majority in parliament, insuring that any measures passed will necessitate support across party lines. Such a development is also conceivably a royal intention.[8]

The Contracting Periphery

Other than large coastal cities such as Casablanca and Rabat, where party politics were significant since the 1950s, politics for Morocco has often been analyzed as an extension of the patronage system of local notables, a swirl of microcosms centering upon predominately local concerns. Until the mid-1970s, such an appreciation was reasonably correct, although the rising participation of students and teachers in smaller centers in nationwide strikes and demonstrations was a harbinger of significant change. Distinctly Moroccan means were often used to gain victory in these elections: the sacrifice of a sheep at the door of an opponent to oblige him by a conditional curse ('ār) to withdraw from the race; the offer of one shoe of a pair to prospective voters, with delivery of the other on election day; or the promise of clothing (Daoud 1976:22-29; see also Rosen 1972). These tactics can be used directly by candidates. In rural areas, the threat of the selective distribution of public works opportunities or the selective enforcement of tax laws and communal land regulations can be used as official leverage, as in the past.

Yet one of the most significant developments in recent years has been the progressive politicization of Morocco's smaller urban centers and a growing disenchantment with existing vehicles of political expression. The January 1984 riots in the smaller centers of the interior, where they were least anticipated, is a sign of this trend. In the late 1960s, when I chose to work in one of these towns, a then middle-range official in the Ministry of the Interior sought to discourage me, saying that the town was dead and politically backward. He predicted that politics would come to it only after twenty years. Now a more senior official, he acknowledged that his timetable was much too conservative (interview, October 25, 1984).

The politicization of Morocco's smaller communities is a direct result of the growing size and sophistication of their educated, politically active population. It is complemented by a corresponding incease in the skill of local representatives of the Ministry of the Interior. The parapolitical role of these "agents of authority" was formally recognized a decade ago by Driss Basri (1975:17, 20, 77, 81), the current Minister of the Interior. In 1975 he wrote that much of the Moroccan population has only a vague idea of the state and public authority. Consequently, the agents of authority must serve as educators of the masses, a role that he claimed was not properly performed by the political parties. Unfortunately, he continued, the Makhzan had in the past been ill-equipped to fulfill this role. Of 322 senior agents of authority in 1960, 32 had only a primary school education, 39 were trained only as interpreters, 101 had some elementary education but no diploma, and 8 were illiterates. As of 1970, only 41.5 percent of the 500 received more than perfunctory formal training by the Ministry and many were borrowed from other services. Fully 222, or 44.5 percent had no prior administrative experience.

By the mid-1970s, older officials were being steadily replaced by younger, specifically trained cadres who recognized more fully than their predecessors the changing requirements of representing authority. Even the lowest level of officialdom, the shaykhs and mqaddams, were being replaced by younger, more educated persons. The Makhzan can now be said to know its subjects all too well in the sense that it can exercise more subtle control. In strategic planning at the local level, political activists recognize that they must now not only outmaneuver their electoral opponents but also local government officials.

Boujad: 1976-77

As an example of political change in the periphery, I draw upon Boujad, a town of 30,000 located on Morocco's western plains at the foothill of the Middle Atlas Mountains, and its immediate region (see Eickelman 1976:65-88; 1980). Boujad cannot be taken as directly representative of Morocco, but it suggests the processes of political change affecting the country as a whole and how state authority is practically elaborated and experienced.

The intensification of state authority in Boujad parallels similar developments elsewhere. At the outset of the protectorate, the French appointed local notables to positions of authority. In the countryside, taxes were systematically exacted, and pastoral movements and disputes were strictly controlled. In the town, a myriad of controls and regulations were elaborated and gradually intensified. Permits and regulations were established for trades and crafts, building construction and land use. Schools and a small hospital were established. In the war years, complex rationing regulations provided opportunities for shrewd speculators to make massive profits in the black market, often in connivance with local authorities. After the war, efforts were made to discourage emigration from the countryside.

With independence, the expanded educational system provided a new point of contact between the state and ordinary Moroccans independent of the direct control of local notables. Nonetheless, the results of expanded access to education were ironic. The rapid inflation of academic credentials broke the former link between education, employment, and advancement. For all but notables, for whom government actions were more predictable and less onerous, the state apparatus remained unpredictable, to be approached cautiously through intermediaries capable of securing favorable decisions on one's behalf.

Local electoral politics in the Boujad area were moribund until 1976. The tutelage of the local representatives of the Ministry of the Interior and the lack of an independent budget left no room for local initiative, and the conduct of local elections was visible. In 1969, several large black rectangles were painted on the side of several buildings for campaign posters that never materialized. On election day, those who tried to vote were sent away and told that the government had already taken care of the matter. Government-appointed shaykhs, like their predecessors in the protectorate, remained all-powerful and arbitrary, using their control over permits and the selective enforcement of regulations as levers to hold even the suggestion of opposition in check.

The November 1976 municipal and the 1977 parliamentary elections marked the first time that political accountability and the public debate of at least local issues emerged as an alternative to the politics of notables or dependence upon appointed officials. In part this change in political circumstances was a direct consequence of the post-1956 educational expansion. As elsewhere, major changes in educational systems are felt only decades later. The heightened political awareness of workers who had been to Europe also acted as a galvanizing force.

Three formal political groupings were significant in the Boujad region in 1976: the Istiqlal party, the USFP, and various groupings of "independents" (*ahrār*). The two organized parties had contrasting bases of support.[9] The local branch of the Istiqlal party dates almost from the party's national founding in January 1944. Local leadership consists of key merchants, together wilth an older generation of artisans and craftsmen, most of whom had joined the party prior to independence or in its immediate aftermath. Because of oaths sworn on the Qur'an in their pre-1956 youth, a standard feature of Istiqlal recruitment, many persons now in their forties and fifties continue to vote for the party in spite of subsequent disenchantment with its policies. New recruits to the party in the last two decades have been negligible.

Local USFP support is more complex. Party strength was originally confined to the large coastal cities and included an important component of organized labor. Party leadership made few efforts to expand its base into small towns and rural areas in the 1960s (Waterbury 1970:198). In Boujad, its handful of cadres was nominally represented by a merchant educated at the Qarawiyin mosque-university in Fez. His brother was head of the local branch of the Istiqlal party, a reminder that politics do not necessarily follow family lines.

Following the brief interlude of liberalization after the 1972 attempted coup, the USFP reorganized and began to recruit nationwide. A Rabat-based university teacher was entrusted with reorganizing party cadres and recruiting new supporters in towns throughout the region, including the nearby mining center of Khuribga. Although the organizer was the French-educated grandson of one of the more notoriously pro-French rural qaids of the protectorate era, his father was a merchant and early contributor to proto-nationalist causes. Rural ties established by the father were successfully used by the son to muster local support. When several USFP leaders were arrested in 1973 following an uprising in the nearby Middle Atlas town of Mulay Bu 'Azza, local recruitment efforts concentrated upon the formation of clandestine cells (*khaliyas*). Each consisted of three to eleven persons, and the local old guard of the USFP was only marginally involved. After the Green March in November 1975, restrictions were again lifted and party expansion resumed in earnest.

Local USFP success among older merchants and artisans was minimal, since most of this group had sworn early allegiance to the Istiqlal party.

Among the younger, educated population, especially schoolteachers, the largest category of employment for educated persons available locally, party success was substantial. Efforts to recruit women were limited but significant.

By 1976, just prior to the municipal elections, the USFP had a local membership of 110 (Ma'ruf 1978). These elections were the first local practical test of USFP appeal. The attitude of most Boujadis toward party politics was that they were a sham (*kizb*), masking personal interest with abstract slogans. Memories were still fresh of the Istiqlal party's crude use of patronage and influence in the years immediately after independence. Both the town and the countryside were divided into electoral districts, roughly determined by population units of 1,000 to 1,500 persons each. Each of Boujad's twenty-one districts provided a delegate to the municipal council. The Istiqlal and USFP each fielded twenty-one candidates, one for each district. There were an additional sixty-three "independent" candidates.

One Istiqlal party tactic to win votes was to distribute cloth and sugar cones to voters, a technique imitated by the wealthy "independents." Following a national directive, the USFP pointedly avoided material incentives. Although the party distributed its formal ideological platform in booklet form to its adherents (USFP 1977), it emphasized specific local issues, a major innovation in local party politics. The leaflets distributed for USFP candidates stressed an improved water supply to replace the overtaxed one installed by the French in 1920, construction of a new school, sewers, and an upgraded health clinic. These were all matters that could be decided or recommended by the municipal council, although some matters were clearly beyond their fiscal and technical means.

Local government attempts to manipulate the election suggest how the state seeks practically to manifest its authority. Government interference was most pronounced in the countryside, where fewer party cadres were present. One tactic was to convene tribesmen in mosques at the weekly markets, at which an administrator declared that the USFP was "against Islam." A USFP candidate was immediately told to desist on the one occasion when he met tribesmen in a mosque. The government was adamant against the use of religious symbols by the parties, although no such restriction applied to its own cadres. Although government spokesmen invoked Islamic values, they also clearly hinted that they could express displeasure by calling in agricultural loans, withholding government assistance or, in one instance, prohibiting a tribal group from making its annual collective "visit" (*ziyāra*) to a maraboutic shrine in Boujad. More subtle intervention, including gerrymandering, which requires a high level of skill, prevailed in urban quarters.

Party workers quickly realized that mass rallies were ineffective. Few persons understood or trusted the speakers, many of whom were poorly known. Public campaigning was an unfamiliar genre, viewed with singular mistrust. The USFP then decided to locate party members of local origin living elsewhere in Morocco and bring them back to talk with fellow tribesmen. This tactic proved successful. Indeed, all candidates extensively used ties of kin, neighbors, and clients to win votes, approaching voters whenever possible through trusted intermediaries. Nonetheless, its tactic of reminding the state of what it formally declares to be the rights of citizens is beginning to alter the conduct of local politics. It captured the enthusiasm of younger voters, especially educated ones.

In the town, candidates went from house to house, pointing out the correct color to use in voting for their candidates, an important consideration for illiterate voters. (In the 1977 parliamentary elections, the government switched colors at the last moment in crucial rural regions.) Women called on neighborhood houses to explain voting procedures to other women. This tactic was especially important. Women have an equal franchise and the registration of women locally outnumbered that of men, many of whom work elsewhere in Morocco or abroad. Electoral rosters indicate long lists of "Fatimas," suggesting that husbands or guardians frequently registered women, not revealing their names, and then voted for them by proxy, an illegal practice but tolerated by some electoral supervisors. Indeed, women officially cast 60 percent of the votes in Boujad's 1976 elections (Ma'ruf 1978). Of 5,501 registered urban voters, 3,683 votes were cast, a 67 percent turnout. Comparable figures are unavailable for the rural regions. Since election days are not holidays, persons absent elsewhere in the country as students, servicemen, and workers were unable to vote.

A significant distinction emerged between voting in quarters in which longtime residents predominate and those composed of recent rural immigrants. A frequent pattern in the latter and in the rural vote was a tendency toward bloc voting (Ma'ruf 1978). Tribesmen met together among themselves prior to the election and decided on how to cast their ballots. Occasional split votes firmly mirrored prevalent local social divisions.

The urban election results (Table 8.2) surprised both the USFP and local officials. Nine seats of the municipal council went to the USFP, ten to the Istiqlal, and two to wealthy local merchants who were "independents." As a group, the USFP delegates were the best educated: five teachers, a university-educated engineer, a postal clerk and an electrician, ranging in ages from twenty to forty. The Istiqlal candidates were of an older generation, including four teachers, four merchants, and two illiterate workers. Because the USFP delegates had a better notion of how to formulate local

TABLE 8.2
Election Results for Boujad Region, 1976-1984

Party	1976 Municipal (Seats)	1983 Council (Seats)	Urban	1977 Rural (Votes)	Total (Votes)	1984 Total
Constitutional Union	NA	16	NA	NA	NA	9,249 (51.44%)
"Independents"[1]	2	0	720 (9.78%)	1,169 (8.88%)	1,889 (9.54%)	NA
Union of Socialist Popular Forces	9	1	3,392 (46.09%)	5,082 (40.88%)	8,474 (42.82%)	4,317 (24.01%)
Istiqlal	9	4	3,248 (44.13%)	6,182 (49.76%)	9,430 (47.64%)	1,143 (6.35%)
Popular Movement[2]	NA	NA	NA	NA	NA	3,074 (17.09%)
Progressive Party	NA	NA	NA	NA	NA	196 (1.09%)
Total valid votes			7,360	12,433	19,793	17,979
Registered voters			8,686	19,615	28,301	32,858

Notes: 1. Combines total vote for three separate candidates in the 1977 parliamentary elections. 2. This party is primarily active only in Berber regions. Its 1984 candidate in the Boujad region was a local Istiqlal party member whom the party passed over in favor of the incumbent member of parliament, who wanted to run again.
NA=Not applicable.
Sources: Ministry of Interior files, Boujad; *Le Matin du Sahara*, September 15, 1984, p. 4.

issues, they took the initiative on most council matters over the next few years, the first time that any significant initiative had been taken in the seventeen years of the council's existence.

Government response to the defeat of preferred candidates in 1976 included the dismissal of some government-appointed shaykhs who did not sufficiently deliver the results which the government, formally neutral, anticipated. The message of these dismissals was presumably not lost on remaining cadres. In the 1977 parliamentary elections, government involvement was more pronounced. The USFP carried the town and several rural regions by a slight majority, but the government's preferred candidate won in the most heavily populated and therefore decisive rural region. Gendarmes reportedly blocked travel to this region on election day, so that party observers permitted by law at the polling places were unable to monitor balloting and the tabulation of results. Such interference contributed to the USFP's defeat, although it nonetheless attracted a surprising 43 percent of the total vote, in large part through its suggestion of an alternative to the politics of government-controlled patronage. For its part, the government's newly developed skill in "managing" the outcome of elections resulted in persistent reports of irregularities in only one crucial rural district, for which conclusive evidence was much harder to come by than in the town itself. In earlier elections, heavy-handed tactics would have been used throughout the region. The rising educational level of Morocco's population and a corresponding tendency to hold the state to the letter of what it formally declares to be the rights of its citizens had begun to alter the conduct of local politics.

Despite government interference, the 1976 local elections offered significant choice. For the first time, municipalities and rural communes had their own budgets, employees, and control of local patronage. A considerable latitude was created for the conduct of politics at a level below that of rule at the top.

Reversals: Elections in 1983-84

If the USFP made a strong showing in the 1976-77 elections in Boujad through its emphasis upon local issues, the same factor contributed to its defeat in 1983. The projects it proposed to Boujad-area voters in 1976 could not be achieved through local resources and initiative alone, and the party's local representatives lacked demonstrable working ties with key officials in Rabat. In 1983, Boujadis remembered the promises, and returned only one USFP member to the municipal council. The USFP was paid the highest compliment: the UC borrowed its most successful campaigning tactics for the 1983-84 elections.

In 1976-77, USFP cadres learned that what counts is not so much how the ideological tenets of its national leaders were locally understood, but their ability to convince people that the USFP organizational framework could work for them. The hope inspired by the discourse was more important than its specific content. In this sense, the leading UC candidate for the municipal elections in 1983, who subsequently became president of the municipal council and successfully ran for parliament in 1984, had a decided advantage. He left Boujad in the mid-1950s to become in succession a leader in the Casablanca labor movement, president of a major association of businessmen, and director of a local transportation company. He nonetheless maintained local ties in Boujad and over the years provided employment for several generations of Boujadis. Although not a school graduate himself, he assumed leadership of the local association of school graduates in 1983 and local leadership of the UC. During the campaign, the orange color of the UC proliferated in scarves, tee shirts, jackets, and tunics distributed to his supporters. He constructed a house locally, intensified his kinship and patronage ties with Boujadis, cultivated excellent relations with local authorities, and instilled the hope in many of his supporters, especially the young, that he could find jobs for them through private connections or public influence. In rural areas, his supporters set up video cassette players for tribesmen, none of whom had regular exposure to television. A videotape showed the UC candidate speaking with Maati Bouabid, the party leader and former prime minister, about Boujad's problems. Unlike the USFP candidate, the UC one readily convinced voters that their connections with national political leaders could get things done on a local level.

The rhetoric of the campaign was far from the lofty words and decorative, religiously evocative script of the party newspaper. In Boujad, the USFP charged tht the UC was the party of the middle class and the capitalists, terms that carried no specific meaning for most voters. The UC candidate repeated these charges in a campaign meeting, pointedly held in the spacious courtyard of a leading merchant, and retorted to the USFP that "their heads are full of shit" (Sharfawi Muhammad, September 8, 1985). The earthy language passed without remark from the townsmen of the quarter where the meeting took place and tribesmen brought in from adjoining regions. Unlike talk of "classes" (*tabaqat*) and "bourgeoisie" (*al-būrjwāziya*), it was understood. The UC candidate then spoke of local issues exclusively, although he carefully avoided specific requests for assistance, such as assistance in collecting unpaid bills, made by listeners.

The USFP activists distributed no gifts, invoked no religious themes, and campaigned principally in the public gardens and door-to-door. Most of their candidates were young and lacked the financial resources of the leading UC candidate. The USFP continued to offer an alternative to the politics of notables, but this alternative was perceived as holding promise more for the distant future than the present. In contrast to 1976-77, the USFP had begun to shrink into a party of schoolteachers and university graduates, at least in Morocco's periphery. The momentum of the politics of quarters, carefully learned in 1976, was not carried forward. The party asked to be judged pragmatically by what it could accomplish at the local level. It was.

Conclusion

Morocco's most recent elections suggest that one result of intensified local political activity is a heightened level of awareness of the responsibilities of the state and the capacity of its citizens to shape their own future. The practical example of conduct of affairs at the local level suggests that the experience might one day be widened. Government interference in electoral politics is widely acknowledged, but so is the responsibility of the government to live up to its promise of delivering public services and serving as exemplars of public service. This expectation, once confined to an educated minority, is now more widespread.

For rural and small town notables, formal electoral politics are now a major concern. Unlike in the past, local offices can be a source of local projects and patronage that must be more actively sought. With the rise in the number of educated voters has come a major increase in politicization. In the smaller towns of the interior and rural areas, the presence of even a single educated person in a household or extended family leads to the political involvement of the others, at least as voters. In the past, women were voted for; now they vote for themselves. In the poorest sections of Boujad, occupied by rural immigrants, the local UC argument that they best represent the interests of the town because their candidates are from "leading" families with urban "roots" (*judhūr*) rings hollow. Yet the UC can convincingly display its national connections and make them work. For those who believe that Islam has a direct role to play in politics, only the UC has sought to elaborate traditional religious themes. This invocation of common values, even if not applied to directly "political" goals, has a more desired effect upon the majority of voters than the more secular appeals of other parties. The UC provides a vehicle for a self-renewing politics of notables, with more openings for the talented young than earlier political creations. It links elected officials more securely with local governmental initiatives and the center. It also holds open the promise for change from the politics of notables. While not excluding a self-declared "avant-garde" (*aṭ-ṭalī'a*) that breaks with accepted ways of doing things from its midst, UC organization and themes provide a political vehicle for younger, educated Moroccans alienated from earlier versions of party politics.

Thus recent elections, even if "managed" by the government, signal an implicit recognition of changed attitudes toward authority, and a heightened recognition of those in authority of shifting popular expectations. A complementary indication of these shifts is the education of the crown prince, Sidi Muhammad. Unlike many of his Middle Eastern counterparts, who have been educated abroad, Sidi Muhammad has remained in Rabat for primary, secondary, and now university studies. Since secondary studies, he has been educated alongside a small cadre of about fifteen cohorts, carefully chosen to represent a wide range of Moroccan society. This group excludes the children of current ministers. The crown prince follows special classes at the university, and remains in touch with the main currents of Moroccan thought and action beyond the confines of the elite and the intelligentsia.

Moroccans are necessarily uncertain about their country's economic and political future, since it is highly dependent upon events beyond their immediate control. This uncertainty is evoked in popular language. Until a few years ago, the common answer to the mundane greeting, "How are you?," was a variation upon "Fine." Now phrases such as "Leave it to God" (*khallīha 'la llāh*) and "Just carrying on" (*ghayr 'addī*) are much more common. A self-conscious movement toward adopting Islamic values is evident in many aspects of popular urban life, connected with a de-emphasis upon that which is Western.

The January 1984 riots, for which no convincing evidence of planning or sinister external control has been brought forward,[10] may retrospectively be regarded as the beginning of a new phase of "participation" in political life and confrontation with existing state authority. As one Moroccan explained, "real" power is not an object of competition in Moroccan politics, but there is considerable latitude in the conduct of affairs below the top. Now that politics at these levels are changing, it remains to be seen how far these new currents will affect political life at the very top. The government recognizes that widened political participation may limit the appeal of both the extreme left and Islamic fundamentalists, self-designated as "the Muslims" (*al-islāmiyūn*). Moroccans may be cynical about the conduct of elections and the monarch's assumed leadership of the Islamic community, but it is possible to be both deeply cynical and profoundly religious at the same time. Through a widened political participation and a continued, often innovative, identification with Islam, the Makhzan and the monarch may well succeed in actively and flexibly responding to long-term shifts in political expectations.

Notes

I wish to thank Hamied Ansari, Myron J. Aronoff, Christine Eickelman, I. William Zartman, and two Moroccan colleagues for comments on an earlier version of this essay. Otherwise unidentified citations from the speeches of Hasan II are taken from Foreign Broadcast Information Service reports for the dates specified.

1. See Leveau 1984, esp. pp. 12-14, 32-34, for a masterly analysis of the "praetorian menace" in Moroccan politics and the monarch's strategies for holding the military in check.
2. For an excellent description of the king's personal style, see Kahn 1984.
3. Every Muslim household that can afford to do so sacrifices a sheep or other animal for this feast (*'Id al-Kabīr*). In a speech commemorating his father's death on August 25, 1984, the monarch explained that to aid the national economy, it would be preferable not to put scarce resources into the feast. Couched in the speech as a "voluntary" act, six days later the sacrifice was forbidden by administrative order. The surprise announcement hurt Moroccans with modest incomes, many of whom purchase animals a few months in advance in order to resell them at a profit just before the feast. Prices for sheep fell precipitously, and in some parts of the country animals were left to die. It was the first time since the deposition of Muhammad V that such a restriction was placed upon the sacrifice. Although inequities in how the monarch's order

was carried out were resented, the order itself was not questioned because it came directly from the monarch.

4. After Yasin sent an open letter to Hasan II in 1973 denouncing moral corruption and injustice in the state, he was imprisoned in a psychiatric hospital for three years, presumably in an effort to discredit him, but subsequently released and allowed to see foreign journalists (Markham 1980:125). In late December 1983 he was again imprisoned for denouncing the conduct of the state. On February 13, 1984, after the January riots, he was rearrested and subsequently sentenced to two years in prison (*Le Monde*, February 15, 1984).

5. In a system begun by the French in the late 1940s, the three professional chambers elect their own regional and parliamentary representatives. At the present, one-third of the seats in parliament are filled by delegates from these chambers. The remaining two-thirds of the seats are chosen by universal suffrage. All Moroccans over the age of twenty-one, both in Morocco and overseas, are eligible to vote.

6. Urban councils had existed since the protectorate, but were reorganized after 1959. For details see Ben Bachir 1969.

7. The USFP is successor party to the earlier Union Nationale des Forces Populaires, formed after a 1959 schism in the Istiqlal Party lead originally by Mahdi Ben Barka, presumed assassinated in 1965. The change of name followed government intervention in the early 1970s and the party's reorganization in 1974.

8. Although certain parties can be said to represent the royal will, they do so indirectly. Moroccan referendums resemble the election results of one-party states, but not its elections. For example, Hasan II formally asked Moroccans to vote "yes" in the August 31, 1984, referendum on the Moroccan-Libyan treaty instituting the "Arab-African Union." The result was a favorable vote of 99.97 percent (*Le Monde*, September 2-3, 1984:3). The lack of such explicit expression of course separates the monarch and the monarchy from direct responsibility for specific political actions.

9. An earlier version of parts of this section appears in Eickelman (in press).

10. In his televised address of January 24, 1984, Hasan II displayed pamphlets seized in Marrakesh that were printed by a Paris-based Marxist-Leninist group. The pamphlets were seized on January 6, well before the demonstrations.

References

'Aqbib, Mustafa. 1976. "Student Attitudes toward Islamic Religion and Religious Beliefs." Thesis for a *license* presented to the Faculty of Arts, Muhammad V University, Rabat. (Typescript, in Arabic.)

Balta, Paul. 1984. "L'Union Constitutionnelle largement en tête." *Le Monde*, September 16-17, p. 2.

Basri, Driss. 1975. *L'Agent d'autorité*. Rabat: Imprimerie Royale.

Ben Bachir, Sa'id. 1969. *L'Administration locale du Maroc*. Casablanca: Imprimerie Royale.

Ben Messaoud. 1976. "Les élections en question." *Lamalif*, no. 83 (October):14-15.

Berrada, Hamid. 1984. "Démocratie dirigée." *Jeune Afrique*, September 26, pp. 29-31.

Burke, Edmund, III. 1973. "The Image of the Moroccan State in French Ethnological Literature: A New Look at the Origin of Lyautey's Berber Policy." In

Arabs and Berbers. Ed. Ernest Gellner and Charles Micaud. London: Duckworth. pp. 175-99.

Daoud, Zakya. 1976. "Analyse des résultats électoraux." *Lamalif*, no. 84 (November-December):22-29.

Eickelman, Dale F. 1976. *Moroccan Islam: Tradition and Society in a Pilgrimage Center*. Austin and London: University of Texas Press.

———. 1980. "Formes symboliques et espace social urbain." In *Système urbain et développement au Maghreb*. Ed. A. Zghal and A. Rassam. Tunis: Ceres Productions. pp. 199-218.

———. In press. "Changing Perceptions of State Authority: Morocco, Egypt and Oman." In *State and Authority in Arab History and Contemporary Reality*. Ed. Ghassan Salameh and Marwan Buheiry. London: Croom Helm.

Escallier, Robert. 1981. *Citadins et espace urbain au Maroc*. Poitiers: Centre Interuniversitaire d'Etudes Méditerranéennes.

Etienne, Bruno and Mohamed Tozy. 1979. "Le glissement des obligations islamiques vers le phénomène associatif à Casablanca." *Annuaire de l'Afrique du Nord* 18: 235-59.

Geertz, Clifford. 1973. *The Interpretation of Cultures*. New York: Basic Books.

Gellner, Ernest. 1973. "Patterns of Rural Rebellion in Morocco during the Early Years of Independence." In *Arabs and Berbers*. Ed. Ernest Gellner and Charles Micaud. London: Duckworth. pp. 361-74.

Hasan II. 1984. February speech to the Higher Council of 'Ulama. Maghreb Arab Presse, French version (telex 141 n.d.).

Kahn, Jr., E. J. 1984. "The King and His Children." *The New Yorker*, July 9, pp. 43-59.

Lamghili, Ahmad el Kohen. 1976. "Lá 'boulitiqué' dúne élection." *Lamalif*, no. 84 (November-December):32-36.

Leveau, Rémy. 1976. *Le fellah marocain: défenseur du trône*. Paris: Presses de la Fondation Nationale des Sciences Politiques.

———. 1977. "The Rural Elite as an Element in the Social Stratification of Morocco." In *Commoners, Climbers and Notables*. Ed. C. A. O. van Nieuwenhuijze. Leiden: E. J. Brill. pp. 226-47.

———. 1984. "Aperçu de l'evolution du systeme politques marocain depuis vingt ans." *Maghrib-Machrek* 106 (October-December): 7-36.

López García, Bernabe. 1979. *Procesos electorales en Marruecos (1960-1977)*. Madrid: Centro de Investigaciones Sociológicas.

McWilliams, Wilson Carey. 1971. "On Political Illegitimacy." *Public policy* 19 (Summer):429-56.

Mannheim, Karl. 1971. "Conservative Thought." In *From Karl Mannheim*. Ed. Kurt H. Wolff. New York: Oxford University Press. pp. 132-222.

Markham, James M. 1980. "King Hasan's Quagmire." *The New York Times Magazine*, April 27.

Marks, Jon. 1984. "All Systems Go for Morocco Elections." *The Middle East*, August, p. 12.

Ma'ruf, 'Abd Allah. 1978. "Report on the Elections in Boujad" [in Arabic]. Photocopy.

Morocco, Kingdom of. 1961. *Population légale du Maroc*. Rabat: Service Central des Statistiques.

Morocco, Embassy of (Washington). 1984. "News Summary" (September).

L'Opinion. 1984. "Cas flagrant de trucage." October 2.

Pascon, Paul, and Mekki Bentahar. [1969] 1972. "Ce que disent 296 jeunes ruraux." In *Etudes sociologiques sur le maroc*. Ed. A. Khatibi. Rabat: Bulletin Economique et Social du Maroc. pp. 145-287.

Ramonet, Ignacio. 1984. "Maroc: l'heure de tous les risques." *Le Monde Diplomatique* (January).

Rosen, Lawrence. 1972. "Rural Political Process and National Political Structure in Morocco." In *Rural Politics and Social Change in the Middle East*. Ed. Richard Antoun and Ilya Harik. Bloomington and London: Indiana University Press. pp. 214-36.

Scott, James C. 1976. *The Moral Economy of the Peasant: Rebellion and Subsistence in Southeast Asia*. New Haven: Yale University Press.

Tozy, Mohamed. 1984. "Champ et contre champ politico-religieux au Maroc." Thesis for the Doctorat d'Etat in Political Science presented to the Faculté de Droit et de Science Politique of the Universities of Aix-en-Provence and Marseille.

USFP. 1977. "The Electoral Platform." Rabat: n.p. (In Arabic.)

Vaucher, Georges. 1962. *Sous les cèdres d'Ifrane*. Paris: Julliard.

Waterbury, John. 1970. *The Commander of the Faithful*. New York: Columbia University Press.

_____. 1976. "Corruption, Political Stability and Development: Comparative Evidence from Egypt and Morocco." *Government and Opposition* 11:426-45.

Yazghi, Mohammed. 1977. "Morocco's Political Experience." Lecture to the North Africanists of New York, September 15.

Zartman, I. William. In press. "The Opposition as a Support of the State." In *The Arab States and Societies*. Ed. Adeed Dawisha and I. William Zartman. London: Croom Helm.

About the Contributors

Myron J. Aronoff is professor of political science and anthropology at Rutgers University. He received his Ph.D. in anthropology from Manchester University and his Ph.D. in political science from UCLA. He is author of *Frontiertown: The Politics of Community Building in Israel*, and *Power and Ritual in the Israel Labor Party*. He had edited *Freedom and Constraint: a Memorial Tribute to Max Gluckman* and all five volumes in this *Political Anthropology* series. He is currently serving as president of both the Association for Political and Legal Anthropology, and the Association for Israel Studies.

Dale F. Eickelman is professor of anthropology at New York University. He received his M.A. in Islamic studies from McGill University and his Ph.D. in anthropology from the University of Chicago. He is the author of *Moroccan Islam: Tradition and Society in a Pilgrimage Center, The Middle East: An Anthropology Approach,* and *Knowledge and Power in Morocco: The Education of a Twentieth Century Notable.* He has conducted extensive field research in the Middle East, especially in Morocco and the Sultanate of Oman, and is presently writing a book on leadership and authority in Oman. His long-term concern is in developing comparative studies of religion and politics in Muslim societies.

Douglas B. Emery received his B.A. from the University of Maryland and is currently a doctoral candidate in political science at Rutgers University. His research interests include the study of the relationship between culture and political change and the application of work being done by the object relations school in psychoanalysis to the study of politics. His major areas of concentration are political philosophy and political economy.

Don Handelman is associate professor of anthropology at The Hebrew University of Jerusalem. He received his B.A. and M.A. from McGill University, continued his graduate studies at the University of Pittsburgh, and received his Ph.D. from the University of Manchester. He is the author of *Work and Play Among the Aged: Interaction, Replication and Emergence in a Jerusalem Setting*, coauthor of *Bureaucracy and World View: Studies in the Logic of Official Interpretation*, and coeditor of *Administrative Frameworks and Clients*, and of *The Social Anthropology of Israel*. Handelman has published extensively in leading professional journals and collections of scholarly essays on a wide range of theoretical topics analyzing the results of fieldwork he has conducted in Quebec, Nevada, Israel, Newfoundland, Sri Lanka, and the Los Angeles Olympic Games.

Lea Shamgar-Handelman is a fellow senior lecturer in the Department of Sociology and the School of Education at The Hebrew University of Jerusalem. A graduate of the Henrietta Szold-Hadassah Hospital School of Nursing, Shamgar-Handelman received her B.A., M.A., and Ph.D. in sociology from The Hebrew University of Jerusalem. She is the author of *A Survey of a Town of New Immigrants*, and coauthor of *The Absorption of New Immigrants in a Development Town*, and *Coordination of Services in a Development Town*. Her forthcoming book, *War Widows of Israel: Beyond the Glory of Heroism*, is currently in press. She has also published numerous articles on various aspects of Israeli society.

Smadar Lavie received her B.A. from the Hebrew University of Jerusalem in sociology, social anthropology, Islamic civilization, and musicology. She received her M.A. in cultural anthropology and is presently a Ph.D. candidate in the Department of Anthropology, University of California at Berkeley. Her primary research interests are symbolic anthropology, performance, humor and play, modernization and social change, and the Arab world. Lavie has published "The Fool and The Hippies: Ritual/Play and Social Inconsistencies Among the Mzeina Bedouin of the Sinai," and coauthored, with William C. Young, "Bedouin in Limbo: Egyptian and Israeli Development Policies in the Southern Sinai." She is currently editing, together with Kirin Narayan and Renato Rosaldo, *Persuasions and Performances: The Poetics of Self and Society*, which is dedicated to the memory of Victor Turner.

Frank E. Manning is professor of anthropology and Director of the Centre for Social and Humanistic Studies, University of Western Ontario. He has done field research in Bermuda and in several countries in the eastern Caribbean. He is author of *Black Clubs in Bermuda and Bermudian Politics in Transition*, and has edited a volume on cultural performance, *The Celebration of Society*.

George E. Marcus has degrees from Yale and Harvard universities, and is currently professor and chairman of the Department of Anthropology at Rice University. His early work was in the Polynesian Kingdom of Tonga, where he focused on contemporary elite culture and politics in the monarchy. Later, he developed an interest in dynastic families in business, politics, academia, and the arts, among other fields, not only in the United States but in modern nation-states generally. He has recently been appointed editor of the new journal *Cultural Anthropology* (of the Society for Cultural Anthropology), and is interested in the reconciliation of theories of culture in anthropology with a pervasive sensitivity to issues of political economy and historical change. His major publications include *The Nobility and the Chiefly Tradition in the Modern Kingdom of Tonga, Elites: Ethnographic Issues* (of which he is the editor) and *An Experimental Moment: Toward Anthropology as Cultural Criticism* (with Michael Fischer).

Helen Fung-har Siu is assistant professor of anthropology at Yale University. She received her B.A. from Carleton College and her M.A. and Ph.D. from Stanford University. Before coming to Yale she taught at the Chinese University of Hong Kong and Williams College. She has done fieldwork in rural China since 1976, and is the coauthor of *Mao's Harvest: Voices from China's New Generation.* She is currently working on two book projects. One is a study of economic development and political change in a Chinese commune, the other an anthology of stories describing peasant-state relationships in contemporary China.

Index